Therapeutic Practice in Behavioral Medicine

A Selective Guide
to Assessment, Treatment,
Clinical Issues,
and Therapies
for Specific Disorders

David I. Mostofsky
Ralph L. Piedmont

Therapeutic Practice
in Behavioral Medicine

Jossey-Bass Publishers

San Francisco • Washington • London • 1985

THERAPEUTIC PRACTICE IN BEHAVIORAL MEDICINE
A Selective Guide to Assessment, Treatment,
Clinical Issues, and Therapies for Specific Disorders
by David I. Mostofsky and Ralph L. Piedmont

Library of Congress Cataloging in Publication Data
Main entry under title:

Therapeutic practice in behavioral medicine.

(Guidebooks for therapeutic practice) (Jossey-Bass
social and behavioral science series) (Jossey-Bass
health series)
Concise digests of previously published articles.
Includes bibliographies and indexes.
1. Medicine, Psychosomatic—Addresses, essays,
lectures. 2. Psychotherapy—Addresses, essays,
lectures. 3. Medicine and psychology—Addresses,
essays, lectures. I. Mostofsky, David I. II. Piedmont,
Ralph L. (date). III. Series. IV. Series: Jossey-
Bass social and behavioral science series. V. Series:
Jossey-Bass health series. [DNLM: 1. Behavioral Medicine
—collected works. 2. Behavior Therapy—collected works.
WM 425 T398]
RC49.T44   1985   615.8′51   84-43031
ISBN 0-87589-638-3 (alk. paper)

JACKET DESIGN BY WILLI BAUM

FIRST EDITION

Code 8507

A joint publication in
The Jossey-Bass
Social and Behavioral Science Series
and
The Jossey-Bass Health Series

GUIDEBOOKS FOR THERAPEUTIC PRACTICE
Charles E. Schaefer and Howard L. Millman
Consulting Editors

Therapies for Children: A Handbook of Effective
Treatments for Problem Behaviors
Charles E. Schaefer and Howard L. Millman
1977

Therapies for Psychosomatic Disorders in Children
Charles E. Schaefer, Howard L. Millman,
and Gary F. Levine
1979

Therapies for School Behavior Problems
Howard L. Millman, Charles E. Schaefer,
and Jeffrey J. Cohen
1980

*Therapies for Adolescents: Current Treatments
for Problem Behaviors*
Michael D. Stein and J. Kent Davis
1982

Group Therapies for Children and Youth
Charles E. Schaefer, Lynnette Johnson,
and Jeffrey N. Wherry
1982

Therapies for Adults
Howard L. Millman, Jack T. Huber,
and Dean R. Diggins
1982

*Family Therapy Techniques for Problem Behaviors
of Children and Teenagers*
Charles E. Schaefer, James M. Briesmeister,
and Maureen E. Fitton
1984

*Therapeutic Practice in Behavioral Medicine:
A Selective Guide to Assessment, Treatment,
Clinical Issues, and Therapies for Specific Disorders*
David I. Mostofsky and Ralph L. Piedmont
1985

Preface

Since the inception of the "Guidebooks for Therapeutic Practice" series, each volume has reflected emerging developments and the corresponding need to acquaint professionals with new publications. In multidisciplinary areas, the relevant literature often appears in obscure journals or sources not usually consulted by the harried practitioner. Such is the case with behavioral medicine, a relative latecomer to the enterprise of psychotherapy. We trust that this volume will help bring behavioral medicine before the wider audience of therapists and other health specialists and relate the broad panorama of activities, disciplines, and technologies that provide an appreciation for what it is all about.

The present volume largely follows the format, level, and

presentation of other volumes in this series. Although none of the articles appearing in this work has been reviewed in any of the earlier volumes, the reader will find some overlap in themes and messages, particularly with a volume such as *Therapies for Psychosomatic Disorders in Children.* We regard this overlap as useful and beneficial. We have attempted to retain the obviously positive features of succinctness with a minimum of theoretical excursions.

This approach is particularly important for this area, since, with the exception of pathology, every specialty within medicine and dentistry has been affected by behavioral medicine. At times this may take the form of incorporating behavioral principles to enhance public awareness, prevention, or compliance. It may also take the form of patient preparation and stress reduction, as well as some version of frank physiological, musculoskeletal, or similar treatment. The literature is vast. Aside from the ocean of journals and periodicals in which such reports appear, the decade from 1973 to 1983 has seen the publication of well over 100 authored and edited *books* that either carry the title or the message of behavioral medicine.

Our purpose in this volume was to cull a representative sampling from the available population of topics. Certainly we never planned to be exhaustive. Because of the collaborative and interdisciplinary nature of behavioral therapies as they relate to medical practice, we began with an introduction to the literature that is concerned first with conceptualizing health and illness and then with assessing them. We then selected areas of application where the professional community shows confidence and acceptance and where professional and public policy priorities lie. For this reason, we omitted many legitimate topics, for example, in neurology and dermatology, and instead emphasized cardiovascular conditions, pain, and chronic ailments in both children and adults. We planned to make this a practical reference for professionals and students in psychology, medicine, social work, nursing, and allied health fields.

In addressing behavioral therapy in the context of medical care (that is, nonmental health), we follow the popular convention of maintaining a body–mind distinction while simultaneously arguing for an interdependence between mind and body. No matter. It is perhaps more important to note that various psychotherapeutic techniques had already been shown to be effective in treating some "medical problems" years before behavioral medicine became a buzzword. However, what is now novel is the explosion of interest in using traditional psychotherapy and behavioral therapies (including biofeedback) to treat a wide range of hitherto *purely medical* problems. This interest has led to enthusiasm among many clinical psychologists, suggesting new roles, skills, and ways to apply conventional therapy forms. Above all, the professionalization and institutionalization of behavioral medicine has attracted interest and promoted collaboration not only with medicine but also with other specialties dedicated to health and healing. Such interdisciplinary collaborations are often necessary to realize success.

A therapist must be informed about the range of possibilities in behavioral medicine in order to achieve self-actualizing goals and to maintain competency. However, the clinician must also develop a perspective and an appreciation of the style of behavioral medicine activities. Not infrequently, the diversity and dynamic quality of published reports are lost when one restricts his or her search to well-known psychology periodicals. We have therefore gone to extra effort to include reports from sources that might be unfamiliar to the novice.

We are also particularly aware that both the private and independent clinician (psychologist, nurse, counselor, teacher, and physician)—as well as the team member of a health and medical organization who wants to employ behavior treatment as an adjunctive component to traditional practice—will value having more information than a terse description of a clinical success story can provide. Very often the suggestion of a behavioral tactic for dealing with a *real* medical condition is met with suspicion, skepticism, and resistance by the patient, if not outright disbelief and hostile rejection. Uninformed physicians and hospital administrators react similarly—perhaps differing only in their overt and higher levels of intensity. We think it is important, therefore, to supply not only the main story line of each publication but also some of the supporting data and analysis. This explains why we have included more technical data and statistical results than might have been expected from other volumes in this series. We hope that the added details in our summaries will facilitate such thoughtful consideration and provide the convincing support that may be needed for program approval and implementation.

We chose not to belabor certain fundamentals. For instance, we have not cited studies in which college students are used as patient analog subjects simply to demonstrate some of the basic principles in operant conditioning or biofeedback. The principles have been adequately and repeatedly tested, confirmed, and reported. To restate this material in this volume would be at best costly and redundant and, more seriously, would cast aspersions on the professional competence of this readership. Similarly, we have not focused attention on psychosomatic theory or the psychiatric components of numerous physical ills. One primary goal is to help the clinician or advocate be well informed about the exciting advances and optimistic outlook that are reported in various behavioral medicine publications. But enthusiasm should be tempered with the realization that research findings may not always be generalized and that they need to be carefully evaluated against the particular conditions described in the published report, as well as other criteria. Since we have retained the digest format common to other volumes in this series, we urge the serious reader to consult the source documents for a thorough evaluation of a given topic.

Behavioral medicine represents a point of view, a collection of procedures, and a corps of health professionals who share a common conviction that social science and medicine are joint partners in the understanding and management of disease and illness. Patients (consumers) as well as physicians (providers) increasingly recognize the scientific, economic, and humane benefits that such a union can provide.

Many people share in the credit for what is valuable and enjoyable about this volume. Our thanks to the gracious and talented authors, clinicians, and researchers who gave us permission to digest their articles. We also thank Barbara Shukitt for her invaluable assistance through the many phases required to bring this manuscript to its final form.

Boston, Massachusetts   David I. Mostofsky
January 1985   Ralph L. Piedmont

Contents

The Authors

David I. Mostofsky is professor of psychology at Boston University. He was awarded the B.A. degree (1953) from Yeshiva College and the M.A. degree (1957) and the Ph.D. degree (1960) from Boston University—all in the field of psychology. An experimental psychologist, Mostofsky's teaching and research interests include learning, conditioning, and quantitative techniques. He has had a special interest in the problem of epilepsy, having established a behavioral neurology clinic at the Children's Hospital Medical Center in Boston. When behavioral medicine was later formally recognized as an area of inquiry and practice, he was an organizing founder of the Academy of Behavioral Medicine Research and a charter member of the Society of Behavioral Medicine. He is a fellow of the American Psychological Association and other national and international societies related to behavior, neuroscience, and health. His publications include journal articles, book chapters, and monographs on a variety of topics.

Ralph L. Piedmont received his B.A. degree (1980) in psychology and history from Iona College and his M.A. degree (1984) in psychology from Boston University, where he is a doctoral candidate in personality psychology. His research interests center on person-situation factors that influence behavior. Some of his other interests concern the investigation of hypnotic phenomena (in particular, the use of hypnosis to potentiate performance on biofeedback tasks) and cognitive systems. He has published several papers in these areas, including "Effects of Hypnosis and Biofeedback upon the Regulation of Peripheral Skin Temperature" (1981) and "Subject's Selective Learning: An Insight into the Depth-of-Processing Framework" (1980). His most recent work (coauthored with G. Gonyea and D. Ozer) is "The Effects of Achievement Motivation on Performance on a Recognition Task" (1984). Piedmont is a member of Psi Chi, Phi Alpha Theta, and Delta Epsilon Sigma, as well as an affiliate of the Society for Clinical and Experimental Hypnosis and the American Psychological Association.

Therapeutic Practice
in Behavioral Medicine

A Selective Guide
to Assessment, Treatment,
Clinical Issues,
and Therapies
for Specific Disorders

Introduction

Throughout history, the social sciences have kept constant company with medicine. The recent past has witnessed a new chapter in this relationship—a chapter that marks a union and collaboration between the two often diverging (if not warring) cultures. These developments promise striking changes in the clinical practices that encompass health delivery services. Such changes —and some are already integrated into standard medical practice—include not only caring attitudes and sensitivities but also altered, alternative, and adjunctive treatment protocols.

This particular union of behavioral science and medicine has been given various labels, including behavioral medicine, health psychology, medical psychology, and clinical psychophysiology. Although these terms reflect historical, philosophical, and subtle connotative differences, the essential meaning is clear, namely, the utilization of concepts and techniques that have been developed in the behavioral sciences in treating a wide range of problems and disorders that have long been the province of traditional (nonmental health or nonpsychiatric) medicine. Such collaborative programs between the social sciences and medicine are logical extensions of the longer history of collaborations in basic research issues and in the evolution of theories.

No practitioner of the healing arts, no matter how committed to organicity, "bug theory" etiology, or faith in the primacy of drugs and surgery could fail to acknowledge the presence of nonorganic factors that affect the course of disease and its expression. No mental health specialist, no matter how focused on intrapsychic or environmental conditions, could fail to observe the interdependence between mind and body. But however common it was to adopt a perspective that mind and body are united and integrated (at least on the verbal level), it was only recently that we have witnessed practical translations from the laboratory and from the mental health clinic to the wider domain of traditional medicine. These applications have already proven themselves and hold continued promise for improving the quality of therapeutics in general medicine. The selections that follow reflect some of the advances in this area. However disparate the techniques or pathologies described, the discussions in this volume share common ground in the overall philosophy and development of behavioral medicine.

Where It Comes From, Where It Is Going

The historical antecedents of behavioral medicine may be found in numerous corners of the scholarly world. It may perhaps best be regarded as the applied or clinical extension of psychophysiology, psychosomatics, the experimental analysis of behavior, and psychotherapy. The techniques that are incorporated into the service plans of behavioral medicine draw freely from a variety of theoretical orientations and stylistic strategies.

Included are hypnosis, cognitive therapies, behavioral protocols, dynamic systems, and milieu and eclectic therapies. In short, pretty much everything that has been developed in the social sciences—and in psychology in particular—is pressed into service for meeting the challenges presented by medical disorders.

Such a sweeping assertion should eliminate any misguided impression that behavioral medicine is some shopworn revision of conventional mental health theories. To be sure, a lot of what has proven successful in treating mental health problems seems to be successful when adapted to the treatment of physical illness. But behavioral medicine seems to embrace far more than just treatment or intervention. The domain of behavioral medicine ranges from purely social and behavioral science issues to molecular biophysiological mechanisms. Clearly, treatment and therapy dominate the field—in terms of the interest that its advocates show, the striking advances that they offer to the practice of medicine, and the added relief and comfort that behavioral medicine gives suffering patients. But however important or dramatic the treatment component of behavioral medicine, it is but one of many components. Others include medical sociology and public health, including the concerns of public policy and the economics of health care delivery systems. (Who knows how much health can be improved if an administrative action provides third-party payment or hospital privileges to providers of behavioral treatments?) Another component is epidemiology—with the latest innovation of "behavioral epidemiology"—which not only represents concern with description and demography but also helps in the design of treatment programs that reach into broad segments of the community and its populace.

Next, we shall consider the glamorous phase of treatment or therapy—about which we shall have more to say shortly. As we move toward the "hard," scientific areas of behavioral medicine, the emphasis is placed on variables in physiology and the life sciences. Research activities focus on biochemical and neurophysiological substrates that interact with behavior, stress, and personality factors.

Behavioral Treatment in Medicine:
Primary and Adjunctive

Admittedly, the most dramatic change in the delivery of health services has been the application of behavioral technologies to medicine. Although liaison psychiatry and dynamic psychotherapy have contributed in an important way to the management of many health problems, protocols derived from the behavioral therapies and biofeedback technologies have provided the most striking results. Even though frank organic pathology is present and clearly suspect for causing the symptoms, such procedures provide relatively permanent behavior changes that are beneficial to health. The application of the behavioral systems invariably begins with diagnostic and assessment phases; these include detailed monitoring and delineation of antecedent behaviors, environmental conditions, and patient and family characteristics, as well as a summary of the medical history. Behavior that interferes with health—or that is itself the undesired "symptom"—is identified, together with the behavioral objectives that the therapy seeks to achieve. These objectives depend on the nature and severity of the disorder.

On occasion, an objective may be to shape a patient's behavior to prevent a disorder or crisis. For instance, a behavioral objective might be to assure compliance with instructions for exercising, taking medications, or similar medically mandated activities. The dazzling performance of the behavior therapies is clearly shown by cases in which symptoms or dysfunctions were altered, remedied, or even eliminated. Dominant among such achievements are the successes achieved in treating pain, incontinence, and insomnia. There is always added excitement and satisfaction when such functional changes are accompanied by a normalization of the physiological machinery. But whether or not there is such a fortunate outcome, the ability of behavioral tactics to provide relief—often when a drug treatment or surgery has failed—is in itself a major development in the medical arts.

The beneficial changes that might be expected when modifying a symptom need not be restricted to reducing the frequency of occurrence. The careful therapist must also be sensitive to conditions where symptoms continue to appear with unchanged frequency but with improvements in duration, severity, topography, predictability, discriminability, or "abortability." Often conventional medical interventions can do no better, but whether as adjunctive to pharmacologic treatment or as a treatment of choice, behavioral treatment programs offer the hope of reducing drug dependency and lessening restrictions on a patient's activities. Not insignificantly, behavioral medicine specialists collaborating with physicians, nurses, and other medical specialists improve the prospects of restoring and rehabilitating a patient. Even when symptoms are refractory to the best treatment available, behavioral medicine may significantly improve the overall health status and quality of life by enabling a patient to cope with illness and suffering, to comply with instructions despite discomfort, to preserve a viable self-image, and to promote socializing and personal as well as interpersonal functioning.

Components of Treatment and Comprehensive Management

A behavioral treatment program is usually not what the average patient seeking medical aid expects. The patient will often allow the physician to do what must be done to the affected limb or organ without becoming involved in the process herself. This reflects the view that the variables of the patient's personality, history, family, and so on are not relevant. Not so with behavioral treatment. Behavior is not untreatable—it can be taught, strengthened, altered, or in some way modulated, but only in a very active and participating patient. Treatment is no longer restricted to a bone being mended or tissue being removed. Whether the objective is symptom reduction or adaptation to a life-style, a variety of special considerations become of paramount importance. For example, the particular environment in which treatment (or care) is delivered must be considered, including the physical resource (whether the patient's home, a clinic, or a hospital), the nature of the family constellation and its dynamics, the working or school setting, and the medical and psychosocial history of the patient.

To design an effective intervention properly, a program of activities is often required that is not in itself usually considered as primarily therapeutic. Not infrequently the patient, family, and attending staff may require information and education for which printed, audio, or visual materials may have to be developed. If specific therapy techniques or procedures must be administered by people unfamiliar with them, a training program will have to be established. Similarly, the package of technologies that comprises an effective treatment system will include (1) diagnostic, measurement, and analytic strategies; (2) biofeedback and other therapeutic tactics to address behavioral, psychodynamic, and physiological performance; and (3) hardware and instrumentation (including electronic and telemetric devices) necessary for response monitoring, data capture, and stimulus or environmental control.

Overview of Book

The selections that follow were included with several purposes in mind. One was to present a representative sampling of the clinical activity that characterizes the practice of behavioral medicine as well as a sampling of the literature that raises important issues. Ideally, this collection will be useful to the interested specialist, who will then be better informed and better prepared to take the next step. A second purpose is to provide a resource for the different professionals who desire to upgrade their competencies and to become familiar with yet other problems in behavioral medicine. We hope that such a reader will not only benefit from the material at hand but also find the volume useful as a bibliography.

Finally, we hope to provide the basis, support, and documentation that many readers require when they start up clinics, programs, or units in behavioral health. Although we have not belabored the rationale or justification for behavioral medicine, we trust that even a cursory review of this volume will validate this area quite easily. Again we emphasize that behavioral treatment, in its broadest meaning, is increasingly being seen as a development whose time has come. Our faith in its utility is not at all weakened in the face of a disorder or dysfunction having an obviously organic pathophysiology. This position has been argued by many other authors, but we hasten to remind our readers of the accumulation of scientific data that show biochemical and anatomical changes following behavioral alterations. Certainly, such laboratory demonstrations provide a strong argument and encouragement for the clinical counterparts. Even when evidence of a physiological response to a behavioral intervention cannot be produced for a given disorder, the remission, cure, or relief that behaviorally based programs have already provided has assured clinical behavioral medicine of a serious place in the health system.

Not every important topic within behavioral medicine will be found in this book. Among such topics are training and supervision, material development and public communication, fundamentals of theory and practice in test construction, basic theory and technique in behavioral modification and biofeedback, and drugs and psychopharmacology. In addition, the careful reader will realize that the organization of the book is only partially successful. A number of therapy issues are common to many of the chapters, including the use of placebos, compliance, depression, stress, self-reporting, secondary gain, and interaction of behaviors and symptoms with drugs and drug effects. Because of their great significance, some of these issues are allotted their own intensive discussion, but the especially important message is that there is more that unites problems and solutions in behavioral medicine than is suggested by the fragmentation introduced by using the classifications of the medical specialties. We invite each reader to formulate his or her own position on each of the issues and, above all, to be a partner in the efforts of the social sciences as they join other health specialties in providing better health and more effective relief from suffering.

1

Assessing
Individual
Health

Treatment never proceeds independently of assessment. Assessment in behavioral medicine includes conventional issues in psychology, psychometrics, and test construction as well as special features that accompany measurement in the traditional medical and health centers. This chapter outlines some of the problems involved in introducing behavior-based therapies for the treatment of non-mental-health disorders. Representative papers discuss selected symptom groups, such as pain and insomnia, as well as methodological isues and standardized test batteries. Proper appreciation for the value and limitations of current health measurement technologies is important both for the practicing clinician and for research or program development groups engaged in multidisciplinary treatment strategies.

Diagnostic and Assessment Criteria

Health complaints are often disguised and may present as mental health problems, and vice versa. Although psychology has made substantial gains in developing assessment procedures for educational and psychiatric objectives, comparable gains in assessing purely medical disorders lag far behind. Conventional wisdom is to adopt the compromise position of adapting procedures from the mental health arena and applying them to the treatment of various somatic disorders. Such adaptations include the use of MMPI, TAT, and other instruments. In addition, various self-report questionnaires and inventories are used together with observer ratings and automated recordings of behavioral events. The variety of methodologies reflects the complexity of the task facing the clinician, and every strategy must be evaluated separately for its strengths and weaknesses.

10

Psychological Profile of the Pain-Prone Individual

AUTHORS: Dietrich Blumer and Mary Heilbronn

PRECIS: Presentation of the psychological correlates of the distinct psychopathological condition termed the pain-prone disorder.

INTRODUCTION: Individuals suffering from chronic pain present themselves for treatment with complaints that do not follow neurological patterns, nor do these individuals respond to traditional interventions such as prescribed analgesics and surgery. Research examining the intrapsychic characteristics of these individuals has found that they possess neurotic conflicts centering on dependency and guilt. Many studies have concluded that psychogenic pain causes the underlying emotional disturbances. Other studies contend that since chronic pain sufferers usually deny overt depression, the physical symptoms are a displacement of underlying anxiety and guilt. Still others have emphasized the masochism and guilt present in these individuals as well as their tendencies to exhibit traits of depression, conversion hysteria, hypochondriasis, paranoia, schizophrenia, or combinations thereof. Yet all of this research has not done much to develop a clear profile of the pain-prone person that would establish the condition as a distinct nosological entity. The purpose of this article is to present the results of a study that address these issues of clarification and definition.

CLINICAL PROFILE: This profile was developed as a result of a 10-year study in which over 234 chronic-pain patients were observed and evaluated. The average age of these patients (149 females and 85 males) was almost 50 years. Most were blue-collar workers with an average educational level of 12.9 years.

All participants received a comprehensive battery of psychological tests including the Questionnaire of Pain Syndromes (QPS), which was developed by the authors. It contains short-answer questions relating to the patient's illness, habits, family situation (past and present), emotional life, and past and present activities. Other tests in the battery were MMPI, Rorschach, TAT, WAIS, Sentence Completion Test, and Szondi Experimental Diagnostics of Drives (SEDD). All participants were also interviewed.

Some of the salient results from the QPS indicated that the majority of patients reported that the pain experienced had a sudden onset and was not limited to a single focus. Over 90% of the patients reported pain in multiple locations. Also of interest is that 63% of the patients reported having a family member or close friend with a chronic physical handicap. More than half denied having any emotional difficulties; when such disturbances were acknowledged, the patient related it to his or her pain. Two thirds of these patients stated that they never lost control of their temper, and 64% said that they were rarely depressed.

The interview data indicated that these patients appeared to present a "supernormal" picture of mental health. In general, they were found to be stoic, overly controlled, and unable to verbalize affect. The MMPI revealed rigidity, lack of insight, needs to present a positive self-image, and a tendency to develop somatic symptoms under stress. The projective tests (Rorschach, TAT, and Sentence Completion) indicated definite depression in 83% of the patients along with substantial underlying rage, aggression, and dependency. Idealization of family members and sexual difficulties were also evidenced. The major defense mechanisms were denial and repression. The general profile on the SEDD suggested that pain-prone individuals had a greater tendency to be good-natured and conscientious than to be angry and vengeful. The prevalent ego patterns were those of inhibition and repression. Hypochondriasis, with its associated guilt-related anxiety, were also frequently found in these profiles.

The characteristic profile of the pain-prone disorder comprises two components, the clinical features and the psychological features. Clinical features center on overt symptomology, such as continuous pain, desire for surgery, denial of emotional and interpersonal difficulties, idealization of family relationships, excessive activity prior to the onset of pain (ergomania), excessive passivity after the onset of pain (anergia), and other major depressive traits (anhedonia and insomnia). The psychological features focus on intrapsychic dynamics. These include concealment and denial of conflict, infantile needs to be dependent and cared for, marked passivity and masochism, inability to cope with anger and hostility, and guilt complexes.

Of important therapeutic interest, the authors maintain that although these individuals must be prevented from undergoing surgery, they are not candidates for psychotherapy. It would be more beneficial if they could be managed in a pain clinic where the treatment deemphasizes pain, encourages physical activities, and avoids the use of analgesics. The prescription of antidepressants for outpatients can also benefit many individuals with chronic pain.

The pain-prone disorder is a type of depressive condition, as manifested in the clinical symptoms of anhedonia, frequent insomnia, despair, and a dominant preoccupation with somatic complaints. These individuals use pain as a displacement of internal conflicts and the resulting anxiety. The pain serves the additional purpose of masking these emotional disturbances and allowing the individual to maintain a positive self-image. It is these underlying aberrations that are presumed to be the primary disorder. The conflicts of guilt dependency and masochism are different aspects of this depression. Preliminary data from related research by the authors suggest that pain-prone individuals come from families whose members are alcoholic or have unipolar depressive disorders. The pain-prone condition can be categorized as a "depression spectrum" disorder. The high success rate in treating these individuals with antidepressant medications seems to support this position.

COMMENTARY: An important psychosocial aspect of the pain-prone disorder is that many of these patients have family models of pain and disability in their early life experiences. These models may be the only avenue of emotional expression available to these individuals. The results of this study are also significant in that they clearly indicate that these people are a homogenous and diagnostically unique group. Having a clear and accurate profile will facilitate the early detection of pain-prone individuals, which may help to prevent unnecessary and ineffective treatment interventions.

SOURCE: Blumer, D., and Heilbronn, M. "The Pain-Prone Disorder: A Clinical and Psychological Profile." *Psychosomatics,* 1981, *22,* 395-402.

Evaluation of Assessment Techniques for Insomnia

AUTHORS: Richard R. Bootzin and Mindy Engle-Friedman

PRECIS: Evaluation of the different assessment techniques used in the treatment of insomnia.

INTRODUCTION: Research has shown that insomniacs are not a homogenous group and that there are a multiplicity of factors involved in the cause, development, and maintenance of a disturbed sleep pattern. Each diagnostic category of insomnia has a related set of variables that can be measured in a variety of ways. Bootzin and Engle-Friedman present the advantages and disadvantages of different assessment methods, including self-reports, use of observer ratings, polysomnography, awakening thresholds, and next-day performance tests. All of these measures contribute important information about the differential diagnosis and treatment approach to a particular insomniac's condition.

DIAGNOSTIC MEASURES: A popular method of assessing sleep disturbances is the use of self-report inventories and sleep questionnaires. One of the advantages of this method is that a person's responses reflect how the individual perceives the problem, its severity, and the effectiveness of treatment, information that is important to both researcher and clinician. However, its disadvantages are substantial. Sleep inventories are retrospective and therefore prone to either conscious or unconscious distortion by the respondent. Correlations between these self-reports and other, more objective measures (such as EEGs) are often very low. Yet the authors contend that this type of measure does give sufficiently important information to justify its use, especially as a screening device or as a convergent check on treatment effectiveness.

Sleep diaries are another self-report measure, and they are more reliable and valid than sleep questionnaires. This method calls for subjects to monitor their sleeping patterns and are therefore prone to the same biases as other self-report measures. Yet this approach does offer an inexpensive, nonintrusive way to obtain sleep data from individuals in their own homes and beds.

The use of observers has also been widely used to assess an individual's sleep condition, both in an institutional setting and the patient's home. Some researchers contend that observer ratings are more valid than self-reports; however, available data on ratings by others show that reliability and validity are poor. Problems inherent in this approach include rater drift (which is a frequent problem) and the lack of agreement among raters of target behaviors. In institutional observation, observer availability is another concern. Nurses, who are responsible for these observations, are sometimes distracted from this duty by more pressing demands. Therefore, they are unable to make some crucial ratings. Videotaping a patient during sleep and having it rated at a later time can avoid this problem. These videotapes can also be used as training material for potential observers in an attempt to reduce rater drift.

Observers in the home are useful during treatment, since either a spouse or roommate is usually very aware of the patient's problem, its severity, and the amount of change that may occur as a result of treatment. They can serve, therefore, as a good convergent source of data about the success of treatment. However, spouses or roommates are usually not troubled by insomnia and may fall asleep long before the insomniac does. As a result, they may not be able to provide reliable information about a patient's total sleeping patterns during the night.

An objective measure of sleep depth is awakening thresh-

olds, the intensities of a stimulus (most commonly auditory)
needed to awaken a subject. Research has shown that these
thresholds vary reliably with the depth of sleep as defined by
EEG stages (with the exception of thresholds for REM sleep,
which is variable but equivalent to stage 2 thresholds). This apparent relationship has led to the development of other sleep-
related measures. However, the authors present three possible
limitations to this approach: First, the relationship between
stage of depth and awakening thresholds may not be as clearly
defined as currently assumed. Although an individual may be
more prone to respond to a stimulus at one stage than at another, subjects do respond to auditory stimuli in all stages of
sleep. Second, after repeated exposure to a stimulus, subjects
can learn to respond to less intense stimuli. Third, awakening
thresholds do not differ between good and poor sleepers. Subjective reports of sleep depth were better related to some aspects of sleep than were awakening thresholds.

One of the best measures of sleep is polysomnography,
although the authors stress that it is not the only true measure
of sleep. It consists of the continuous, all-night measuring of
EEG, electrooculogram, and EMG. This protocol has come to
be the standard with which other measures are compared. Research has shown that different stages of sleep can be discerned
from changes in EEG patterns. Research has begun to use the
EEG as a means of ascertaining treatment outcome. Polysomnography offers some substantial advantages. Primarily, it is the
only way to accumulate detailed information on a variety of
sleep variables continuously during an individual's sleep time.
This method is also the best way to rule out physical disorders
that may underlie the insomnia. Finally, it enables one to discriminate between individuals with subjective complaints of insomnia and those with physiologically documented sleep disturbances. Some of the drawbacks to this method center mainly on logistical issues. In particular, the equipment is expensive,
an enormous amount of sleep data is generated (which can
make its interpretation and analysis difficult), and subjects must
become adapted to the laboratory environment in order to be
examined. On this final point, research has indicated that sleep

can become stimulus controlled. Individuals who have a sleep problem at home may not experience one during laboratory testing. However, there are methods available for home polysomnography, which may circumvent this latter difficulty.

A final approach outlined in this paper deals with next-day effects. These are objective tests given to the patient after a night's sleep. These are basically indirect measures in that they do not actually focus on actual sleep patterns and are mostly tests of performance skills or affective states. The authors state that this is not a frequently used approach to insomnia, even though the degree to which poor sleep interferes with a person's daily functioning level is part of the insomniac's presenting complaint. These tasks can be useful in determining the effect that sleep deprivation has on an individual's general arousal level and performance abilities.

All of these methods can contribute vital information about an individual's complaint of insomnia. All of the data compiled from these methods are complementary and provide insights into the condition and therefore are useful for differential diagnosis and treatment approaches. The measures can help clarify not only the physiological concomitants of insomnia but also the possible cognitive and perceptual problems that may be associated with the disorder.

COMMENTARY: Bootzin and Engle-Friedman provide a detailed review of both the methods used to assess insomnia as well as the practical and theoretical issues that are related to the methods. Any assessment approach has advantages and disadvantages that must be considered before any method is applied. This article is useful in presenting the strengths and weaknesses inherent in insomnia research. The evaluation of physiological measures, self-reports, observer ratings, and objective tests within insomnia research have broad and far-ranging implications for many areas of behavioral medicine.

SOURCE: Bootzin, R. R., and Engle-Friedman, M. "The Assessment of Insomnia." *Behavioral Assessment,* 1981, *3,* 107–126.

Environmental Bias in Behavioral Observations

AUTHORS: Thomas R. Cunningham and Roland G. Tharp

PRECIS: Examining the bias imposed by unrelated environmental stimuli upon the accuracy and reliability of behavioral observations.

INTRODUCTION: Behavioral observation has become an increasingly popular form of assessment in behavioral medicine. However, research has shown that there are factors that influence the ratings of observers, thus confounding pre- and post-treatment evaluations. There are five general areas of biases that affect observer reliabilities: induced expectancies and feedback, the complexity of the observation method and the behaviors to be coded, observer drift, the nature of observer training and reliability assessment, and the observational medium (such as videotape or direct observation). Much research in locating possible sources of observer error has centered on manipulating observers and subjects and the environments in which they are presented for observation. The present study manipulated two different modes of observation: global (in which the observer watches a subject for a period of time and then makes an assessment after the observation) and systematic (in which the observer checks for the target behavior at fixed intervals throughout the observation period). Also manipulated were the quality and quantity of behaviors exhibited by nontarget individuals in the same setting. The two major hypotheses were: (1) Observers' perceptions of the target person can be manipulated by varying the behaviors of others in the observational setting, and (2) the type of observational method employed influences perceptions of the target person.

METHOD: One hundred and twelve subjects, 40 males and 72 females, participated in this study as observers. They ranged in age from 18 to 35 years (mean age was 21.4).

The stimulus materials for observation were five black-and-white, silent, 10-minute videotapes of three third-grade boys at their desks. For each tape, the target boy sat in between the other two boys and spent 50% of his time working on a task, 25% quietly off-task, and the remaining 25% disruptively off-task. On-task behaviors were operationalized as looking at his workbook and either reading or writing while holding a pencil in his hand—anything not meeting these criteria was defined as off-task. Off-task behaviors were differentiated between quiet off-task (simple inattention to work materials while the boy was at his desk and making no gross body movements) and disruptive off-task (gross body movements such as banging hands or books on the desk and pretending to play).

Different behavioral environments were created around the target boy. This was accomplished by having the two non-target boys follow different scripts. On two of the five tapes, the nontarget boys were on-task 85% of the time; on two other tapes, they were on-task only 15% of the time. In one of each of these two pairs of tapes, the nontarget boys engaged in quiet off-task activities; on the other pair, they engaged in disruptive off-task activities. A fifth videotape was used for practice and shown to all subjects. In this tape the three boys acted much like the target boy. The sound of the boys was not recorded for any of the tapes, but an audio track was added later that emitted signals every 5 seconds to denote an observational period for subjects in the systematic observation group. The boys' scripts called for them to engage in on-task behaviors for durations between 15 seconds and 2 minutes. Intervals of on- and off-task behaviors were randomly arranged. Also, within each tape, the two nontarget boys engaged in the same amount of on-task behavior and the same kind of off-task behaviors as each other, but their scripts were staggered so that they did not appear to be moving in unison.

Two observational modes were manipulated. Half the subjects used a global method, which required them to watch the entire videotape before estimating the percentage of on-task time each boy exhibited. The other half of the participants used a systematic approach, where they determined if the boy was either on- or off-task every 5 seconds. They observed all three boys in sequence; the first 5-second period they were to focus

on the boy on the left, the next 5 seconds the boy in the middle, and so on. This study used a three-way factorial design with
two levels of each independent variable: quantity of on-task behavior (85% versus 15%) × quality of off-task behavior by the
nontarget boys (quiet versus disruptive) × observational method
(global versus systematic).

There were two dependent measures, which were based
on the observers' estimates of the target boy's on-task behavior.
The first measure was accuracy. This was determined by computing the number of percentage points that an observer's estimates differed from 50%, the true value of the target child's on-
task behavior. Reliability was determined by computing the
number of percentage points that an observer's estimate differed from the mean estimate of all subjects in the same experimental condition. Accuracy .and reliability scores for individual
subjects were correlated at +.662.

A three-way analysis of variance yielded a significant
main effect for observational method and a significant interaction between quality of off-task behavior and observational
method. A Neuman-Keuls analysis yielded the following conclusions: (1) The systematic observation group had almost
equally accurate estimates of percentage of on-task behaviors
regardless of the quality of the off-task behaviors of the nontarget boys; (2) those in the global observation group were
much less accurate than those using the systematic observation
method; and (3) observers using the global method were far less
accurate in estimating the percentage of on-task behavior when
the quality of off-task behavior in the nontarget boys was quiet
rather than disruptive.

The authors contend that global observation was not only
less accurate and reliable than systematic observation but that
those in the global condition were influenced by a "pattern" of
bias, which was influenced by the social context of the target
boy. In other words, there was a major contrast effect present
in the global observation group. This effect evidenced itself in
the two global observation groups when the nontarget boys
were disruptive during their off-task periods. Judges under these
conditions estimated the target boy's percentage of on-task time

more accurately than did judges under the two global conditions where the nontarget boys were quiet during their off-task
periods. The mean estimates of percentage of on-task behavior
were 40.93 and 53.79 versus 29.43 and 32.93, respectively. The
authors hypothesize that the judges in the global observation
conditions saw the disruptive boys as being worse and the target
child as better. When the nontarget boys were quietly off-task,
such a contrast was not present and therefore the percentage of
on-task behavior was greatly underestimated. No clear pattern
of bias was detected for the systematic observation group.

The authors argue for the robustness of systematic observation in preventing any biasing effect due to the behaviors
of the nontarget boys. The authors also note that it was not
necessary to train extensively the observers in the systematic
observation group so that they could obtain the reported sound
level of accuracy and reliability.

COMMENTARY: It appears that in observing specific behaviors
in a particular individual, people who use a global approach depend on the total social context within which the individual is
observed. This study has shown that accuracy is enhanced as obvious discrepancies between the behaviors of the target and the
nontarget persons increase. Systematic observers are not as dependent on the entire social context for their evaluations. These
observers focus on specific stimuli within the social environment. An important variable is the amount of time elapsed
before an evaluation is made. Global observers made their evaluations after viewing a 10-minute videotape. The systematic observers made their evaluations every 5 seconds. The amount of
information an individual must retain and sort through before
making an evaluation may play a critical role in creating observer bias. Finally, two important procedures were used in this
study that are essential to any successful use of observational
methods. The first is the standardization of the vocabulary of
the ratings, that is, the exact meaning of each term (such as *off-
task* and *disruptive*). The second is the clear and exact opera-
tionalizing of the behaviors to be evaluated (in this case, on-task
behaviors being defined as looking at a workbook and either

reading or writing while holding a pencil). These considerations take on special importance for many activities in behavioral medicine. Many situations demand the discrimination of symptom behaviors such as pain, sleep, asthma, and other conditions. Appropriate diagnostic decisions and treatment designs require the precondition of unbiased observations.

SOURCE: Cunningham, T. R., and Tharp, R. G. "The Influence of Settings on Accuracy and Reliability of Behavioral Observation." *Behavioral Assessment,* 1981, *3,* 67–78.

A Diagnostic Model of Pain

AUTHORS: Allan A. Maltbie, Jesse O. Cavenar, Elliot B. Hammett, and John L. Sullivan

PRECIS: Presentation of a therapeutically useful diagnostic model of the pain process.

INTRODUCTION: The experience of pain, especially chronic pain, results from the activation of an individual's physiological and psychological systems, which work together to find relief from the noxious stimulus and to develop appropriate coping strategies. It is proposed that there are three components to this model: a reality trauma (physical or emotional), an affective-cognitive reaction, and a coping reaction (both conscious and unconscious). This model synthesizes the mind and body processes by illustrating how physical and psychological "injuries" can both initiate and/or maintain the pain process. In approaching the pain patient, all levels of the pain process, both psychological and physical, must be considered independently and jointly. The authors contend that pain can no longer be conceptualized in terms of physical injury alone. Consideration must be given to both the patient's reaction to the pain and the role that the pain plays in protecting or maintaining the individual in his or her social environment.

COMPOSITE MODEL: The first component to this model is the reality trauma. The stimulus can be either a physical injury or an emotional loss, such as the death of a close family member or spouse. Interfaced with the noxious stimuli present in the perceptual field is a gate or threshold mechanism that screens out relatively unimportant stimuli or responds to them reflexively, without activating other components of the system. Thus, minor irritants are easily tolerated without distracting a person from other activities. When a stimulus is of sufficient intensity, it breaks through this gate and creates an afferent impulse that is perceived as a hurt. This hurt in turn activates the second component of the model, the affective-cognitive reaction.

At this level, the individual recalls similar past experiences in an attempt to develop a defensive response to the pain and to eradicate it. When the afferent impulse persists in spite of efforts to eliminate it, an escalation of the affect may occur. Associated memories and worries emerge over the pain. The person manifests anxiety in anticipation of further pain, which serves to create additional anxiety. The protracted afferent impulses escalate into a repetitive cycle of pain-related memories and associated anxieties, which can become all consuming and drain the individual of the ability to cope with the pain. In emotionally healthy individuals, even after a protracted pain experience, the cessation of afferent impulses is followed by a de-escalation of this cycle of affective expectation. The authors equate this natural process with Freud's pleasure principle. The individual attempts to achieve a state of psychic equilibrium, minimizing the energy expended for pain defense and maximizing free, adaptive energy.

The third component is the coping reactions to pain, which may be both conscious and unconscious. It is a defense process whereby the individual behaves so as to avoid the pain-producing stimuli (fight or flight reaction) and adapts internal psychic structures to establish a new dynamic equilibrium. In the case of acute pain, the reaction is one of avoiding or eliminating pain.

Chronic pain often accompanies the emergence of infantile, dependent types of behavior and is often associated with decreases in self-esteem. This process may not be reversible when afferent pain impulses cease. Whether it is reversible largely depends on premorbid personality characteristics. In approaching the chronic pain patient, it is important to assess the role that the pain serves in the person's defensive coping structures. Pain or illness may bring out unconscious latent drives, provoke a neurosis, or become an integral part of a preexisting neurotic or psychotic adaptational organization. The experience of pain may provide a particular interpersonal status with which the person feels secure; the removal of the pain may jeopardize that position. The pain may also serve as a buffer, protecting the individual from confronting personal inadequacies. The inability to perform tasks is then blamed on the pain condition rather than on one's shortcomings. Central to these illustrations is the maintenance of psychic equilibrium through the use of pain. Loss of the pain disorder is seen as a threat, perhaps depriving the person of a useful defense mechanism.

Other research has identified six conditions characteristic of persons vulnerable to protracted pain: (1) the prominence of guilt and the tendency to use pain as a way to relieve guilt feelings; (2) childhood history of pain regularly associated with disciplinary measures; (3) an inability to directly express anger and a disposition to turn anger in against the self; (4) a history of defeat and suffering and an inability to tolerate success; (5) strong, unconscious sexual conflicts that appear symbolically as pain; and (6) a reflection of loss or potential loss of another person. In these six conditions, pain maintains support for preexisting behavior patterns. For such patients, adaptation to life's demands requires a chronic pain perception, with or without a physical component.

Any experience with extended pain requires some type of adaptation, regardless of whether the patient seeks relief or whether an afferent pain source is located. The authors contend that the best measure of the patient's success in coping with the pain is to examine the effectiveness of adaptation and coping as reflected by self-esteem, appropriate independent functioning, and interpersonal relationships. More sensitive indicators are the ability to work, the quality of family and sexual relationships, and the ability to sleep. The more fully these capacities are actualized in a chronic pain patient's daily activities, the more successful the adaptation.

Each of the three levels of the pain experience deserves specific diagnostic and therapeutic considerations. Because of the intimate interrelationships between physical and psychological processes, one can no longer evaluate the effects of these dimensions independently of the others. In the chronic pain sufferer, all aspects of the pain experience must be evaluated—physical, intrapsychic, and psychosocial—as well as the interactions among them. Similarly, clinical interventions must address all levels of the pain experience.

COMMENTARY: This article presents an important reaffirmation of the reality of an interlocking psychophysical system associated with the pain process. Of importance is not the discrete components but rather the functioning of the system as a whole. This model emphasizes the role that pain plays in maintaining adaptational equilibria. Consequently, the design of treatment programs for chronic pain patients should address the various components of the pain experience. The authors support the use of an interdisciplinary, organized team approach to treatment, in which the various specialties can articulate more fully the problems at different levels and provide appropriate interventions.

SOURCE: Maltbie, A. A., Cavenar, J. O., Hammett, E. B., and Sullivan, J. L. "A Diagnostic Approach to Pain." *Psychosomatics*, 1978, *19*, 359–366.

Assessment Issues

AUTHORS: Dennis C. Russo, Bruce L. Bird, and Bruce J. Masek

PRECIS: A discussion of issues relating to the reliability and validity of dependent measures that are derived from behavioral and biomedical technologies.

INTRODUCTION: The development of behavioral medicine is characterized by attempts to integrate behavioral and biomedical knowledge and techniques to develop more effective strategies for the prevention, diagnosis, treatment, and rehabilitation of health care patients. The authors contend that for behavioral methods to be accepted within medicine, it will first be necessary to demonstrate a compatibility between behavioral and traditional medical assessment practices. The authors focus on the reliability and validity in selected assessment areas (for example, diagnosis and treatment outcomes) and the status of reliability and validity within each discipline. Because of philosophical and procedural differences, reliability is of greater concern to behavioral science, and validity to medicine.

RELIABILITY: Considered are three reliability problems for behavioral techniques that can have an important effect on medical research and treatment. The first centers on poor test-retest reliabilities in presumed objective measures of physiological status. The authors cite as an example chemical assays used to determine drug levels, a technique that heavily relies on the proficiency of technicians. Research has shown that the results of such assays can vary from one hospital to another, thus confounding outcome measures of treatment effects. This same research suggests that behavioral techniques for increasing observer reliabilities (in this case, of the technician) can be used to increase the accuracy of such procedures.

A second problem area focuses on the reliability of assessing the influence of behavior on disease as well as on behaviorally expressed symptoms. Problems here may relate to the influence of personality variables on the course of a disease or the selection of a treatment program. Another problem is the utility of drawing on behavioral performance to locate organic dysfunction.

The third area concerns reliability in the context of compliance behaviors. Noncompliance with medication regimens is a pervasive medical problem, and researchers may find solutions to it through developments in behavioral technologies. Self-report measures are the popular medical approach for assessing compliance, but research has shown that they are the least reliable. Traditionally, the most objective method is the use of blood or urine analyses to determine levels of the drug. Also used are tracer substances and the metabolites of drugs. Yet, as mentioned earlier, there are limitations to such assaying procedures. Also, not all drugs can be easily detected by such methods, and it is difficult to specify therapeutic levels. Bioassay techniques do not allow a detailed analysis of adherence to dosage schedules. The introduction of behavioral techniques can help to increase the reliability of compliance assessment. Such technologies include actual observation of medication ingestion, penalty procedures, and chemical tracers. The authors contend that behavioral assessment procedures can make three significant contributions to understanding drug effects in medicine: (1) making the determination of therapeutic drug levels more precise; (2) making the results of clinical drug trials more valid by enhancing patient compliance; and (3) providing direct evaluation of relevant, behavioral parameters when studying psychopharmacologic drugs.

VALIDITY: Traditional medical criteria can be incorporated into behavioral approaches to provide new measures of outcomes, to validate behavioral outcomes, and to make the measurement of treatment effects more precise.

The authors suggest that the traditional behavioral dimensions of frequency, duration, and intensity of overt responses may be inadequate indicators of outcome. Such gross assessment variables may not always allow direct observation of the psychophysiological process of interest. The authors provide two cases involving urinary retention that illustrate this point.

They point out how existing medical procedures can be adapted to serve as a dependent variable that is more sensitive and relevant to behavioral treatment methods for this disorder.

Medical treatments can also be valuable in validating behavioral treatment effects. An example given by the authors relates to "observer calibration," which employed EEG readings to validate a behavioral treatment of seizures in a 4½-year-old girl. Behavioral medicine can also be useful in validating medical interventions. Significant contributions can be made by clearly defining homogenous patient categories and the functional significance of behavioral symptoms. Clearer assessment and nosological systems will greatly aid in selecting and refining treatment interventions.

The combination of behavioral medicine and traditional medical approaches can help develop new conceptualizations of disease processes. Of particular interest is the area of chronic pain. The authors trace the growing interest of medical practitioners in pain management. This interest has been prompted by the increasing inability of medically based treatments (such as analgesics and nerve blocks) to provide relief as well as the recognition of a complex interaction between pharmacologic, physiological, and psychological factors in the perception and experience of pain. Using the technologies of behavior medicine assessment adds a meaningful and new perspective. Diagnosis can be facilitated by manipulating behavioral or environmental variables. Information gathered from behavioral medicine assessment can also be useful in detailing the relative contribution of various factors to the etiology of the presenting complaint. This information coupled with medical data can be useful in making more accurate diagnoses.

Areas of interest in the field of behavioral medicine center on the assessment of stimulus and response generalization. The authors highlight two important issues. The first concerns the selection and measurement of various responses (for example, behavioral and psychophysiological) and the determination of their general and specific effects. In designing economical therapies, it is necessary to improve our understanding of how a particular treatment will affect a patient. The second issue addresses the need to ensure the generalization of a treatment effect beyond the treatment setting. The generalization and maintenance of treatment effects are major problems for behavioral scientists.

COMMENTARY: The potential for interdisciplinary cooperation in refining reliability and validity is sure to provide new advances in the etiology, pathology, treatment, and rehabilitation of disease. As the authors point out, there are differences in the philosophical, assessment, and therapeutic approaches between behavioral medicine and traditional medicine. Yet these differences can be important in developing new conceptualizations and approaches in both fields.

SOURCE: Russo, D. C., Bird, B. L., and Masek, B. J. "Assessment Issues in Behavioral Medicine." *Behavioral Assessment,* 1980, *1,* 1-18.

Diagnostic Categorization of Persistent Insomnia

AUTHORS: Frank J. Zorick, Thomas Roth, Kristyna M. Hartze, Paul M. Piccione, and Edward J. Stepanski

PRECIS: Clear differentiation among various sufferers of insomnia on the basis of polysomnographic recordings, the Cornell Medical Index, and the MMPI.

INTRODUCTION: Insomnia is characterized by difficulty in initiating and maintaining sleep. Individuals who present themselves with this complaint are frequently treated with sedative-hypnotic medications that provide relief from the disturbed sleep patterns. However, the use of chemotherapy presents long-term health risks to the individuals. The excessive use of sedatives among most insomniacs emphasizes the imprecision in the diagnosis and treatment of their condition. Other research has shown that insomnia may be associated with a variety of psychological and physiological conditions. The authors contend that the application of the broad label *insomnia* obscures etiological factors that may be treatable without medication, the use of which in certain circumstances may exacerbate the patient's problem. The purpose of this research was to differentiate insomniacs on the basis of psychological characteristics and polysomnographic recordings.

METHOD: Eighty-four insomniac patients and twenty normal subjects (comparison group) were used. None of the normal subjects had a history of sleep disturbances. All subjects completed a sleep disturbance questionnaire, the Cornell Medical Index, and the MMPI. All subjects were given at least one night of polysomnographic recording. The measurements used for analysis included an EEG (C3-Oz), an electrooculogram (EOG), and an electromyogram (EMG). Airflow was monitored with oral and nasal thermistors, heart rate was recorded with a V5 EKG lead, and EMG activity was measured with electrodes placed over the right and left anterior tibialis muscle. Only the first-night recordings were analyzed. The tibialis EMG and respiration recordings were evaluated by two clinical polysomnographers, who made a consensual diagnosis. On the basis of the entire clinical evaluation (including interview, questionnaires, and nocturnal polysomnography), each patient (not including the comparison group) received a specific diagnosis. Patients were classified according to the following problems: a psychophysiological problem ($n = 5$), a psychiatric disorder ($n = 12$), a disorder related to drug or alcohol use ($n = 10$), respiratory impairment ($n = 6$), nocturnal myoclonus ($n = 9$), restless leg syndrome ($n = 9$), a disorder associated with medical disease ($n = 6$), atypical polysomnographic features ($n = 4$), subjective complaints without objective polysomnographic findings ($n = 16$), circadian rhythm disorder ($n = 7$), and no problem (normal subjects) ($n = 20$).

There were six polysomnographic parameters against

which all diagnostic categories were measured: total sleep time, wake before sleep, wake during sleep, wake after sleep, percent awake, and percent stage 1 sleep.

The ten diagnostic categories were subsequently divided into "good sleep" and "poor sleep" groups on the basis of their similarity to the normal comparison group on the six polysomnographic parameters. The poor-sleep group consisted of patients in the psychiatric disorder, restless leg syndrome, and respiratory impairment categories (they differed from the normal group on at least two of the six parameters). The good-sleep group consisted of patients in the nocturnal myoclonus, subjective complaint, atypical polysomnographic feature, and circadian rhythm disturbance classification. Patients in these categories did not show any significant differences from the normal comparison group. The three remaining diagnostic categorizations—psychophysiological disorder, disorder related to drug or alcohol use, and disorder associated with medical disease—were not definitively placed in either group since they varied from the comparison group on just one of the parameters.

In the poor-sleep group, patients in the psychiatric disorder category appeared to have the most disturbed sleep of all; they had less total sleep time, more percent awake, more awake before sleep, and more awake after sleep than the two good-sleep groups. Those in the nocturnal myoclonus, subjective complaint, and circadian rhythm disorder diagnostic categories had consistently better sleep than patients in any other group.

With regard to the MMPI findings, the most frequently elevated scale was the depression scale (a T score of 70 or above on any scale was considered to be elevated in this study). Patients in the psychiatrc disorder, disorder related to drug or alcohol use, and atypical polysomnographic feature categories were significantly different from the normal subjects on this measure. No such differences were found in the remaining seven diagnostic categories. According to the authors, these results suggest that the presence of elevated MMPI scales in large numbers of insomniacs may reflect abnormalities characteristic of certain diagnostic categories (or even subcategories) but that psychological distress may not be characteristic of all individuals suffering from insomnia.

The preeminent finding of this study was that individuals complaining of insomnia in some diagnostic categories may experience disturbed nocturnal sleep while others may not, thus confirming the premise that insomniacs do not constitute a clinically homogenous group. Furthermore, the categories may be differentiated from each other on the basis of polysomnographic and psychological features. The MMPI is useful in diagnosing some categories of insomniacs, for example, the psychiatric disorder, disorder relating to drug and alcohol use, and atypical polysomnographic feature categories. Zorick and others stress that by overemphasizing the psychological profile of an individual, other salient features of the person's disorder can be overlooked; consequently, one should not assume that all individuals suffering from insomnia are psychologically troubled. Thus there is a need for a broad-based approach to the differential diagnosis, evaluation, and treatment of insomnia.

It is noted that muscle relaxants and antidepressants are indicated for treating patients in the diagnostic categories of nocturnal myoclonus, restless leg syndrome, and atypical polysomnographic features. Sedatives, on the other hand, are of no therapeutic value for patients with persistent subjective complaints of insomnia that are unaccompanied by objective findings.

COMMENTARY: This study specifies many salient factors relevant to the diagnosis and treatment of insomnia. The diagnostic categorizations are direct and center on the overt psychophysiological features of the individual's condition. It is also interesting to note the perspective taken by these researchers, namely, that insomnia is a symptom rather than a specific disorder. This diagnostic system is useful in indicating whether the insomnia is of a primary sleep disorder (one that has an organic etiology) or a secondary disorder (in which there is an underlying psychological difficulty). In either case, it is the underlying condition that must be treated rather than the symptom alone.

SOURCE: Zorick, F. J., Roth, T., Hartze, K. M., Piccione, P. M., and Stepanski, E. J. "Evaluation and Diagnosis of Persistent Insomnia." *American Journal of Psychiatry,* 1981, 6, 769–773.

Additional Readings

Armentrout, D. P., Moore, J. E., Parker, J. C., Hewett, J. E., and Felz, C. "Pain-Patient MMPI Subgroups: The Psychological Dimensions of Pain." *Journal of Behavioral Medicine,* 1982, 5, 201–211.

The MMPI and an extensive pain history questionnaire were given to 240 male chronic pain patients. Three distinct pain profiles were noted: (1) a normal profile, (2) a profile revealing the hypochondriasis configuration, and (3) highly elevated scores on the psychopathological dimensions. These three groups did not differ on variables such as age, income, IQ, type of pain, or duration of pain, but did differ on the pain history questions relating to pain severity and the effect of pain on their lives. The latter group reported significantly more distress than the hypochondriasis group, which in turn reported higher levels of distress than the normal group. The authors contend that these results have an important bearing on differential treatment approaches for these groups and are likely to be important in the design of effective pain treatment programs.

Kremer, E. F., Block, A., and Gaylor, M. S. "Behavioral Approaches to Treatment of Chronic Pain: The Inaccuracy of Patient Self-Report Measures." *Archives of Physical Medicine and Rehabilitation,* 1981, 62, 188–191.

This report examines the accuracy of patient self-reports of physical activity, social behavior, and pain intensity. While they were making their ratings, the four patients were unobtrusively observed hourly by staff, who rated the behaviors of interest. The results indicated that the patients reported significantly lower levels of physical activity and social behavior than observed by the staff. The authors contend that this under-reporting of "well" behaviors results from patients' selective attention (remembering) to those events that are most compatible with their perceived role. Because of such a possible bias, the authors suggest that determining the effectiveness of an intervention is best done by the use of systematic observational data rather than by patient self-report.

Snyder, D. K., and Power, D. G. "Empirical Descriptors of Un-elevated MMPI Profiles Among Chronic Pain Patients: A Typological Approach." *Journal of Clinical Psychology,* 1981, *37,* 602-607.

A most difficult task for a clinician is to evaluate the contribution of psychological factors to a patient's pain disability. This is especially so for patients with unelevated MMPI profiles in whom physical findings are minimal or absent. These authors applied a multivariate, quantitative taxonomic procedure to such a group of patients to delineate homogeneous subgroupings of chronic patients. The results indicate five separate subgroupings of patients. Only one group, which comprised but 9% of the total sample, was found to be free of significant psychological components in pain behavior. The most obvious issue these findings raise is the need to develop more precise diagnostic and assessment criteria for evaluating pain patients. The broad categorizations that now exist cannot make the necessary discriminations needed to provide effective intervention.

Tursky, B., Jamner, L. D., and Friedman, R. "The Pain Perception Profile: A Psychophysical Approach to the Assessment of Pain Report." *Behavior Therapy,* 1982, *13,* 376-394.

These authors contend that current methods to assess clinical pain provide only qualitative information about the pain experience. This report presents a quantitative, multidimensional method for assessing pain. The Tursky Pain Perception Profile consists of four parts: (1) measures of sensory threshold and verbal descriptions of pain, (2) a measure of an individual's ability to estimate the magnitude of controlled nociceptive stimuli, (3) quantified pain descriptors, and (4) a pain diary format useful for ongoing assessment. This profile can provide clinicians with a wide variety of information about the pain experience that is both reliable and objective. Such information can assist therapists in making more accurate diagnoses and in developing better evaluations of treatment.

Statistical Methods

Clinical studies often present staggering problems for traditional statisticians. The small sample sizes of special clinical populations may be inadequate for many popular tests and models; error inflation is a constant danger; univariate analyses are used more because of unfamiliarity than because of conscious design; and even a strategy for testing significance is too often selected because of inertia and the lack of any clear alternative. Recent developments have come to the aid of the health scientist and practitioner. Alternative (and often quite simple) solutions are available and are particularly useful for various research efforts in behavioral medicine.

Methodological Issues in the Design
of Nontherapeutic Trials

AUTHORS: Carol Buck and Allan Donner

PRECIS: Conventional statistical designs that were applied to drug trials need to be revised considerably when applied to non-therapeutic trials.

COMMENTARY: Extending design methodology from clinical drug trials to controlled trials of surgical procedures requires substantial revision. When the experimentation is not therapeutic, the problems become greater still. One class of nontherapeutic interventions concerns prevention and life-style—exercise programs, eating habits, and smoking, for example. A second class concerns innovations in the delivery of health care.

Partly out of necessity and partly due to administrative matters, it is often compelling to randomize groups of people rather than individuals. This raises the problem of reduced sample size imposed by group randomization. Another problem involves a control group. Usually there is no established method of intervention—and no suitable placebo—with which to compare the experimental strategy. The decision whether to have one or more control groups is a complex one that depends upon the availability of subjects, the importance of identifying a Hawthorne effect, and the extent to which the latter can be controlled analytically by covariance adjustment. Finally, the issue of blindness (being unaware of the particular nature of the therapy) is often difficult to ensure for either the patient or the therapist.

There is no simple analog of the techniques for achieving blindness in drug trials where identical placebo and experimental medications are available. The problem is made easier, however, by separating the two purposes for which blindness is desired, namely, the control of nonspecific responses and the control of subject expectancies.

This paper highlights several considerations that are important not only for the researcher but also for the clinical practitioner. For the latter, many decisions about the revision of therapeutic procedures, the termination of treatment, and general confidence in the reliability of behavioral protocols are an integral part of the treatment process.

SOURCE: Buck, C., and Donner, A. "The Design of Controlled Experiments in the Evaluation of Nontherapeutic Interventions." *Journal of Chronic Diseases*, 1982, *35*, 531–538.

Indexing the Disease Activity of Rheumatoid Arthritis

AUTHORS: R. K. Mallya and B. E. W. Mace

PRECIS: A simple multiple-variable method for grading the objective and subjective status of rheumatoid arthritis (RA).

COMMENTARY: Therapeutic criteria for evaluating RA patients have always been imprecise, time consuming, and impractical. The present report describes the combination of two objective parameters (hemoglobin level and sedimentation rate), two semiobjective parameters (grip strength and articular index), and two subjective parameters (morning stiffness and pain-scale rating) to provide a single index of disease activity (IDA). In essence, the procedure consists of grouping the respective measures into four possible categories (grade levels). A single person's index is computed by (1) converting the dependent-variable measure to a grade level score and (2) summing and averaging the six grade levels to yield the IDA. IDAs are themselves assignable to one of four grade levels, yielding a mean disease activity grade (MDAG). It is important to note that the IDA correlates strongly with all the facets used and with other measures that are occasionally used in rheumatological assessments but not included in the construction of this index (such as pain grade, on-set of fatigue, platelet count, and the Rose-Waaler test score). Although the procedure does not rely on multivariate analysis procedures and is based on much subjectivity in grouping and scoring, it does suggest a direction for developing similar instru-ments that would be easy to use and have wide applicability.

SOURCE: Mallya, R. K., and Mace, B. E. W. "The Assessment of Disease Activity in Rheumatoid Arthritis Using a Multi-variate Analysis." *Rheumatology and Rehabilitation,* 1981, *20,* 14–17.

<hr>

Signal Detection Analysis
of Myofascial Pain Dysfunction

AUTHORS: Robert M. Malow, Laurence Grimm, and Ronald E. Olson

PRECIS: The use of a signal detection theory analysis to deter-mine differences in pain perception between myofascial pain dysfunction (MPD) syndrome patients and normals.

INTRODUCTION: MPD syndrome is best understood as a con-dition that results from tension due to emotional stress and anx-iety. The purpose of this study was to determine if there are differences between MPD sufferers and normals in their ability to discriminate between sensations and in their tendency to re-port different sensations as painful. These behaviors are func-tions of both sensory-perceptual variables and attitudinal, judg-mental, and learning (response) factors. Research has shown that MPD patients have a greater reaction to pain than normals, but the extent to which this is due to sensory or response vari-ables is not fully known. Traditional psychophysiological tech-niques do not fully permit one to discriminate between these two aspects of pain perception. However, the use of a signal detection measurement approach would allow such discrimination and thereby enable a more detailed analysis. In research on pain perception, signal detection theory would aid in analyzing data produced when subjects rate the painfulness of stimuli of differing intensity. The stimuli are usually presented in pairs, the more intense stimulus being the signal event. It is characterized as being rated as painful on a large number of trials. The less intense stimulus is the noise event and is characterized as not being rated as painful over a large number of trials. Also examined in this study was the relationship between pain thresholds and anxiety and social desirability. MPD patients scoring high on social desirability may be altering their behavior to comply with what they perceive to be appropriate behavior for a pain patient.

METHOD: Subjects consisted of twenty normal undergraduate, female psychology majors with a mean age of 19 years. The MPD sufferers consisted of twenty female patients with a mean age of 28 years. The severity, location, duration, and experience of pain was homogenous for the patient group.

The apparatus employed was a Forgione-Barber Focal Pressure Stimulator. This device has a dull Lucite edge that applies a continuous pressure to the second phalanx of any finger. It produces a slight pressure that gradually builds into a dull, aching pain. The rate at which this sensation becomes painful can be varied by placing different weights on the apparatus, which in turn changes the intensity of the pressure applied to the finger. For the purpose of this research, a 100-gram (heavy) weight, an 85-gram (medium) weight, and a 70-gram (light) weight were used to vary pressure intensity. The weights were visually identical so that subjects could not tell which weight was attached to the apparatus on a given trial. Other research has shown that this device can produce sensations that very closely resemble clinical pain.

All subjects were seen individually and required to complete the Kubrick Anxiety Scale, Spielberger State-Trait Anxiety Scale, and the Marlowe-Crowne Scale of Social Desirability. They were also given two tasks that involved the pressure stimulator. First was the rating-scale task. On each of six experimental trials (there were two additional practice trials), subjects rated their reactions to the stimulation on a 10-point scale, with 0 meaning no sensation and 9 meaning definite pain. Ratings were given every 5 seconds until either the subject gave a rating of 9 or 60 seconds had elapsed. Over these six trials, both the finger stimulated and the weight used were varied.

The second task was a forced-choice discrimination test. Here, the pain stimulator apparatus was used on subjects for eight trials. On each trial, the light weight was applied to one finger and the heavy weight was applied to the same finger on the opposite hand for 5 seconds. At the end of a trial, subjects were asked to determine which hand was stimulated by the heavy weight. The order of stimulation was counterbalanced according to hand, weight, and finger.

Pain thresholds were calculated for both groups according to the number of seconds required for a subject to give a rating of definite pain (a 9 on the rating scale). This served as a dependent measure for a multivariate analysis of variance. It was found that MPD patients had significantly lower pain thresholds than normals. This was true over all trials of the pain stimulation.

MPD patients were found to have a significantly lower sensitivity to pain and a significantly greater tendency to report pain than normal subjects. The results of the discrimination task also supported the conclusion that MPD patients are less able to discriminate among painful stimuli.

Of all the personality measures used, only one yielded a significant relationship, namely, social desirability. MPD patients with high social desirability scores had lower pain thresholds. The authors believe that this finding is consistent with contemporary conceptions of psychogenic pain patients. Patients with high social desirability scores are sensitive to the demand placed on them by health care professionals—in this case, to the behaviors they are expected to exhibit as pain patients. To comply with these expectations, these patients are freer and more open in their reports of pain (that is, have lower pain thresholds) and do so in a less discriminating manner.

Aside from these social dynamics, the authors also contend that chronic pain can increase the sensitivity of the entire nervous system to stimulation. The central nervous system may process afferent sensory information inadequately, so that the cortex receives information that is usually responded to by lower brain centers.

COMMENTARY: This study is important for the diagnosis and treatment of chronic pain patients. It illustrates that these individuals experience and respond to pain very differently from normal individuals. Also of interest was the use of a signal detection theory as an analytic strategy for chronic pain patients, in which a pain stimulus similar to chronic pain is manipulated. Although not commonly used, this approach appears to offer a valuable method for understanding the physiological and cognitive components of pain as they mediate the perception and experience of noxious stimuli.

SOURCE: Malow, R. M., Grimm, L., and Olson, R. E. "Differences in Pain Perception Between Myofascial Pain Dysfunction Patients and Normal Subjects: A Signal Detection Analysis." *Journal of Psychosomatic Research*, 1980, *24*, 303-309.

Quantifying the Concept of Health

AUTHOR: Harri Sintonen

PRECIS: A disease-independent approach to the measurement and valuation of health states.

PROCEDURE: The quality of life is viewed as consisting of three major components: perceived health, psychophysical functioning, and social functioning. The description of social functioning may be divided into two dimensions, social participation and ability to work. Nine dimensions define psychophysical functioning (eating, moving, intellectual or mental functioning, hearing, seeing, speaking, incontinence, sleeping, and breathing). For each of the twelve dimensions (perceived health, the two social functioning dimensions, and the nine psychophysical functioning dimensions) six or seven discrete levels, ranging from normal functioning to dead, were defined by example. Forty-three healthy subjects and 77 hospital patients were given the questionnaire. Of these 120 subjects, 59 were asked to assign a magnitude estimation, and the other 61 assigned a category rating from 0 (least desirable or important) to 10 (most desirable or important). Subjects also judged their own health status as well as the comprehensibility of the valuation task itself.

The results suggest an approach to the measurement and valuation of health states that is both viable and worthy of further testing. The task is cost effective, efficient to administer and analyze, and disease independent.

COMMENTARY: The history of psychometrics is noteworthy for the enormous effort and major refinements that have led to numerous measuring instruments in the areas of intellectual functioning and mental health. In dealing with health, however, there remains a paucity of materials. Many of the measurement strategies that have proved successful for other activities cannot be easily applied to health. This article suggests an important approach for clinicians to use in designing assessment instruments that may have wide applicability and that may be easily constructed.

SOURCE: Sintonen, H. "An Approach to Measuring and Valuing Health States." *Social Science and Medicine,* 1981, *15C,* 55-65.

A Simple Statistic for Spotting a Trend

AUTHOR: Warren W. Tryon

PRECIS: A simple method for doing time-series analysis by hand with as few as eight points per experimental phase.

PROCEDURE: In the best designs for therapeutic programs, a dependent variable during a pretreatment or baseline phase is later compared with one or more interventions and/or follow-up. The length of the treatment phase may depend on some measure of stability, while evidence for the successful effect of a treatment may be inferred by the presence of a trend in the captured data. Trend analysis usually requires rather complicated statistical routines and is often limited to data sets with at least 50 to 100 points. The conventional treatment setting, however, may permit considerably shorter baseline and experimental phases. Under such circumstances, the application of regression models or polynomial curve fitting is inappropriate. This article describes a simple ratio of the summation of squared successive differences to variance that is simply transformed to a statistic, C, having a standard error that is entirely a function of the sample size. (The latter point implies that entirely trivial effects can be found to be statistically significant if enough data points are collected, but this defect is characteristic of all statistical analyses and not just the C statistic.)

COMMENTARY: This article enables the clinician or researcher to apply a simple yet elegant quantification tool to test the presence of changes due to treatment interventions in serially dependent time-series data. It tests for both abrupt changes in the level of a time series as well as for gradual changes in its slope (but not for the separate effects). Among its great advantages are the simplicity of hand calculation and its use with much smaller data sets than are normally required for comparable analyses.

SOURCE: Tryon, W. W. "A Simplified Time-Series Analysis for

Evaluating Treatment Interventions." *Journal of Applied Behavior Analysis*, 1982, *15*, 423–429.

Additional Readings

Donner, A., and Bull, S. "The Mean Versus the Minimum as a Criterion for Hypertension Screening." *Journal of Chronic Diseases*, 1981, *34*, 527–531.

From both a practical and a theoretical perspective, there is no general reason to prefer the mean to the minimum as a criterion for hypertension screening. This is especially true if readings from only one patient visit are available. Given such circumstances, as well as the variability in blood pressure recordings and conventional Type I considerations, the advantages of using minimum measurements to prevent a false diagnosis can greatly outweigh the advantages of using the mean to identify a true hypertensive. The authors' arguments should have implications for other areas in medicine and behavior.

Wells, K. C., Connors, C. K., Imber, L., and Delamater, A. "Use of Single-Subject Methodology in Clinical Decision-Making with a Hyperactive Child on the Psychiatric Inpatient Unit." *Behavioral Assessment*, 1981, *3*, 359–369.

The efficacy of various stimulant medications and behavioral interventions in treating hyperactive children has been well documented. These authors report the use of a single-subject methodology to determine which treatment or combinations of treatments are the most effective for a particular individual. An A-B-A-C-CD-A1B-CD design was employed, in which the effectiveness of Dexedrine (B), Ritalin (C), behavioral self-control (D), and their combinations in a hyperactive child was compared. Assessment was performed across two response dimensions, behavioral and physiological. The results indicated that a combination of Ritalin plus behavioral self-control procedures was clinically the most effective. The authors contend that single-subject methodologies provide important information for the clinical decision-making process for an individual client. When properly designed, such studies can provide experimentally rigorous information even though only one subject is used.

Tests, Inventories, and Scales

Certain medical conditions require their own specialized instruments for evaluation. Usually these conditions involve pain and distress. The design of intervention programs for such problems rests on an informed and careful delineation of factors: organic, intrapsychic, and environmental. A number of heroic attempts at measurement have been proposed and have met with widespread acceptance. More important, the diverse strategies that are employed may well be used for other medical settings and patient populations.

Predictive Value
for Three Low Back Pain Measures

AUTHOR: Frank Leavitt

PRECIS: Determining the predictive value of three measures aimed at detecting psychological disturbances in individuals with low back pain: the MMPI Low Back scale, the Conversion "V" MMPI profile, and the Back Pain Classification Scale.

INTRODUCTION: There is a growing population of individuals who present themselves for treatment of low back pain symptoms with no underlying organic component. Research has led to the belief that such a complaint often reflects a psychological disturbance. Since the medical approach has been unable to provide an effective intervention, attention is now focusing on how to identify such individuals early in the diagnostic process and how to direct them to a treatment that addresses their needs. The development and use of psychological inventories that are able to identify individuals whose presenting pain symptoms may be related to psychological problems are necessary for reducing the risks and costs of inappropriate diagnostic procedures. This article attempts to establish the predictive validity of three scales that have traditionally been used to detect mental disturbances. The three scales are the Low Back scale and the Conversion "V" profile from the MMPI and the Back Pain Classification Scale (BPCS).

METHOD: The subject sample consisted of 175 patients, 83 men and 92 women, treated for low back pain over a 3-year period by six neurosurgeons and orthopedic surgeons.

All subjects received a comprehensive medical and laboratory workup. Findings were reviewed by surgeons, who assigned individuals either an organic or nonorganic diagnosis. There were 91 patients in the nonorganic group, and they comprised the experimental sample for this study. The subjects were administered a comprehensive psychological examination including an extended clinical interview, projective tests, and the Inventory of Recent Life Experiences. The results of these test batteries were reviewed by two clinical psychologists and used to identify patients having significant emotional disturbances. Of the 91 patients screened, 59 manifested symptoms of psychiatric disorders. These disorders ranged from reactive depressions to neurotic conflicts with issues such as dependency, sex, aggression, and identity. These patients were labeled as the psychologically disturbed group. The remaining 32 patients were classified as the nondisturbed group.

Each category served as its own criterion group against which individuals' scores on the three pain measures were compared. The profiles obtained were then compared with the diagnoses made by the clinical psychologists (that is, disturbed or nondisturbed). Three scales were employed. The first was the Low Back scale, which is a twenty-five-item true/false self-report questionnaire taken from the MMPI. A score of 11 or above indicates psychological disturbances. The second scale was the Conversion "V" profile, consisting of above-average scores on the Hypochondriasis (Hs), Depression (D), and Hysteria (Hy) scales of the MMPI with the Hs and Hy scales greater than the D. The criterion for defining this profile is as follows: Hs and Hy score more than 70; D scores less than the Hs and Hy scales; and all other MMPI scales score less than 70. The final scale used was the BPCS, which is a self-report checklist of thirteen adjectives descriptive of pain embedded in a 103-item questionnaire. Each adjective has a specific weight attached to it, so that negative weights tend toward nonfunctional categories and positive weights toward functional categories.

The profiles obtained were interpreted with regard to any psychological disturbances the individuals manifested on the pain measures. This result was then compared with the individual's diagnostic classification as determined by the psychologists. Agreement between results on the profiles and the clinical diagnosis was indicative of the accuracy of the scale in predicting psychological disturbances in low back pain sufferers.

The Low Back scale predicted patients classified by the clinicians as being nondisturbed with 46.9% accuracy (53.1% error). The scale predicted with 32.2% accuracy patients classified as disturbed (67.8% error). The Conversion "V" profile predicted subjects in the disturbed group with 64.5% accuracy (35.5% error). There are no data on this measure that can be used to predict patients classified as nondisturbed. The BPCS was clearly superior to the other two scales. The BPCS correctly identified seventy-one out of ninety-one cases, for an overall accuracy rate of 78.0%. It had an accuracy of 87.5% in predicting nondisturbed patients (12.5% error) and a 72.9% rate of accurately predicting disturbed patients (27.1% error).

In comparing the ability of the three instruments to detect psychological disturbances, base rate levels become an important issue. Base rate refers to the natural occurrence of a specific condition in a given population of individuals. Of the ninety-one patients tested, fifty-nine, or 64.8%, were classified as disturbed by the psychologists. With this serving as the base rate, only the BPCS substantially increased the number of accurate decisions over the baseline—by 13.2% (64.8% baseline to 78.0% overall accuracy).

However, not many practitioners are confronted with such a homogenous sample of individuals (that is, all patients determined as having a nonorganic cause of back pain); as a result, most practitioners have a different base level of individuals having a nonorganic etiology for their complaint. When considering such a base level for all subjects in this group (this includes both organic and nonorganic patients, $N = 175$), the author determined the base rate to be 48%. Assuming this level reflects the incidence of low back pain sufferers in the general population, the Conversion "V" profile can have some therapeutic value when used in a general orthopedic practice. This scale provided an increase in the accuracy of prediction by almost 16% over baseline. However, the author points out that there are some weaknesses inherent in the use of this scale. Primarily, this study illustrates the rather large error rate in predictions made with this instrument. Strict reliance on this scale will produce a high rate of false classifications. Second, physicians are not well trained in interpreting MMPI profiles, particularly when there are other clinically elevated scales aside from the Hs and Hy profiles. Finally, the MMPI is very time consuming to administer and asks questions that some patients may find objectionable.

The Low Back scale does not appear to be an effective measure for discriminating between disturbed and nondisturbed patients. The percentage of accurate predictions was substantially less than the base rate. This finding seems to agree with the conclusions of other studies, which found very little utility for the instrument.

In conclusion, the author contends that the BPCS offers a way to identify psychological disturbances in low back pain sufferers at clinically useful levels. It also appears to offer a parsimonious approach to the issues in question; it is brief, nonthreatening to patients, easy to interpret, and potentially useful to practitioners who are not sophisticated in the use of psychological tests.

COMMENTARY: In addition to demonstrating the statistical and heuristic value of the Back Pain Classification Scale, another important issue is highlighted in this study: that of base rates of occurrence. When attempting to develop or select a measure that discriminates individuals on a particular dimension, it is crucial to know the natural frequency with which the condition presents itself in the population of interest. The usefulness of an instrument, especially in the context of low back pain, must be evaluated by the degree to which it increases accuracy in prediction over the baseline rather than by its relationship to some theoretical construct (as is the case with the MMPI). The efficacy of the BPCS may be attributable to its nonreliance on the relationship between various intrapsychic and physical functions and its focus on the patient's experience of the presenting symptoms.

SOURCE: Leavitt, F. "Comparisons of Three Measures for Detecting Psychological Disturbances in Patients with Low Back Pain." *Pain*, 1982, *13*, 299-305.

Use of Content Analysis
with Medically Ill Patients

AUTHORS: Allen H. Leibovits and Jimmie C. Holland

PRECIS: Description of the use of the Gottschalk-Gleser Verbal Content Scales to measure mood states in medically ill patients.

INTRODUCTION: The authors note the growing interest among medical practitioners in determining the psychological consequences of advanced medical therapies (such as germ-free environments and coronary care units) upon patients. Yet the systematic investigation of this particular population has been hampered by (1) the lack of assessment measures appropriate for this specific population, (2) an insensitivity of the measures currently used to the normal stressors inherent in any illness, and (3) the absence of a measurement instrument that can be administered repeatedly to patients over the course of treatment. Two of the more common assessment approaches, self-report inventories and observer rating scales, are subject to severe limitations. Self-reports are easily influenced by a patient's defense mechanisms of denial and rationalization. These mechanisms, which are triggered by the illness, may distort a person's perception of internal experiences and make the patient insensitive to his or her current psychological status. Observer ratings require special training for the observer, the establishment of interrater reliabilities, and a clear operationalization of the behaviors to be rated. The Gottschalk-Gleser scales (G-G) appear to be an instrument well suited for psychologically assessing medically ill patients through the course of treatment.

TEST INSTRUMENT: The procedure employs content analysis to derive a measure of immediate emotional states. It is easily administered and can be repeated frequently. Underlying the use of the G-G is the assumption that psychological states are greatly influenced by biological conditions. Each emotional state is defined by an associated biological characteristic of the patient.

The test procedure is simple. The person is instructed to talk into a tape recorder for 5 minutes. The instructions are general and basically nondirective. The individual is free to discuss any interesting or dramatic personal life experience(s). Directions can be tailored to suit any medical situation. These recordings are then transcribed verbatim, and the transcript is scored by a trained technician for up to sixteen psychological dimensions. The scoring is done on a strictly empirical basis. Each clause is scored using well-delineated linguistic categories to define each verbal behavior scale. A prescribed mathematical formula is then applied to determine the final score for each category.

This analysis evaluates syntax, semantics, and the choice of words. Different semantic and linguistic cues that reflect the magnitude of a subjective experience are weighted. Reliability increases with the number of words in a verbal sample (samples with less than 300 words cannot be scored). The most reliable and widely used scales include anxiety (which has six subscales: death anxiety, mutilation anxiety, separation anxiety, guilt anxiety, shame anxiety, and diffuse or nonspecific anxiety), hostility (which has three subscales: hostility outward, hostility inward, and ambivalent hostility), depression, hope, cognitive-intellectual impairment, and social alienation–personal disorganization.

The authors then discuss some of the variables that critically affect the G-G. As with any projective test, administering procedures must be strictly followed. Research has shown that the sex of the interviewer can influence the content of the elicited response. Furthermore, some interviewers can elicit greater emotional content than others, although the G-G test situation attempts to minimize experimenter sources of variability (for example, the entire test time is limited to 10 minutes and instructions are standardized).

One important strength of this approach is that completing the test requires no physical exertion by the patient such as writing, which could be a problem for this population. In addition, patients easily accept the short administration period; many would be unwilling to complete extensive psychological test batteries. The only requirement for subjects is that they speak intelligibly and be willing to speak into a tape recorder. The liability of the G-G approach is the scoring, which is complex and requires extensive training and practice. However, commercial scoring services are available.

The G-G scale has been used with a wide variety of patients (including cancer and coronary patients) and its utility is clearly justified. The authors present a sampling of studies where the G-G was used and where some interesting features of the test emerged. In some studies where other assessment measures were used in conjunction with the G-G, the G-G was the only instrument to show any significant results (in all the studies presented, the G-G yielded significant results). Other research findings have shown that the G-G is very sensitive to pharmacologic-physiological relationships, treatment effects, environmental effects, and psychological factors related to specific disease states. The anxiety and hostility scales are valuable in evaluating medical patients, and the G-G can be useful in identifying high-risk patients. Finally, the G-G is very amenable to longitudinal studies, since it has excellent test-retest reliability. Above all, the G-G avoids many of the limitations inherent in the self-report and observer rating measures.

COMMENTARY: The authors provide summaries of research in which the G-G scales were administered to a variety of medically ill patients. The results of these studies show that the G-G scales are sensitive to immediate mood states of patients and versatile enough to assess individuals over a wide range of dimensions. The authors believe that the G-G can be a valuable tool in evaluating patients' psychological reactions to new medical technologies and treatment modalities, and in helping to identify high-risk patients. Although content analysis techniques have existed for a long time, it is an approach to assessment that deserves further investigation and increased application in the field of behavioral medicine.

SOURCE: Leibovits, A. H., and Holland, J. C. "Use of the Gottschalk-Gleser Verbal Content Analysis Scales with Medically Ill Patients." *Psychosomatic Medicine*, 1983, *45*, 305–320.

The McGill Pain Questionnaire

AUTHOR: Roland Melzack

PRECIS: A presentation of the major properties of an instrument designed to quantify clinical pain.

INTRODUCTION: The objective measurement of pain is critical for diagnosis and for pre- and posttreatment assessments. Because pain is a complex phenomenon, many assessment instruments are severely limited. Most notable among the deficiencies is that they treat pain as if it were a specific sensory quality that varies only in intensity. Yet pain has many qualities, and there are many aspects to pain aside from intensity, each pain type having its own qualities. The McGill Pain Questionnaire (MPQ) is an attempt to specify these qualities and to translate them into quantitative measures that can be statistically analyzed.

THE MPQ: The MPQ consists of three classes of descriptive words that are used by patients to describe their subjective pain experience. These classes are (1) sensory qualities, which relate to temporal, spatial, pressure, and other properties; (2) affective qualities, which relate to the tension, fear, and autonomic properties that are part of the pain experience; and (3) evaluative qualities, which relate to the overall intensity of pain.

The instrument takes between 5 and 20 minutes to administer. It should be given by either a nurse or other health care worker who can read the questions and descriptive words to the patient. This procedure has been found to reduce unreliability in the scale associated with patients' misinterpretations of the instructions and with response set (such as being compelled to select a descriptor from every category). It is important that the test administrator be patient and understanding, since impatience may cause the subjects to make hurried decisions.

Analysis of the MPQ yields four types of data: (1) a pain rating index based on the scale values of all the words chosen in a given category; (2) a pain rating index based on the rank values of the words; (3) the number of words chosen; and (4) present pain intensity, or the subjective experience of pain at the time of administration. Each type of data is a quantitative index of pain and can be used to measure changes in pain quality or intensity resulting from therapeutic intervention.

Continued research has found that the MPQ can detect changes in the pain experience due to different interventions and can provide important information about the effects of the intervention on the sensory, affective, and evaluative aspects of pain. The present pain intensity scale has also been used for self-monitoring pain levels at home.

COMMENTARY: The MPQ provides a uniform method for assessing an individual's pain experience. It allows clinicians and/or researchers to quantify a qualitative experience in a meaningful manner. It also provides a way for patients to classify their unique pain experience comprehensively, going beyond the more traditional, unidimensional approach of assessing pain intensity.

SOURCE: Melzack, R. "The McGill Pain Questionnaire: Major Properties and Scoring Methods." *Pain,* 1975, *1,* 277-299.

The Millon Behavioral Health Inventory

AUTHORS: Theodore Millon, Catherine J. Green, and Robert B. Meagher

PRECIS: A presentation and outline of a psychodiagnostic instrument developed primarily for a medical population.

INTRODUCTION: As the field of behavioral medicine grows, there has developed an increasing need for psychologists to assess their treatment approach, the patients' responsiveness to therapy, and prognoses. Clinicians have routinely employed test

batteries that are not entirely appropriate for such a population (such as the MMPI or the 16PF). Such instruments were
developed on psychiatric populations, and the authors contend
that evaluating medical patients with traditional psychiatric
constructs may not be valid or useful. To address this need,
some behavioral-medical tests were developed (such as the Cornell Medical Index and the Jenkins Activity Survey). However,
these tests are either very broad in scope or extremely narrow,
evaluating single dimensions and excluding other significant
variables that may contribute to maintaining a patient's problem. This article describes the Millon Behavioral Health Inventory (MBHI), which is claimed to be a comprehensive, easy-to-
administer psychodiagnostic test that is relevant to important
health dimensions.

THE MBHI: There are four major areas covered by the instrument, each addressing the disease process from a different perspective. The first is *personality style.* Here the underlying contention is that understanding an individual's intrapsychic
organization can provide important therapeutic insights into the
development of a disease and the patient's coping mechanisms
as a response to the disease. This approach emphasizes particular psychogenic attitudes, such as the impact of stress on the
incidence of various diseases and premorbid attitudes toward
diseases.

The second area is *social alienation,* which describes the
amount of familial and/or social support an individual has while
ill. Research has shown this to be an important variable in moderating the impact of life stressors. Strong social support networks help patients to cope effectively with a disease and to
moderate levels of somatic anxiety (that is, a patient's concern
about his or her body).

The third health area is concerned with establishing clear
psychosomatic correlates of disease. Here the goal is to differentiate individuals with a common disease according to the relative contributions of psychological and physiological factors.
Understanding an individual's predisposing characteristics is important in determining the major therapeutic intervention

(whether it should center on psychotherapy, surgery, medication, environmental management, or something else).

The fourth area is concerned with a *patient's response to treatment* and how the person's psychological makeup affects the efficacy of that treatment. The development of such prognostic indicators are important because they enable clinicians to anticipate problems a patient may experience during the course of treatment and to counteract them, thus reducing the likelihood of a poor outcome.

The MBHI incorporates twenty clinical scales under these four categories and consists of 150 self-descriptive true/false items. Eight scales comprise the section on personality styles. These scales are considered normal variants of personality in that they were derived from a pathological view of personality. These scales on personality style include introversive, inhibited, cooperative, sociable, confident, forceful, respectful, and sensitive. Six scales examine sources of psychosocial stressors and attitudes toward illness and their somatic effects. These scales evaluate chronic tension, recent stress, premorbid pessimism, future despair, social alienation, and somatic anxiety. Three scales evaluate patients in terms of the contribution of social and emotional factors to the etiology of their disease. These three scales are allergic inclination, gastrointestinal susceptibility, and cardiovascular tendency. In these scales, which were empirically derived, high scores are associated with psychosomatic patients. The three scales in the final set were also empirically derived and serve as prognostic indicators. They attempt to identify possible difficulties that may occur over the course of treatment. These scales are pain treatment responsivity, life threat reactivity, and emotional vulnerability.

Reliability coefficients were obtained in two ways: First, the Kuder-Richardson formula, which assesses the internal reliability of the scales, revealed reliabilities ranging from .66 to .90, with a median of .82. Test-retest reliabilities ranged from .72 to .90, with a median of .83. Validational measures were obtained by comparing the scales of the MBHI with other scales measuring the same construct. These coefficients for the psychogenic scales with other instruments (including the California

Personality Inventory and the MMPI Depression, Psychasthenia, Social Introversion, Hysteria, and Hypochondriasis scales) provided correlations ranging from −.40 to +.65. Cross-validational samples were also used to establish the validity of individual scales.

COMMENTARY: Although only recently developed, the MBHI is being used in a variety of medical settings and is proving to be a very useful tool in developing treatment interventions for patients. The MBHI is a brief, easy-to-administer instrument that patients find acceptable (that is, it does not ask intrusive questions that some people find offensive, like those commonly found on the MMPI) and can provide important information about an individual's predisposing personality characteristics that are relevant to treatment.

SOURCE: Millon, T., Green, C. J., and Meagher, R. B. "The MBHI: A New Inventory for the Psychodiagnostician in Medical Settings." *Professional Psychology,* 1979, *10,* 529-539.

Additional Readings

Cox, G. B., Chapman, C. R., and Black, R. G. "The MMPI and Chronic Pain: The Diagnosis of Psychogenic Pain." *Journal of Behavioral Medicine,* 1978, *4,* 437-443.

This study investigated the ability of the MMPI to discriminate among groups of patients with different types of pain. Results indicated the MMPI to be effective in discriminating between chronic and acute pain sufferers. The scales most sensitive to this difference are those of the neurotic triad (Hypochondriasis, Depression, and Hysteria). However, the MMPI was not able to differentiate between chronic pain patients of differing etiologies (surgical or iatrogenic versus unknown). The authors conclude that the MMPI is unreliable for differentiating among different kinds of chronic pain sufferers. However, these findings may be specific to the characteristics of the special subject population. The authors suggest that researchers should exercise caution when generalizing results to populations other than those from which the original samples were drawn.

Doyle, D. V., Dieppe, P. A., Scott, J., and Huskisson, E. C. "An Articular Index for the Assessment of Osteoarthritis." *Annals of Rheumatic Diseases,* 1981, *40,* 75–78.

These authors present an index for osteoarthritis that assesses changes in joint tenderness during the natural course of the disease or during treatment. The index includes forty-eight joints or joint groups that are assessed for tenderness either by applying firm pressure over the joint margin or by passive movement. Tenderness is rated on a four-point scale, 0 meaning no tenderness and 3 meaning that the patient complained of pain, whined, and withdrew the joint. The articular index is the sum of the scores for the forty-eight joints tested. This measure was shown to be reliable and sensitive to changes in patients' conditions due to various types of treatments. Although the articular index is not intended to measure arthritic severity, the authors contend that it is a useful addition to current methods of assessment.

McCreary, C., and Turner, J. "Psychological Disorder and Pain Description." *Health Psychology,* 1983, *2,* 1–10.

Descriptions of the pain experience in 233 chronic low back pain patients are analyzed. Responses from the Pain Experience Questionnaire (derived from the McGill Pain Questionnaire) were factor analyzed, revealing three dimensions of pain expression: sensory, affective, and evaluative. Significant multiple correlations were found with MMPI scales reflecting somatic preoccupation most related to the pain description. Certain MMPI scales relating to psychological disorder were more related to the affective and evaluative dimensions than to the sensory dimensions.

Meadow, M. J., Kochevar, J., Tellegen, A., and Rohects, A. H. "Perceived Somatic Response Inventory: Three Scales Developed by Factor Analysis." *Journal of Behavioral Medicine,* 1978, *1,* 413–426.

These researchers report the development of three new scales that assess autonomic reactivity and voluntary control of autonomic responses. The scales are autonomic response frequency (to assess spontaneous fluctuations in autonomic responding), autonomic response to stress (to determine the amount of autonomic arousal perceived by a person in stress situations), and somatic response control (to measure the capacity to control both autonomic and fine muscle responses). The authors contend that these scales can be useful in examining relationships between behavioral and psychophysiological indicators of responses to stress and useful as well in predicting successful voluntary control over autonomic responses. The scales may also be useful in assessing relationships among stress reactions, somatic control, and the development of physical dysfunctions.

Zung, W. W. K. "A Self-Rating Pain and Distress Scale." *Psychosomatics,* 1983, *24,* 887–894.

This report describes the utility of the pain and distress (PAD) scale. The scale consists of twenty self-report items that patients complete on a four-point index. The items relate to a variety of pain-associated areas, such as mood changes, behavioral changes, sleep disturbances, and decreased alertness. The author contends that the PAD can be used in clinical and research settings to (1) provide an overall index of experienced pain, (2) provide a pain profile based on the dysfunctions experienced by the patient, and (3) evaluate the efficacy of various therapeutic interventions for pain treatment. Research reported by the author substantiates the validity of this measure, in that it can accurately differentiate between normals and pain patients.

2

Major
Treatment
Techniques

Behavioral therapies have evolved from learning theory, where changes in mental health behaviors are affected (treated) by operations developed through human and animal research. Just as the first applications of these therapies rested on the assumption that neurotic and psychotic behaviors follow the laws of learning, the extension of these techniques to nonmental problems retains the same assumption; that is, medical symptoms may undergo change by the same operations that govern mental health symptoms. The main theoretical and procedural variations among the behavior therapies are presented in this chapter, which presents reports on various medical problems treated with biofeedback, behavior modification, and cognitive-behavioral therapies.

Biofeedback

By transducing an otherwise nondiscriminated physiological signal, biofeedback procedures allow a patient to monitor a body function and consciously control it. This has proven to be particularly valuable in treating a number of medical problems, among them urinary and fecal incontinence, migraine headaches, and cardiovascular functioning. The technologies for the various transductions have allowed changes in temperature, pressure, and muscular tension to be rewarded and consequently learned. Although relaxation procedures may be equally effective for some of these problems (without requiring cumbersome, expensive instrumentation), it is quite clear that for certain medical conditions, a well-designed electronic biofeedback protocol is the treatment of choice.

Hypnosis and Biofeedback
in the Treatment of Hypertension

AUTHORS: Howard Friedman and Harvey A. Taub

PRECIS: A report on the effectiveness of hypnosis and biofeedback, used alone and in tandem, in the control of essential hypertension.

INTRODUCTION: Biofeedback and hypnosis are each effective in decreasing both systolic and diastolic blood pressures. As the authors point out, there is a paucity of research in which these two techniques are combined into a single treatment. This report examines the possibility of hypnosis and biofeedback used together in a treatment package.

METHOD: Forty-eight subjects, with a diagnosis of essential hypertension and a minimum diastolic pressure of 85 Hg were randomly assigned to one of four conditions: (1) hypnosis only (HO), (2) biofeedback only (BO), (3) hypnosis and biofeedback (HB), and (4) control measurement only (MO).

All subjects first had baseline measures taken of their blood pressure and hypnotic susceptibility. Two days later the first training session, consisting of fifteen automatic measures of blood pressure, was given. Thereafter, all subjects received two training sessions a week for 3 weeks (for a total of seven sessions), which were held 2 days apart at the same time of day as the first session.

Subjects assigned to the biofeedback groups (HB and BO) were instructed to observe a clearly lit visual display of their blood pressure readings, while those in the HO and MO conditions did not view these readings. Subjects in the latter two groups were instructed to relax and sit quietly in a reclining chair while their blood pressure was recorded several times. Subjects in the HB and BO groups were given basic instructions for lowering their blood pressure readings; in addition, the HB subjects were maintained in a hypnotic trance. After the training trials, subjects in the HO and HB conditions were taught autohypnosis and were instructed to place themselves in a relaxed position and enter a trance twice a day for 3 minutes each time. They were instructed to visualize with eyes closed their last training session. Subjects in the BO and MO groups were given the same instructions, but no mention was made of hypnosis. Follow-up evaluations were conducted at 1-week and 1-month intervals.

The results indicated that the HO group showed the greatest decrease in diastolic blood pressure, significantly lower than subjects in the MO and HB groups. Diastolic reductions in the BO group were not significantly different from any of the other conditions. These differences were maintained at the 1-week follow-up. At the one-month evaluation, only the BO and HO groups differed significantly from the baseline measures. More detailed analysis revealed that for the BO group, only the seventh training session and 1-week follow-up were significantly different from baseline. However, in the HO group, all measurements were significantly different from baseline.

The authors conclude that hypnosis alone is more effective than the other procedures examined for lowering diastolic blood pressure. Although biofeedback alone is also capable of such changes, it seems to be less effective than the HO conditions and not significantly different from any of the other procedures. The combination of hypnosis and biofeedback did not support the contention that together they provide a more effective strategy than either protocol alone. It appears that the HB group offered no advantage over simply taking repeated measures. The authors suggest that when used together, biofeedback and hypnosis seem to cancel each other's effects. Similar results were found for systolic measurements, even though no explicit training program was designed.

COMMENTARY: These results indicate the efficacy of hypnosis in treating essential hypertension. Hypnotic techniques offer a simple procedure for effecting important changes in diastolic blood pressure without the use of extensive technical equipment. As the authors note, the durability of these results over time without further training remains to be established.

SOURCE: Friedman, H., and Taub, H. A. "The Use of Hypnosis and Biofeedback Procedures for Essential Hypertension." *International Journal of Clinical and Experimental Hypnosis*, 1977, *25*, 335–347.

Migraine, Biofeedback Training, and Skin Site

AUTHORS: Janel Gauthier, Richard Bois, Denis Allaire, and M. Drolet

PRECIS: An evaluation of the effectiveness of two different skin sites in thermal biofeedback as used in the treatment of migraine.

INTRODUCTION: Skin temperature biofeedback is the most common technique used to treat migraine headaches. The most popular site for electrode placement is usually the finger. However, in light of the changes in intracerebral hemodynamics occurring before and during a migraine attack and the successful use of a cerebral placement for blood pulse volume feedback training, it is appropriate to ask whether it is better to teach subjects control of temperature in the local area of the migraine rather than at a location distant from the headache site (finger). A related issue deals with the possible anatomic specificity of this learned response. Research has shown that the better a person can control dermal temperature, the more specific the response is to the trained part of the body. This study assesses the effects of temporal artery and finger temperature biofeedback in treating migraine. It also examines the effects of dermal warming or cooling on migraine activity at each site.

METHOD: Twenty-four patients (four men and twenty women aged 21 through 65), selected on the basis of high frequency and regularity of migraine attacks, were randomly assigned to one of four biofeedback groups: (1) finger warming (FW), (2) finger cooling (FC), (3) temporal artery cooling (TAC), and (4) temporal artery warming (TAW). All sessions were conducted in a climate-controlled environment. Subjects were seated in a padded chair and given auditory feedback consisting of a steady pulsating tone whose frequency changed as a function of skin temperature.

Biofeedback training sessions were held once per week for 8 weeks. Each training session lasted 50 minutes. The first 15 minutes were used to establish a baseline, followed by five 3.5-minute periods of training separated by 3.5-minute rest periods. All subjects were instructed about their experimental condition but were not given any suggestions about how to control temperature. Instead they were encouraged to develop their own strategies. They were instructed to practice the techniques at home for two 10-minute periods daily and to employ these strategies after the onset of a migraine attack. Patients were also required to keep a headache diary, recording intensity of pain and the type and quantity of medications consumed. These diaries were completed for 4 weeks prior to treatment, for 4 weeks after the termination of treatment, and for 4 additional weeks at the 6-month follow-up.

Four variables of interest were the number of headaches, the total duration of headaches, the mean headache intensity, and the number of pills consumed. Skin temperature was recorded before and after biofeedback training and at follow-up to evaluate the patient's ability to control the targeted physiological response. No feedback was provided during these sessions.

The results indicate that improvement in thermal regulation skills from pre- to posttreatment and from pretreatment to follow-up was significant for the FW and FC conditions. All gains made by subjects to control temperature were maintained at the follow-up evaluation. With regard to the number of pills and headache intensity, duration, and frequency, all groups benefited equally from participating in the study.

The authors conclude that temperature biofeedback can produce significant therapeutic gains for migraine sufferers.

However, the direction of dermal temperature regulation (warming versus cooling) and the different sites of application (temporal artery versus finger) did not result in any significant differences in migraine activity. These authors also contend that the finger warming and cooling conditions could have a common effect by stabilizing the cerebral vascular system by providing a physiological condition incompatible with extreme vasomotor activity. However, further research is necessary to substantiate this hypothesis and to rule out nonspecific and placebo effects.

COMMENTARY: Although biofeedback is a commonly used technique, there is always the need to evaluate its relevant parameters. Particularly in the area of migraine treatment—where its application has been valued and recognized—there are likely to be accepted myths about the modalities of the feedback procedure. This report contributes to our appreciation of the salient features of the technique and points to directions where research may further simplify the routine and extend the utility of this important therapeutic option.

SOURCE: Gauthier, J., Bois, R., Allaire, D., and Drolet, M. "Evaluation of Skin Temperature Biofeedback Training at Two Different Sites for Migraine." *Journal of Behavioral Medicine,* 1981, *4,* 407–420.

Treatment of Urinary Retention with Biofeedback

AUTHOR: R. J. Hafner

PRECIS: Increasing sensitivity to detrusor reflex through manipulation of intrinsic bladder pressure in a 29-year-old female.

INTRODUCTION: The author posits that reflex urethral instability is psychogenic in origin, developing as a result of inhibition by certain cerebral mechanisms of sensory input from the bladder to the brain. The absence of such input presumably prevents the voluntary activation of neural systems appropriate to releasing bladder inhibition. To provide information regarding bladder tumescence, two probes were inserted into the patient: A 1-millimeter fluid-filled catheter was inserted into the bladder, enabling the measurement of the total pressure in that organ; the second, a 2-millimeter fluid-filled catheter, protected from blockage by a finger stall, was placed into the rectum to obtain a measure of intraabdominal pressure. Subtraction of the latter pressure from the total bladder pressure yielded the "intrinsic bladder pressure," the measure used for the biofeedback. Increases in this measure indicated contractions of the bladder.

CASE HISTORY: The patient in this study was a 29-year-old, white, single female who had suffered from urinary retention for 11 months following her second pregnancy termination. A detailed urological examination excluded an organic basis to this condition.

The patient had been performing self-catheterization one to three times a week for 9 months. Every 2 to 3 weeks this routine was replaced by severe, urgent, and frequent micturition. In addition, she would pass small amounts of urine involuntarily at least fifteen times a day.

After a psychiatric workup, she was seen for 5 months of individual psychotherapy, after which the patient reported no change in bladder functioning. At this point she received the biofeedback training. She received eleven 1-hour biofeedback sessions over a period of 15 weeks.

TREATMENT: The patient was given auditory feedback throughout all sessions. The pitch of this feedback rose and fell in relation to increments and decrements, respectively, in intrinsic bladder pressure.

At the beginning of each session, the patient was encouraged to increase the auditory signal after a measured amount of

0.9% saline solution was infused into her bladder. A rise in pitch was indicative of active detrusor muscle movement. Throughout the course of treatment, the patient kept a detailed record of the frequency of self-catheterization, spontaneous voiding, and the volumes of urine obtained.

During the first three sessions, there was a large amount of urine present in the bladder. Also during these three sessions, the patient was unable to increase the pitch of the auditory signal, even though over 800 milliliters of saline solution were infused into her bladder. Throughout this period the patient recorded no sensations in the bladder.

During the third session, the author reports an interesting observation. The patient had a mild case of diarrhea, and when the bowel would contract, she would report her bladder as contracting. However, her intrinsic bladder pressure would not vary. There was an obvious confusion by the patient in discriminating between bowel and bladder contractions. The next two sessions were devoted to discrimination training so that the patient would be better able to respond to bladder activity.

By the sixth session, the patient was beginning to perceive sensations in the bladder area and was able for the first time to increase the pitch of the auditory signal (after 750 milliliters of saline solution were passed into the bladder). Over the remaining sessions, the amount of saline required to induce a voluntary contraction of the bladder began to decrease. The amount declined from 750 milliliters at the sixth session to 370 milliliters at the eleventh. The patient was also exhibiting greater voluntary control over urination outside the treatment setting, thereby reducing the need for self-catheterization.

After the eleventh session, the patient was voluntarily voiding twice a day, and a 6-month follow-up indicated that the treatment had been entirely satisfactory for at least 3 months.

COMMENTARY: The systematic sensitization method outlined in this study is an accurate and simple procedure that can present sensory information concerning bladder pressure.

The difficulty the patient experienced in differentiating

between bowel and bladder contractions illustrates the need for better treatment instructions. Instructions to a subject should be very specific; some type of pretraining exercises may be beneficial in aiding patients to become more aware of specific physiological systems and less distracted by other extraneous "noise" factors. Close monitoring of patients and the strategies they employ during the feedback sessions may greatly facilitate the treatment process by giving the therapist early indications that the patient is having difficulties in interpreting (or responding to) internal stimuli. Also, it may be necessary to provide periodic refresher sessions in order to extend the effectiveness of the treatment and to help the patient to develop a more appropriate pattern of behaviors outside the treatment environment.

The author also presents a schematic diagram of the biofeedback apparatus that has been used successfully in other related research, which is so noted.

SOURCE: Hafner, R. J. "Biofeedback Treatment of Intermittent Urinary Retention." *British Journal of Urology*, 1981, *53*, 125–128.

Utility of Thermal Biofeedback for Raynaud's Disease

AUTHORS: Richard H. Sundermann and John L. Delk

PRECIS: A case study of thermal biofeedback in treating Raynaud's disease.

INTRODUCTION: Raynaud's disease is a vascular disorder where dermal temperature in the extremities decreases. Constriction of the arterial pathways causes cyanosis along with sensations of unpleasant coldness, numbness, and/or tingling.

The cause of this disorder is unknown, and traditional pharmacologic and surgical interventions are often of limited value. This report presents a case history evaluation of the effectiveness of temperature biofeedback as a treatment intervention.

CASE HISTORY: The patient was a 40-year-old white female whose condition developed at the age of 25, several months after the birth of her one and only child. Symptoms began as a painless blanching in one finger on the left hand. This occurred during a period of mental depression associated with weight loss and sleep disturbance. Ambient temperatures below 72°F usually precipitated her attacks. Although no severe pain was associated with her attacks, throbbing sensations during recovery caused considerable discomfort. Review of the patient's life history revealed no serious past illnesses. The patient had a history of being anxious. Rheumatological evaluations showed no significant abnormalities. Although various medications had been prescribed over the years, they brought little relief. Significant depressions were associated with the use of reserpine.

METHOD: Treatment consisted of temperature biofeedback over 13 consecutive months. Sessions were scheduled from one to three times weekly and were 40 minutes in duration.

During these sessions, a thermistor was attached to the middle finger of the preferred hand and occasionally applied to the nonpreferred hand. The patient was provided with both visual (blinking lights and a temperature dial) and auditory (high versus low intonations) feedback. The only instructions given were to keep the appropriate temperature light on and the tone as high in pitch as possible (that is, maintaining a rise in temperature in the fingertip). No specific instructions were given to her about how to accomplish this task. The task remained structurally open, and she was free to try any subjective state, imagery, or cognitions that produced the desired effect. The patient found that reading the Bible during these sessions led to increases in skin temperature. This practice was encouraged for two reasons: (1) It worked, and (2) it represented a highly defined task that could be performed outside of the treatment setting, thereby increasing the generalizability of the treatment effect.

Finger temperature below 75°F was considered evidence of poor circulation, while temperatures above 90°F were regarded as signs of excellent peripheral blood circulation. The criterion for adequate vasodilation was set at 85°F since no unpleasant sensations were associated with this dermal temperature.

Performance was erratic during the initial stages of treatment. The patient was later able to raise the dermal temperature consistently to the desired levels by the end of the session. During the final stages of the treatment period, she had begun to register higher finger temperatures at the beginning of the sessions. Although a slight trend, it was interpreted as reflecting a generalized treatment effect that was continued after the termination of treatment. At this point, the patient was encouraged to purchase an inexpensive home temperature trainer on which she practiced daily for 1 month. Average finger temperature at the beginning of these exercises was 86.9°F (as compared with the 75°F temperature recorded at her first treatment session), and average temperature at the end of these sessions was 93.7°F. Aside from improved vascular functioning, the patient did not experience any of the symptoms from which she had suffered for the previous 15 years.

COMMENTARY: Although only a case study, this report highlights a variety of important factors that are crucial to a successful biofeedback intervention. As the authors point out, a high degree of motivation and determination are necessary for retraining a complex physiological response. The authors also suggest that a supportive patient-therapist relationship was crucial to this patient's successful completion of the program. Such emotional support and encouragement may also have positively influenced her compliance with the regimen. Having the subject purchase a home temperature trainer to continue her mastered ability was useful in maintaining the therapeutic effect in the home environment. Such a device can also be used by the patient for booster sessions should the need arise. Also of interest was the very specific and salient task for the patient to perform while increasing her temperature. Such a specific task makes the procedure more concrete to the subject and thus promotes more consistent performance.

SOURCE: Sundermann, R. H., and Delk, J. L. "Treatment of Raynaud's Disease with Temperature Biofeedback." *Southern Medical Journal*, 1978, *71*, 340-342.

The Use of Biofeedback
with Gastrointestinal Disorders

AUTHOR: William E. Whitehead

PRECIS: An examination of the effectiveness of biofeedback techniques in treating a variety of gastrointestinal disorders.

COMMENTARY: The author reviews the literature on the application of biofeedback techniques to various gastrointestinal disorders, such as peptic ulcer, esophageal motility disorders, irritable bowel syndrome, inflammatory bowel disease, and fecal incontinence. In all of these areas, biofeedback was an effective therapeutic intervention. It is suggested that the conditioning principles inherent in biofeedback can be applied to any physiological system successfully.

The balloon system, used in the treatment of fecal incontinence, is believed to be the treatment of choice for this disorder. Electromyogram biofeedback for skeletal muscle relaxation may be an important treatment for peptic ulcer sufferers. Both specific and nonspecific techniques can be applied to a variety of complaints. This volume details many of these approaches for a variety of disorders.

As the author notes, this area of treatment is still developing. For some disorders (such as esophageal motility), there is a need to develop more effective procedures for carrying out a treatment and for measuring the patency of the physiological system.

Biofeedback is still an emerging area in the field of behavioral medicine. The need for controlled studies that compare the effectiveness of the technique with that of other interventions remains great. The evidence to date appears to suggest that biofeedback is a promising approach warranting further applications and investigation.

SOURCE: Whitehead, W. E. "Biofeedback in the Treatment of Gastrointestinal Disorders." *Biofeedback and Self-Regulation,* 1978, *3,* 375–384.

Additional Readings

Basmajian, J. V. "Biofeedback in Rehabilitation: A Review of Principles and Practices." *Archives of Physical Medicine and Rehabilitation,* 1981, *62,* 469–475.

Biofeedback is a technique that communicates the status of physiological processes to an individual and enables him or her to control otherwise involuntary biological events by responding to correlated and clearly discriminable signals. This procedure has gained wide acceptance in the field and has been used successfully with a variety of disorders. Electromyogram feedback is most popular and serves as a useful tool in both diagnostic and rehabilitative applications. This article reviews the application of biofeedback techniques in treating upper motor neuron lesions, cerebral palsy, and spasmodic torticollis. This author concludes that EMG feedback is well established in rehabilitation and is very effective in the treatment of upper motor neuron lesions.

Keefe, F. J. "Biofeedback vs. Instructional Control of Skin Temperature." *Journal of Behavioral Medicine,* 1978, *4,* 383–390.

The purpose of this study was (1) to determine the effects of instructions versus biofeedback on the development of skin temperature self-control and (2) to assess the retention of such skills over time. Subjects either received biofeedback or not with one of three instructional sets: (1) response specific (specifying a particular finger in which to raise temperature), (2) thermal (raising finger temperature by repeating a given phrase), and (3) intructions to rest (sitting quietly during the session). Five training sessions were given with two follow-up sessions at 1-week intervals. Subjects receiving feedback with the response-specific and thermal suggestions and those not receiving feedback with the thermal instructions consistently produced significant increases in digital temperature after three training sessions, as well as being able to retain these skills at follow-up. The remaining groups showed no evidence of acquired central over dermal temperature. This study illustrates the important role that instructions play in biofeedback training (those receiving thermal instructions without feedback performed like subjects who did not receive feedback).

Keefe, F. J., Surwit, R. S., and Pilon, R. N. "Biofeedback, Autogenic Training, and Progressive Relaxation in the Treatment of Raynaud's Disease: A Comparative Study." *Journal of Applied Behavior Analysis,* 1980, *13,* 3–11.

The relative efficacy of autogenic training, progressive muscle relaxation, and a combination of both to control Raynaud's disease is compared. All subjects were trained to raise digital temperature using these techniques after receiving three training sessions. The results indicated significant improvement for subjects in all three groups. No differences were found between the groups. Improvements were all maintained over time. The authors interpret these results as support for the contention that individuals suffering from Raynaud's disease can utilize simple behavioral self-control techniques to maintain dermal temperature. These procedures appear to be viable treatment options for individuals suffering from this condition.

Turk, D. C., Meichenbaum, D. H., and Berman, W. H. "Application of Biofeedback for the Regulation of Pain: A Critical Review." *Psychological Bulletin,* 1979, *86,* 1322–1338.

These authors review the biofeedback literature on the regulation of pain. They conclude that there are conceptual and methodological deficiencies in its present applications. An important finding is that comparisons of biofeedback with other less expensive and less instrument-oriented treatments for migraine and chronic pain (such as progressive muscle relaxation and coping skills) have not shown biofeedback to be superior. Although the need for more controlled comparisons is noted, the authors strongly caution the blanket acceptance of biofeedback as the treatment of choice for these conditions. In particular, one should identify the active ingredients of biofeedback therapy and assess the generalizability of learning from the laboratory to the natural environment. These authors contend that due to the inconsistencies in the literature and the lack of empirical support for the effectiveness of biofeedback in the area of pain, this technique should only be considered as a research tool at this time.

Behavior Modification

Behavior modification has become the label describing the clinical application of learning principles. The theoretical models of learning differ in their emphasis of the variables that govern changes in behavior, and corresponding differences in emphasis and style are found in the various behavior therapies that are the formalized expression of these models. However, it is important to note that the general definition of learning, "a relatively permanent change in behavior attributable to a prior history of rehearsal and experience," is as valid for an operant conditioning experiment with infrahuman subjects as it is for persons with mental health or somatic dysfunctions. For either case, behaviors may be shown to undergo "relatively permanent change" —hence the importance of learning as both a causal and therapeutic factor.

The Constructional Approach
to Behavioral Modification

AUTHOR: Dennis J. Delprato

PRECIS: An outline of a theoretical alternative to the popular eliminative approach to behavior modification.

INTRODUCTION: There are two approaches to the application of behavior modification techniques. The first is the eliminative model, in which presenting complaints are classified as behavioral excesses and behavioral change techniques (such as extinction or punishment) are used to reduce or eliminate the problematic behaviors. The other is the constructional approach, in which new behavioral repertoires are established through the use of positive reinforcement so that socially acceptable behaviors can replace the problematic behaviors. The author cites four advantages of the constructional approach over the eliminative model: (1) The former is more in accord with a patient's individual rights; (2) it is more likely to satisfy ethical concerns; (3) adherence to the constructional model involves noncoercive interventions; and (4) this model is more effective (although this is an empirical question needing further investigation). This report contrasts these two approaches with regard to behavioral analysis, goals, and change procedures.

MODEL COMPARISONS: In the eliminative model, the approach is to get rid of the problem behavior. The focus is on the particular deficiencies and weaknesses of the person. The constructional approach focuses on developing socially acceptable behavioral repertoires. Consideration is given to the person's behavioral assets that can be used as a starting point from which to guide the person in the desired direction. The presenting complaint is viewed as the individual's adaptation to life's circumstances rather than as a maladjustment that must be overcome. In short, the constructional model attempts to analyze and harness strengths and skills and to use them in developing different behaviors compatible with psychological functioning.

An essential distinction between the two models is in the goals. The constructional approach does not ignore eliminative goals when they are necessary to alleviate distress, but they also include positive behaviors that are socially acceptable alternatives to the behavior that is to be extinguished. This is especially true if rehabilitative rather than merely custodial services are to be offered. In the treatment of psychosis, alcoholism, or delinquency, eliminative goals account for half of the problem (that is, extinguishing the problematic behavior). Constructional goals are necessary for developing habilitative interventions that start the individual on the path of adaptive functioning.

Finally, the two approaches employ different techniques to produce change. Eliminative techniques include time-out, extinction, physical restraint, covert sensitization, flooding, and implosion. All of these methods are designed to eliminate behavior under the assumption that, once the intrusive behaviors are removed, the person's life situation will somehow improve. Behaviors that are more acceptable are not substituted for the maladaptive ones. The constructional approach may incorporate eliminative techniques under certain circumstances, but it goes one step further by specifying and reinforcing socially acceptable alternatives to the problem behavior. Operant counterconditioning procedures are the most typical methods. Modeling can also be used to help the patient develop alternative behaviors. Token economies and overcorrection (when it includes reeducation whereby the person practices the desired response) are still other examples. Systematic desensitization is a more widespread technique that fits the constructional model and that can be effectively applied to a wide variety of health problems.

COMMENTARY: The constructional approach provides a new perspective on behavior modification and prompts us to rethink our goals for behavioral therapy and behavioral medicine. The model presents an integrative, humanistic approach to behavioral change. The issue for future research is to determine whether and how these two models should be combined. As the author notes, the potential for abuse in eliminative programs and the greater sensitivity to patient's rights and the right to noncoercive treatment seem to make development and refinement of the constructional approach imperative.

SOURCE: Delprato, D. J. "The Constructional Approach to Behavioral Modification." *Journal of Behavioral Therapy and Experimental Psychiatry*, 1981, *12*, 49–55.

Basic Concepts in Behavior Modification

AUTHORS: Ovide Pomerleau, Frederic Bass, and Victor Crown

PRECIS: A discussion of some fundamental issues related to the use of behavior modification.

INTRODUCTION: It has long been known that certain lifestyles (involving such factors as diet, smoking, and physical activity) are associated with increased morbidity and mortality. A major task for preventive medicine is to change those patterns of behavior that increase individuals' vulnerability to disease. These authors contend that behavior modification (BM) can provide the necessary theoretical and empirical basis for making such changes. This article presents an overview of the basic concepts of BM as well as some issues relevant to evaluating research conducted in this framework.

OVERVIEW: Although BM is a relatively new concept, it is an extension of the fundamental principles developed by Pavlov and Skinner. BM has been successfully applied in treating a variety of problems, including anorexia nervosa, autism, phobias, chronic pain, and stuttering.

Two basic concepts of BM are contingency management and stimulus control. The former is the process of identifying the behavioral antecedents (stimuli) of a specific behavior (response) as well as the contingent reinforcers that either maintain or increase the probability of the response being produced. Before behavior can be changed, one must know those stimuli that are producing and reinforcing the behavior. Stimulus control relates to how stimuli provide the context for ongoing behavior. Stimuli affect behavior either by signaling a situation where behavior has been associated with a reinforcer or by having its own reinforcement effect. Such analyses of stimulus control are frequently performed to determine how the environment influences the problem behavior.

Emerging out of these two concepts are the use of self-control methods. These procedures help an individual to modify aspects of the environment that influence the problem behavior. With these methods, the patient actively participates in treatment while the therapist devises effective behavioral change techniques and motivates the patient to execute them. These procedures, which attempt to change behavior in order to attain long-range advantages, appear likelier to succeed than attempts at modifying certain environmental cues alone (such as taking a walk after a meal instead of smoking a cigarette).

Research has demonstrated that BM procedures are effective for preventive medicine. They have been successfully employed in the areas of smoking, dieting, alcoholism, and the prevention of cardiovascular diseases.

Either in evaluating or in performing research (treatment), there are some issues to keep in mind. The first concerns the accuracy of self-report data. Central to self-control procedures is establishing what the patient believes to be the stimuli influencing the problem behavior. Establishing the reliability of self-reports has been one of the most troubling issues. There are two possible solutions. One consists of independent observations, where an individual monitors the patient's behavior at specific intervals. Such monitoring should be executed as unobtrusively and objectively as possible. Devices such as wrist counters, wireless microphones, and inexpensive videotape equipment have helped to make this task easier. A second solution is to use physiological indicators, which can be helpful in augmenting self-report data. Indexes such as biological assays of physical capabilities (for example, exercise tests) can be helpful when appropriate to treatment. Further research into the relationships between physiological processes and behavior can help to apply this method to more areas.

The final issue relates to choices of outcome, which has three levels: (1) changes in the target behavior itself, where the person is encouraged to modify a behavior that poses health risks (such as smoking); (2) short-term physiological consequences (such as increased pulmonary functioning after quitting smoking); and (3) long-term changes in morbidity and mortality. It is obvious that the preferred outcome measures should relate to long-term changes in morbidity, and this is especially true in the area of preventive medicine. The goal of this type of treatment is to change a person's behavior because it is having an adverse effect on the person's life.

COMMENTARY: The concepts presented here comprise the basic foundation of BM. This technique has been successfully applied to a variety of behavioral problems that are responsive to this type of treatment. The issues these authors raise are applicable not only to BM but to all areas of behavioral medicine and will reappear in different discussions in this volume.

SOURCE: Pomerleau, O., Bass, F., and Crown, V. "Role of Behavior Modification in Preventive Medicine." *The New England Journal of Medicine*, 1975, *292*, 1277–1282.

Evaluating Behavior Therapy for Obesity

AUTHOR: G. Terrence Wilson

PRECIS: An outline of the strengths and limitations of behavioral interventions for obesity as well as recommendations for future research.

INTRODUCTION: The introduction of behavioral techniques to the treatment of obesity has brought unprecedented success. This approach has been shown to be more effective than other modalities for controlling mild to moderate obesity. However, more recent evaluations have not been as favorable. It has been suggested that behavioral techniques are no more effective than previous psychological techniques. The author contends that such dismissals are premature. He asserts that in the face of growing information about obesity, behavioral techniques can and must be refined in order to treat this condition more effectively. A more important issue centers on the need to increase compliance with the treatment regimens and the development of better maintenance strategies.

APPRAISAL: Research has shown that the basic assumption underlying behavior therapies for obesity is invalid. Obesity is more than just a simple, learned disorder. A variety of genetic, physiological, and metabolic variables are associated with the etiology of obesity, each of which may respond to different therapeutic approaches. No longer can it be assumed that obese individuals are merely more sensitive to external food cues or that there are distinct eating styles characteristic of obesity.

The author presents five conclusions that represent the status of behavioral techniques in this area: (1) Behavioral treatments are significantly more effective in bringing about weight loss than other methods on a short-term basis; (2) there is a high degree of interindividual variability in outcome; (3) there are no accurate predictor variables related to treatment outcome; (4) there is a dearth of evaluations focusing on long-term treatment outcome; and (5) the amount of weight loss reported in the majority of behavioral studies is not clinically significant. However, the author does present several suggestions for improving the effectiveness of behavioral interventions.

First, the author notes that although the goal of behavior therapy is to alter specific behaviors, most researchers focus on weight loss as the dependent variable instead of an independent confirmation of whether a particular behavior has actually changed. Research has shown that there may be a relationship between eating patterns (frequency *and* volume) and weight loss. It is difficult to obtain reliable measures of behavioral change, but these measures could help resolve discrepancies in the research findings. Developing measures of change in eating patterns, total food consumption, and weight loss are necessary not only to improve treatment strategies but to expand our understanding of obesity.

Second, the author contends that behavioral procedures are presently unimaginative, overly standardized, and very brief. It is very difficult to modify ingrained behavioral patterns in a short period of time (most treatments last eight to ten weeks). Instead, treatments should be more sensitive to the progress made by each patient. Therapy should be modified to meet the needs of each individual.

A third suggestion is to expand behavioral treatment programs beyond mere operant conditioning. These programs should incorporate other techniques of effective therapy. Greater attention should be given to increasing physical exercise and controlling caloric intake in behavioral treatments. Research has shown that an exercise component can significantly improve treatment outcome and may be an important factor in maintaining treatment gains. Another important area for improvement is increasing compliance with prescribed regimens. Behavior therapy depends heavily on having the patient do something such as monitoring caloric intake, identifying maladaptive cognitions, or performing specific behaviors.

Another area in critical need of improvement is maintaining therapeutic gains. Research has shown that merely providing booster sessions after the end of treatment is insufficient for maintaining weight loss in the long run. Instead, clients should be taught to monitor their condition and to self-initiate corrective procedures at the first signs of weight gain. This constant vigilance and willingness to correct difficulties at their first appearance are more crucial to successful weight loss than the scheduling of prearranged booster sessions at fixed intervals. Finally, the author suggests the use of social support networks to monitor compliance and maintain high levels of motivation. Research indicates that the inclusion of a spouse in the behavioral treatment program significantly enhances the maintenance of weight loss. Other, more artificial social influences (such as self-help groups or ongoing therapy groups) can be used to help ensure maintenance of treatment effects. Other sources of support worthy of investigation are the work environment and the community at large.

COMMENTARY: Problems with behavioral treatments for obesity do not lie with the approach itself but rather with the therapeutic procedures used. These difficulties can be eliminated by modifying and improving these techniques. Of paramount importance is the development of better maintenance and compliance strategies that will improve long-term changes in eating and exercise patterns. The issues raised in this report are pertinent not only to obesity but to all other areas of behavioral intervention. The need to improve technique, increase compliance, and maintain therapeutic gains are the cornerstones of successful therapy.

SOURCE: Wilson, G. T. "An Evaluation of Behavioral Therapy in Obesity." *International Journal of Obesity,* 1980, *4,* 371–376.

Additional Readings

Innis, N. K. "Ethics of Behavior Modification and Medicine Psychology." *Social Science and Medicine,* 1981, *15F,* 69–73.

There are important ethical questions for both clinicians and researchers. Of particular importance are the rights of the client. It is the clinician's responsibility to inform the client of all possible appropriate forms of treatment so that the patient can select an intervention and grant consent. A related consideration is the need to assess the client's competence to make a selection and to volunteer participating in the treatment. Issues such as civil liberties arise in research projects when aversive stimuli (such as punishment) and deprivation procedures are used. At all times it is necessary to protect the client physically, psychologically, and legally. Often behavioral techniques are misunderstood by the general public and come under criticism. The author suggests some direct courses of action, including the education of the general public and the development of joint experimental-applied programs for training behavior therapists. Individuals would then be well prepared to develop new treatment procedures free of ethical criticism.

Streja, D. A., Boyko, E., and Rabkin, S. W. "Predictors of Outcome in a Risk Factor Intervention Trial Using Behavior Modification." *Preventive Medicine*, 1982, *11*, 291–303.

In a study to identify variables that predict outcome of a behavioral intervention program for cardiovascular risk factor reduction, sixty-five volunteers completed a 20-week program for improving eating habits. Significant decreases in weight, blood pressure, total serum cholesterol, and uric acid were found in subjects after the program. Analyses were performed on the thirty-five subjects who dropped out of the program to identify factors associated with attrition. Variables relating to cigarette smoking, high body weight, large desired weight loss, and psychiatric history were found highly correlated. This report raises the important issue of identifying behavioral variables at the beginning of treatment that indicate poor responders. Other strategies can then be used to maximize response to treatment. These compensating strategies can also be used with the good responders to improve performance even more.

Ziesat, H. A. "Behavior Modification in the Treatment of Hypertension." *International Journal of Psychiatry in Medicine*, 1977–78, *8*, 257–265.

The use of a behavior modification program as an adjunct to a medical treatment for hypertension was investigated. Five adult male patients with medically treated uncontrolled essential hypertension participated in group interaction with peer reinforcement, peer competition, cognitive dissonance, stimulus control, and direct social influence. Five control subjects received only routine medical treatment. The results indicated significant decreases in diastolic blood pressure for the experimental subjects from pre- to posttreatment; no such change was noted for the controls. This author concludes that behavior modification techniques can be used successfully as an adjunct to a standard medical treatment for hypertension.

Cognitive-Behavioral Methods

The effectiveness of behavioral treatment programs attracted many clinicians who, because of their theoretical biases and temperament, required some revisions in the classic behavior modification system. By wedding dynamic concepts (such as self and cognition) with those from behaviorism (such as stimulus and reinforcement), a major style of behavior therapy evolved. Few of the theoretical issues have been resolved to anyone's satisfaction, but the stylistic quality of such treatment programs are noteworthy. Not least among the achievements of cognitive behavior therapy is its ability to embrace self-control strategies and imagery techniques. It is suggested that not only can observable motor or physiological responses be learned or extinguished, but so can covert cognitions. It is indeed reasonable to expect that the treatment of many medical problems will require modifications of behaviors from the domains of observable behavior, cognitive behavior, and physiological responses.

Cognitive-Behavioral Treatment of Chronic Vomiting

AUTHOR: Gregory A. Grinc

PRECIS: A description of a treatment model for chronic vomiting that includes self-monitoring, stimulus control, and cognitive restructuring.

INTRODUCTION: Most research in the area of chronic vomiting has focused on hospitalized infants, retarded patients, or trauma patients. However, there appears to be a lack of information regarding the treatment of "neurotic vomiters," individuals with multiple neurotic symptoms whose vomiting is multideterminted. Also referred to as bulimia, this condition is usually volitional and conceptualized as a self-destructive behavior, weight control strategy, or a maladaptive coping response to anxiety. This report provides a case-study cognitive-behavioral model for treating bulimia.

CASE HISTORY: The subject was a 26-year-old, single, white female professional. She had a 10-year history of vomiting at least once a day. The vomiting normally followed the ingestion of a large quantity of sweet foods (such as cake or cookies), although it sometimes occurred after a regular meal. Initially she had to induce regurgitation manually, but at the time of treatment she was able to induce vomiting by simply bending over the toilet.

TREATMENT: The subject was first given a complete physical examination to rule out any organic cause and to provide her with information about the physical effects of vomiting. The intervention consisted of three phases: (1) self-monitoring, where the subject recorded her food intake, vomiting, and any related thoughts and feelings; (2) stimulus control—where she was instructed to stay away from or limit situations and foods associated with vomiting; and (3) cognitive restructuring— where irrational beliefs related to the vomiting were replaced with more adaptive attitudes (following a rational-emotive model). The subject was seen for twenty sessions over a seven-month period. Initially sessions were weekly; the last ten sessions were scheduled less frequently.

Initial baseline frequencies indicated that the subject vomited twelve times weekly (this was established during the self-monitoring phase). During the next three sessions, the stimulus control phase, she substantially reduced her rate of vomiting to three times a week. After the implementation of the cognitive restructuring techniques, there was a complete stop to all vomiting. This level was maintained for 12 weeks. Then there was a short, 3-week interval when the subject vomited seven times, but she then stopped. One year after treatment began, the subject was having no episodes of regurgitation and claimed to have not vomited for over 5 months.

COMMENTARY: The self-monitoring and stimulus control techniques had a significant influence on the rate of vomiting but by themselves would not have eliminated the vomiting entirely. Research has shown that these techniques are effective interventions in the short term but require additional therapeutic measures in the treatment plan.

The use of the cognitive restructuring techniques in this case, as with any habit disorder, centered on removing those cognitions surrounding or inducing the habit (vomiting) and replacing them with more adaptive attitudes. It is this new cognitive framework that serves as a maintenance component for the new behaviors by providing the person with a new orientation toward the behavior. The author believes that such new cognitions occupy a pivotal role in the treatment process and the maintenance of a successful outcome. A cognitive-behavioral treatment has several advantages over other behavioral treatments: (1) It utilizes no aversive techniques; (2) it can be easily employed on an outpatient basis; and (3) it focuses on a variety of factors contributing to the behavior.

SOURCE: Grinc, G. A. "A Cognitive-Behavioral Model for the Treatment of Chronic Vomiting." *Journal of Behavioral Medicine*, 1982, 5, 135–141.

Cognitive-Behavioral Approaches to Pain Control

AUTHOR: Siang-Yang Tan

PRECIS: A report on cognitive and cognitive-behavioral methods for controlling and reducing pain.

INTRODUCTION: There are three reasons for the increased interest in psychological techniques for pain control over the past decade: (1) New conceptualizations in which pain is seen as a complex phenomenon resulting from the interaction of cognitive, motivational, and sensory components; (2) the inability of traditional medical approaches to alleviate pain in chronic pain sufferers; and (3) the high incidence of psychological illness in chronic pain patients. This article examines the efficacy of both cognitive strategies (techniques that modify thought processes) and cognitive-behavioral strategies (more comprehensive protocols that include both cognitive interventions and some behavioral components) used in the control of pain.

COGNITIVE TECHNIQUES: It is a common procedure to provide a patient with information about a discomforting procedure that is going to be administered. This is done to make the person's cognitive appraisal of the uncomfortable event more positive so that the pain experienced will be minimized. The information concerns either objective aspects of the upcoming event or sensations that the patient is likely to experience during the event. Research indicates that sensory information is more effective than procedural information in reducing pain, although the efficacy of giving these types of information still needs to be established.

Cognitive coping strategies offer other interventions for pain control. Although techniques such as distraction or attention diversion have been known for a long time, only recently have they come under systematic investigation. There are six categories of coping techniques: (1) imaginative inattention—ignoring pain by engaging in imagery that is incompatible with the experience of pain (such as by imagining oneself at a party);

(2) imaginative transformation of pain—acknowledging the unpleasant sensations but interpreting them as something other than pain or minimizing them as trivial or unreal; (3) imaginative transformation of context—acknowledging the pain but transforming the setting or context in which it is occurring (such as by picturing oneself as a secret agent who has been shot in a limb while driving a car down a dangerous mountain while being chased by enemy agents); (4) external attention diversion—focusing attention on the physical characteristics of the environment (such as by counting tiles on the floor or ceiling); (5) internal attention diversion—focusing attention on self-generated thought (such as by mentally performing arithmetic operations); and (6) somatization—focusing on the part of the body receiving the intense stimulation but in a detached manner. Clinical studies of these methods have produced encouraging but equivocal results.

COGNITIVE-BEHAVIORAL TECHNIQUES: A representative approach is the combination of preparatory information and instructions on coping skills or training for the reduction of stress or anxiety reactions during or after the medical procedure. Research has demonstrated this approach to be effective in reducing the level of experienced pain; however, its efficacy in reducing pain per se is not as well established.

More recently, multifaceted cognitive-behavioral treatment regimens have been employed. These include social system interventions, biofeedback, educational lectures, psychotherapy, and stimulus control procedures. The techniques may be combined differently for different pain conditions. With some pain syndromes (such as peptic ulcers), the interventions may be most effective when combined with traditional medical treatments. Multifaceted treatment regimens have been shown effective in controlling clinical pain associated with low back, ulcer, and migraine pain syndromes.

The final area relates to stress inoculation training. It is often used to manage not only pain but also anger and anxiety. This method usually involves three phases: (1) an educational phase, in which the pain experience of patients is explained (usually by means of a didactic presentation about the neuro-physiological mechanisms involved); (2) a rehearsal phase, in which the patient is exposed to a variety of techniques for coping with pain (such as distraction, relaxation, and coping self-statements), from which he or she selects those methods that appear most suitable; and (3) an application phase, in which patients are given the opportunity to test out their newly acquired skills in either a role-playing situation or by exposure to an actual pain stressor (cold pressor task). This approach incorporates both the multidimensional nature of pain and its variations among individuals by providing individuals with a variety of techniques from which to choose.

COMMENTARY: Although there are no conclusive research findings that support the efficacy of these methods, there are some encouraging results, particularly for the more comprehensive cognitive-behavioral methods. Clearly, future research must control for individual differences in coping styles and personality variables and their influence on pain reactions. A question that needs to be addressed is: Which intervention works best for whom? The author contends that these methods warrant further investigation in well-controlled laboratory and clinical studies.

SOURCE: Tan, S.-Y. "Cognitive and Cognitive-Behavioral Methods for Pain Control: A Selective Review." *Pain,* 1982, *12,* 201-228.

The Efficacy of Cognitive-Behavioral Group Therapy

AUTHOR: Judith A. Turner

PRECIS: A report comparing the effectiveness of cognitive-behavioral group therapy to progressive relaxation training in groups for treating chronic low back pain.

INTRODUCTION: Cognitive-behavioral therapies (CBT) have been widely used in managing chronic pain. The underlying rationale for this approach is that pain problems involve affective, evaluative, sensory, and behavioral components. Manipulating the various components may alter the pain experience. Progressive relaxation training (PRT) has also been used successfully with chronic pain patients. In this approach, one attempts to reduce the anxiety and muscle tension that often accompanies and exacerbates the pain experience. The purpose of this report was threefold: (1) to employ both of these procedures in a group format, (2) to evaluate their effectiveness relative to a control group, and (3) to determine if cognitive-behavioral techniques (including a relaxation component) are more effective than relaxation training alone.

METHOD: The subjects were thirty-six patients (three males and thirty-three females), aged 20 to 63 years (mean age 42 years). All had suffered low back pain for at least 6 months and were judged by a physician to have had an adequate trial of conservative medical treatment. The mean time since first back pain was 8.7 years, which is characteristic of those seen in private practice by family practitioners, internists, and orthopedic surgeons.

All subjects completed a comprehensive set of measures that assessed levels of physical and psychosocial functioning, depression, and pain. These measures included the Sickness Impact Profile, medication usage, pain severity scales, and self-ratings of improvement following treatment.

Patients were assigned to either a waiting list control group or to one of two treatment conditions. They were equally distributed across groups by age, sex, and employment status. Those in the waiting list condition were telephoned weekly, at which time they reported their daily pain ratings to the therapist. The therapist conversed with the patients but made no direct suggestions or interventions. Those in the other two groups received five weekly 90-minute sessions for treatment. There were no significant pretreatment differences among the three groups in age, radiology findings, Sickness Impact Profile scores, or pain ratings. Those in the control group, however, were significantly more depressed than patients in the other two groups.

Those in the PRT condition were taught progressive muscle relaxation techniques. Subjects received audiotapes of the procedures, which they were to practice at home at least once a day. Those in the CBT condition were also taught progressive muscle relaxation, but added to their therapy was a stress inoculation treatment for their pain. This therapy included working toward individual behavioral goals; identifying cognitive and affective responses to pain; and learning to use relaxation, imagery techniques, and coping self-statements to deal with pain. Subjects also received audiotapes of these procedures, which they were to practice daily at home.

Follow-up investigations were conducted 1 month and 1½ to 2 years after treatment. Variables of interest included: number of hours per week that the subjects were working, number of times in the past interval that they had seen a physician for back pain, all medications that they were currently taking for pain, and how often they were using the techniques that they had learned in the treatment program.

The results indicated that waiting list patients remained the same or worsened over the course of the program, while patients in the therapeutic groups had improved significantly. Both treatment groups improved on the Sickness Impact Profile, Beck Depression Inventory, and self-report ratings. Those in the CBT group also improved on daily pain severity ratings.

At the 1-month follow-up, patients in the PRT group showed no improvement from posttreatment and rated their pain as being significantly worse. Those in the CBT condition showed further improvement on the Sickness Impact Profile, Beck Depression Inventory, and daily pain severity ratings. Both groups indicated significant decreases in pain ratings from pretreatment to the follow-up at 1½ to 2 years, but only those in the CBT condition showed a significant increase in the number of hours worked per week, which were nearly double the pretreatment figure.

At the 1-month follow-up, patients in the CBT group

reported significantly less pain than those receiving PRT and viewed themselves as having improved more in terms of pain severity, the ability to tolerate pain, participation in normal activities, and anxiety reduction. They also reported the use of less somatic treatments for pain (such as massages and compresses) following treatment and anticipated greater future use of the techniques learned in the program. These differences were not observed at the follow-up investigation at 1½ to 2 years.

COMMENTARY: The results indicate that both PRT and CBT can be effective in reducing pain associated with low back difficulties. However, those receiving CBT did show significant improvements in some areas (such as self-ratings of pain), while those receiving PRT did not. This was particularly true at the 1-month follow-up, where subjects in the CBT condition continued to improve after treatment and those in the PRT group did not. The most impressive finding relates to the number of hours worked per week, which nearly doubled for CBT subjects from baseline to final follow-up. Although both treatments appear equally effective in the long run, one possible advantage of CBT over PRT is that it alters one's perception of pain. Possibly by placing the experience of pain in a different conceptual framework, coupled with techniques to lessen the amount of pain, an individual can adapt to a new life situation more rapidly. PRT, on the other hand, reduces aspects of the pain but does not provide the necessary adaptive strategies for dealing with the new circumstances brought on by the pain. Such individuals need to develop their own strategies; this issue accounts for the initial differences between the two groups at the 1-month follow-up. The use of CBT provides a durable and effective treatment for chronic pain.

SOURCE: Turner, J. A. "Comparison of Group Progressive-Relaxation and Cognitive-Behavioral Group Therapy for Chronic Low Back Pain." *Journal of Consulting and Clinical Psychology*, 1982, *50*, 757–765.

Additional Readings

Arrick, M., Vass, J., and Rimm, D. C. "The Relative Efficacy of Thought-Stopping and Covert Assertion." *Behaviour Research and Therapy*, 1981, *19*, 17-24.

These authors examined the efficacy of thought-stopping and covert assertion, alone and in combination, in reducing arousal to exposure to a fearful object (a snake). All three groups were found to have significantly lower experienced fear and arousal than a control group. There were no significant differences between the three experimental groups. The therapeutic gains were maintained over time. Given the equivalence of the treatment effects, the authors contend that there is a large amount of overlap between thought-stopping and covert assertion. Although effective in treating a specific fear, the experimental groups showed no greater generalization of effect than the control group.

Blinchik, E. R., and Grzesiak, R. C. "Reinterpretative Cognitive Strategies in Chronic Pain Management." *Archives of Physical Medicine and Rehabilitation*, 1979, *60*, 609-612.

The effectiveness of cognitive treatment for clinical pain was examined. The intervention consisted of providing subjects with a conceptualization of their pain, instruction in being aware of their thoughts prior to and during their experience of pain, and training in the use of several cognitive strategies to replace these thoughts and relabel their pain experience. The self-control strategies were presented in a group setting, which allowed subjects to role-play the instructions with one another. Subjects were instructed to reinforce themselves verbally each time they correctly used the procedure. The results indicate that the cognitive strategies were effective in altering the experience of pain.

Carney, R. M., Schecter, K., and Davis, T. "Improving Adherence to Blood Glucose Testing in Insulin-Dependent Diabetic Children." *Behavior Therapy*, 1983, *14*, 247-254.

These researchers present a program designed to increase

compliance with glucose monitoring in insulin-dependent children. The program includes contingent praise by parents and a point system in which points are given for the completion of the monitoring procedure at the scheduled times and for recording the blood glucose values. Controlled evaluation of this program showed improved compliance in the children. These improvements were maintained over a 4-month follow-up period. The authors note that the long-term metabolic control in the observed children greatly improved following the implementation of this program.

Meichenbaum, D. "Cognitive Factors in Biofeedback Therapy."
   Biofeedback and Self-Regulation, 1976, *1,* 201–216.

    A client's cognitions play an important role in each phase of biofeedback therapy. Three identifiable phases are initial conceptualization, skills acquisition and rehearsal, and transfer of treatment. Cognitive-behavioral techniques can be employed to modify an individual's cognitions to potentiate performance at each phase. The author offers a self-control theory that assumes a three-stage mediational change process: (1) The client must become an observer of his or her behavior and physiological responses; (2) this awareness becomes the cue to emit incompatible cognitions and behaviors; and (3) the cognitive content after treatment facilitates both the generalizability and durability of the therapeutic effects. This theory implies that the therapist must have a greater sensitivity to a client's cognitions so that they can be modified and included in the treatment itself. The author contends that a cognitive perspective will make biofeedback training more effective and help clarify the mechanisms that contribute to change.

3

Aiding
Patient Compliance
and Coping Skills

An important aspect of conventional medicine is the diligence with which a patient carries out the recommendations of the primary health care officer. The behavioral perspective does not invoke a simplistic trait approach ("the patient is a noncomplier") but rather treats stress coping and compliance as behaviors that can be learned, controlled, or extinguished, depending on the particular history of the patient, the physician, and the context and environment. The reports in this chapter describe models that teach and foster compliance (rather than simply noting and bemoaning it or its lack) and that indicate ways to carry out uncomfortable medical procedures more efficiently.

Adherence
to Medical Regimens

Compliance is a class of behaviors that resembles the nonhealth behaviors related to conformity, obedience, and being law abiding. Social psychology has had much to say about such phenomena. Additional insights from personality theory have further enriched our understanding about the complex way in which both environmental variables and intrapsychic factors determine how well a person's behavior can be predicted. The advent of behavioral technologies provided a powerful conceptual framework such that environmental, social, and personality factors can be understood and controlled, resulting in more effective patient compliance with medical regimens. This has proven to be of major importance as psychology increasingly addresses issues pertaining to health and medicine.

An Interactional Approach to Compliance

AUTHORS: Kathleen A. Dracup and Afaf I. Meleis

PRECIS: The proposal of a unified theoretical approach to understanding the dynamic and social mechanisms affecting patients' compliance with treatment regimens.

INTRODUCTION: There are several perspectives on compliance and the variables that affect a patient's compliance with a treatment regimen. The authors contend that these theories are limited, either because they are biased or because they do not account for the full range of relevant factors. Since compliance is central to successful health care and since one third to one half of all patients are noncompliant, the need for a comprehensive theoretical framework explaining noncompliance and the conditions that foster it becomes ever more important.

Compliance is defined as the degree to which a person selects behaviors that are consistent with a clinical intervention. The regimen must be one that is consensually developed between the patient and the clinician. Noncompliance describes behaviors that are not consistent with the consensual regimen. There are two categories of noncompliance: behaviors of omission, where the patient fails to perform certain behaviors (such as taking medications or missing appointments), and behaviors of commission, where the individual performs actions that are expressly contraindicated by the regimen (such as taking too many medications or eating restricted foods). The compliance/noncompliance framework presented here takes an interactional perspective, stressing an individual's role adjustment through his or her interaction with significant others.

ASSUMPTIONS: For the patient, compliance with a health regimen entails the development of a new role. There are four essential components to this new role: (1) the behaviors that are appropriate to the health regimen, which may include the enactment of new behaviors or the omission of previously familiar behaviors; (2) how the patient's self-concept is affected in the transition from a well to a sick role; (3) the counterroles played by the health professionals, spouses, and significant others that serve as models and provide specific cues to the maintenance of compliant behaviors; and (4) periodic evaluations of the role by the patient and those in counterroles. For compliance to occur, all four of these components must be present.

The first proposition that the authors present to augment these four essential features is that "to the extent of knowledge and competency a patient has in enacting a proposed role, a higher level of health regimen compliance is expected." This relationship is mediated by the level of complexity and the duration of the regimen. The greater the required behavioral change, the less the compliance.

The second proposition relates to the client's self-concept, which is essentially the compilation of one's repertory of roles. These roles reflect the person's life priorities, family and social roles, and sociocultural responses to wellness and illness. An important component in compliance is the ability of an individual to accept a sick role with regard to his or her illness, which includes behaviors complementary to the treatment regimen. The inability of a client to incorporate such a role into a self-concept results in noncompliant actions. As the authors note, "compliance is maximized when there is evidence that the sick or at-risk roles have been incorporated into the self-concept of the client."

The next two propositions pertain to the patient's relationships with other reference groups (other patients, health care professionals, and significant others). Research has shown that noncompliance is highly correlated with tensions in the physician-patient relationship and with the failure of the physician to explain the purpose of the treatment to the patient. Also, the involvement of other family members as well as the stability of the family constellation have been shown to correlate positively with compliance. These reference groups are useful in clarifying the patient's role within the treatment regimen. They also provide important behavioral cues and reinforcement of that role. Therefore, propositions 3 and 4 state: "Compliance is enhanced when relevant other roles are congruent and/or complementary with the client's roles" and "Compliance is enhanced if the compliance role is reinforced by significant others and other reference groups."

Basic to this role theory approach is the need for both the patient and others in counterroles to evaluate new behaviors. A variety of behavioral techniques are used at this level, including shaping, differential reinforcement, and feedback modeling of self-care procedures; all of these help to maintain or increase compliant behaviors. Proposition 5 is "the level and extent of a client's compliance . . . depends on the degree to which behaviors of compliance are judged valuable by the client and are validated by significant others." The success of attempts to increase compliance depends on a detailed assessment of omissions and commissions by the patient in the four components of role enactment: self-concept, role enactment of compliance, counterroles, and evaluations of behaviors.

COMMENTARY: The authors contend that role theory presents a unifying approach to understanding and facilitating compliance with a treatment regimen. This framework examines an individual's predicament, the impact of a disease or disorder upon one's current psychosocial functioning. It attempts to integrate social demands and internal perceptions of self in a manner that fosters a productive and supportive approach to treatment within the patient and significant others. Role theory focuses on interaction and communication processes and can be applied to both preventive and curative settings.

SOURCE: Dracup, K. A., and Meleis, A. I. "Compliance: An Interactionist Approach." *Nursing Research*, 1982, *31*, 31–36.

Adherence to Medical Regimens

AUTHOR: Jacqueline Dunbar

PRECIS: A presentation of methods for assessing compliance with a medical regimen as well as factors that affect compliance.

INTRODUCTION: Adherence to a prescribed medical regimen is an important issue for all health care professionals. The effectiveness of any therapeutic intervention rests on whether a patient follows the prescribed regimen. Noncompliance rates can range from 20% to 80%. The purpose of this report is to present some ways in which compliance can be assessed as well as to identify factors that are related to adherence.

MEASUREMENT OF ADHERENCE: Several different ways to measure adherence are described. One simple method is biological evaluation. Assays of serum or urine may detect the presence of certain drugs, their metabolites, or markers placed in the drug. This method is a direct way to determine whether a drug was consumed. However, it cannot determine the quantity of the drug taken or the length of time during which the medication was taken. A patient can take only half of a required dosage and still have a positive adherence test. Individual differences in absorption, excretion, and metabolism limit the accuracy of this measure.

Pill counts are another way to estimate the amount of a prescription taken. This method does not reveal the pattern of adherence, for instance, whether the patient is missing doses or which ones are being missed. The author believes that this is a useful method in a research setting, especially if the patient is unaware that it is being performed. However, it, too, can be problematic, especially if the patient shares medications with family or friends or forgets to return the drugs for the count.

Self-monitoring behavior is a technique that can be employed in all health care activities. This method can provide information on adherence patterns over time and can also provide data about problems that lead to noncompliance. It is a very simple technique that can provide rich and detailed information and is suitable for clinical practice. One drawback is that it can be reactive, altering the behavior itself. Although useful in a clinical setting, it can be a source of confusion in an experimental study.

Interviews are essential in assessing all health behaviors, especially in a clinical setting. Although adherence tends to be overestimated by this approach, interviews allow a patient's routine, problems, and errors to be documented in detail. Three shortcomings to this method are: (1) Patients have to rely on their own memory; (2) the more erratic patients are in their habits, the likelier they are to overestimate their adherence; and (3) social desirability and demand characteristics can be a likely source of error.

The final method is clinical estimates. Although they are frequently used, this author contends that they are very ineffective because clinicians tend to overestimate the level of compliance.

FACTORS ASSOCIATED WITH ADHERENCE: In addition to measuring the degree of adherence, there is a more important need to discover the variables affecting compliance. The factor most commonly related to a patient's ability to comply is the ability to remember and understand the clinician's advice. Research has shown that patients tested immediately after an office visit remember about two thirds of the instructions they were given. The more information patients are given, the more they forget. This difficulty can be circumvented by (1) presenting material in natural, logical categories; (2) presenting the regimen *both* verbally and in writing; (3) tailoring instructions to the patient; (4) emphasizing how to execute the regimen rather than why it is prescribed; (5) including the family in the educational process whenever possible; and (6) being aggressive about continued follow-up to ensure that the patient remembers and understands the regimen. Age, race, sex, educational level, marital status, and intelligence are *not* related to patient adherence.

Clinician characteristics also seem to affect adherence. The most obvious is the clinician's ability to instruct the patient in the details of the regimen. Another factor is the approachability of the clinician; clinicians should show empathy and understanding to the patient. Clinicians should not point out dangerous consequences of noncompliance, since raising the patients' level of fear can cause them to abandon treatment altogether.

Factors associated with the clinic also affect adherence, particularly the amount of time spent waiting for one's appointment. The longer the patient waits in the office, the greater the likelihood that the patient will not return for future appointments. The use of reminders by the clinic can help improve appointment keeping. Finally, managing the patient in a personalized, warm manner helps to improve appointment keeping. Compliance is increased when the patient is kept in treatment and makes all scheduled appointments.

Finally, the type of regimen greatly influences the degree of patient compliance. Of all the factors related to compliance, this appears to be the most crucial. Important variables in this regard include: (1) the degree to which the patient is required to change habits (the greater the need for change, the less the amount of compliance), (2) treatment complexity, (3) the number of side effects experienced, and (4) the duration of the treatment. A concerned and thoughtful clinician can help minimize the impact of these factors by providing patients with the necessary information about the regimen, handling complaints carefully, and providing support and reassurance.

COMMENTARY: Although much is known about the factors that influence adherence, it remains a major problem in the health field. Much work still needs to be done in this area. The information presented here can help a clinician provide the necessary support and information to a patient that will improve the patient's compliance with a prescribed treatment regimen.

SOURCE: Dunbar, J. "Adhering to Medical Advice: A Review." *International Journal of Mental Health,* 1980, *9,* 70-87.

The Clinician-Patient Relationship in Compliance

AUTHOR: Thomas F. Garrity

PRECIS: A review of the literature concerning aspects of the clinician-patient relationship that affect compliance with a prescribed regimen.

INTRODUCTION: Medical compliance has been studied most commonly from the perspective of the patient and the prescribed regimen; studies have focused on patient characteristics and the duration and complexity of the regimen. Very little research has addressed the client-physician relationship and the context in which the regimen is prescribed. Although there is only a small body of literature, there is sufficient evidence that the clinical relationship has an important effect upon adherence. A four-category classification is used that examines different elements of the patient-physician interaction.

CLASSIFICATION MODEL: The first element of this interaction is a pedagogical encounter whereby the clinician uses different approaches to convey the specifics of the recommended regimen. This formulation questions the presumption that the recommendations are always clearly communicated and fully understood by the patient. Research has found a link between the comprehensibility of a prescribed regimen and the degree of compliance. Among the factors that hinder the patient from remembering the advice are: (1) a large number of statements presented to the patient; (2) high anxiety of the patient; and (3) a patient's low medical knowledge. The physician can improve the recall by giving medical advice early in the interview, emphasizing its importance, using simple sentences, arranging advice in categories, and giving specific advice. Written advice can greatly facilitate the recall of instructions as well as compliance. The more clearly and specifically medical instructions are conveyed to the patient, the better the patient will comprehend his or her own responsibility.

The second element relates to mutual expectations. Individuals bring to the therapeutic situation certain expectations (the amount of time that the physician spends, the time answering questions, the type of treatment, and so on), as does the clinician. The greater the congruence between these two sets of expectations, the greater the level of compliance. Physicians who can communicate with patients in a way that can reduce discrepancies and promote a commonality of expectations increase the likelihood of patient adherence.

The third element concerns patient responsibility. Three models are identified that characterize the clinician-patient relationship. The first is the activity-passivity model, which is characterized by the physician taking total responsibility for care of the patient. Because of the imbalance of power between the physician and the patient, this model is usually most appropriate when the patient is unable to respond. The second is the guidance-cooperation model, where the physician gives recommendations and the patient is expected to comply. This is the traditional role structure in society and is seen as appropriate in situations where acute infection is the presenting complaint and the prescribed short-term therapy makes only modest demands on patient responsibility. Finally, there is the mutual participation model, where both doctor and patient share in the responsibility of patient care equally. This approach appears most appropriate in treating chronic disease, where the physician relies on information provided by the patient in order to adjust the therapy. The author notes that there is a growing body of research suggesting that greater patient responsibility in executing the therapeutic intervention leads to greater compliance.

The final element of the therapeutic relationship is the affective tone of the interaction. Included in this dimension is social support such as the material, intellectual, and emotional resources that individuals find through others, whether they are goods, services, information, sympathy, understanding, or encouragement. Particularly important is the issue of physician approachability, that is, the physician's signs of friendliness, interest, and respect for the patient. Research has shown that the degree of approachability is directly related to patient compliance; conversely, the greater the tension, disagreement, and antagonism between the doctor and patient, the greater the level of noncompliance.

COMMENTARY: Current evidence suggests that these factors play important roles in determining the degree of patient compliance. There is a need to delineate more clearly the relative contributions of each of these factors as well as their interactions with each other and with characteristics of the therapeutic situation. There is also a need to extend this analysis to different health care workers (such as nurses and health educators) and to understand how physicians try to encourage compliance in individuals with different types of illnesses. This report provides a new perspective on this issue.

SOURCE: Garrity, T. F. "Medical Compliance and the Clinician-Patient Relationship: A Review." *Social Science and Medicine,* 1981, *15E,* 215–222.

Self-Recording of Blood Pressure to Enhance Compliance

AUTHORS: Martin L. Gelman and Cyrus Nemati

PRECIS: A report establishing the reliability of a new method for self-recording blood pressure, which may increase patient compliance with antihypertensive regimens.

INTRODUCTION: Maintaining patient compliance is a major difficulty in antihypertensive control. Often this difficulty centers on controlling blood pressure (BP) after an effective drug treatment program. To rectify this difficulty, usually a family member takes the patient's BP readings at home; in some cases, the patient is taught to take the readings alone. Problems arise when the family member loses interest or the patient has difficulty in self-recording his or her BP. Commercial recording devices are expensive and often inaccurate. This report presents a new method of self-recording that is accurate, reliable, and easily performed by most patients.

METHOD: The authors call this new procedure the sensory detection method (SDM). It consists of inflating the BP cuff to a point greater than the individual's systolic pressure, then slowly releasing the pressure until the person senses a throbbing, rhythmic pulsation in the arm under the cuff. At this point, the pressure in the cuff is recorded as the systolic pressure. As the cuff continues to deflate slowly, the point where the patient no longer perceives this pulsation is recorded as the diastolic pressure. Therefore, individuals only need to inflate their cuff and slowly release the air as they monitor the pressure gauge, noting the levels at which the throbbing sensation starts and stops.

Three groups of subjects participated in this study: twenty-one normotensives (group 1), fourteen hypertensive patients who were receiving antihypertensive medications (group 2), and twenty patients undergoing cardiac catheterization (group 3). The ability to record BP was correlated with the routine indirect BP measurement taken with stethoscope and cuff by the experimenter. For group 3, SDMs were also correlated with the direct brachial artery pressure taken during arterial catheterization.

Three consecutive BP recordings were taken at 2-minute intervals by the experimenter and then averaged. Subjects were not informed of these readings. The cuff was then inflated to about 30 mm Hg over systolic pressure (usually 200 ± 10 mm Hg) and the pressure slowly reduced. Subjects were instructed to report to the experimenter when they first felt the throbbing under the cuff and then when this throbbing disappeared, at which point the systolic and diastolic pressures were recorded. The same extremity was used for all measurements (except for subjects in group 3, in whom brachial artery pressure was obtained in the opposite extremity). All recordings were taken in triplicate.

Subjects were then given instructions in the SDM. All subjects received an explanation and demonstration of the procedure two or three times before performing the method themselves. SDM BPs were taken just after the IBPs to reduce discrepancies due to lability in BP. In a single-blind fashion, the subjects were never informed of any BP readings.

No significant group differences were found between the SDM recordings and those measurements obtained by the IBPs. In group 3, there was no difference between the SDM, IBP, and direct brachial arterial pressure recordings. There were also no significant differences between any of the measurements among the different BP recording techniques for any subject. The authors concluded that the SDM is a reliable method by which patients can take their own BP.

The authors also report that 15% of the subjects (ten out of sixty-five) were not able to use the SDM for recording their BP (these subjects were not included in the study or the data analysis). Of these subjects, six were antihypertensives and also obese. All required a thigh cuff for BP measurements. Two of these subjects could not sense the throbbing sensations, and one could only sense it 75% of the time. The other three reported the sensations but were inconsistent in their judgments. The remaining four subjects were all cardiac catheterization patients who were extremely anxious during the procedure. Although they did report having the sensations, they did not feel that they could participate in the study.

COMMENTARY: The authors suggest that although SDM is a simple method for self-recording BP, it is important to determine a person's success with this technique before allowing him or her to use it. The authors contend that by providing individuals with a simple way to record their own BPs, they will comply with antihypertensive regimens more fully and maintain control of their BP. Obesity may play a role in confounding this technique by preventing individuals from perceiving the flow of blood in their extremities.

SOURCE: Gelman, M. L., and Nemati, C. "A New Method of

Blood Pressure Recording That May Enhance Patient Compliance." *Journal of the American Medical Association,* 1981, *246,* 368–370.

Enhancing Compliance with a Medical Regimen

AUTHORS: Kathleen Lowe and John R. Lutzker

PRECIS: An examination of the efficacy of written instructions and the use of a point system to improve compliance with a medical regimen in a juvenile diabetic.

INTRODUCTION: Noncompliance with a treatment regimen is a common problem in the medical profession. It is believed that over 50% of patients do not comply with prescribed routines. Research has identified some of the variables that are correlated with noncompliant behaviors, such as psychiatric diagnosis, complexity of the regimen, degree of behavior change required, duration of the regimen, and family instability. These authors also suggest that noncompliance may result from stimulus control: Patients learn to perform the required regimen in the physician's office, but the behaviors do not generalize to the home. This report examines two techniques that may reduce compliance difficulties due to reinforcement contingencies in a juvenile diabetic.

METHOD: The subject was a 9-year-old female who was non-compliant with her medical regimen. She was neglecting to test her urine, to engage in foot care, and to follow her diet.

Multiple baselines across three medical regimens (urine testing, dieting, and foot care) were used to evaluate the treatment interventions. The subject was required to make four urine tests daily; to eat all the food on her plate, to cut down on snacks, and to eat at scheduled times; and to maintain proper foot hygiene every evening. Compliance was determined by the completion of these tasks at the prescribed times or within 15 minutes of that time. The subject's mother kept a chart to monitor the degree of compliance.

The two behavioral treatments consisted of a memo program (where instructions for executing the three responsibilities were written down and given to the subject in a pamphlet form) and a point system (where the subject could earn points by correctly completing the medical instructions). Points earned could be exchanged for daily and weekly reinforcers.

A pretest was given to the subject to ensure that her noncompliance did not result from her inability to perform the required tasks. It was found that she did not know how to perform proper urine testing for acetone. When the proper skills were learned, the subject's mother was informed of the data collection methods for the study and a 1-week baseline was then established. Both the mother and the subject's older sister monitored the subject's compliance independently. The experimenter also evaluated the subject's behavior periodically. Reliabilities calculated for these family members' observations of the subject on all three dimensions ranged from 81% to 100% agreement.

Treatments were staggered over time. First, the memo format was initiated, then the point system. The memo system proved very effective for the compliance with diet (a compliance rate of 100% was observed), but it did not work as well for the other two tasks. The experimenter decided to reintroduce this method for the other two behaviors to determine if one more application would produce a change. The point system was also introduced in a staggered manner but not for the diet objective, since the memo technique was already producing satisfactory compliance. For the first month the subject's mother provided daily reinforcers, and the experimenter the weekly reinforcers. At the end of this time, the parents were the sole providers of all rewards as the experimenter gradually reduced involvement with the subject. At the end of 10 weeks, the experimenter formally terminated involvement and the parents continued the program. Follow-up data were collected 2½ months later.

The results indicate that the point system was effective in increasing compliance with foot care and urine testing responsibilities. Although the memo technique was relatively ineffective for these two behaviors, it did greatly facilitate dietary compliance. The point system was able to increase compliance rates for urine testing and foot care from 16% and 72% to 97% and 100%, respectively. The follow-up data indicate that these gains were maintained. It is important to note that over this 10-week period, the subject's mother continued to implement these techniques and apparently did so effectively without any assistance from the experimenter.

COMMENTARY: As the authors point out, the results of this study are promising, but further research is needed to generalize these techniques. By all indications, behavior management techniques appear to be effective for reducing noncompliance in patients. These techniques could greatly help a patient to establish the habits necessary for successfully completing a medical regimen in the person's own home. Gradually, after proper monitoring, responsibility for maintaining the regimen could be transferred from a professional therapist to the patient or the patient's family.

SOURCE: Lowe, K., and Lutzker, J. R. "Increasing Compliance to a Medical Regimen with a Juvenile Diabetic." *Behavior Therapy,* 1979, *10,* 57–64.

Additional Readings

Epstein, L. H., and Cluss, P. A. "A Behavioral Medicine Perspective on Adherence to Long-Term Medical Regimens." *Journal of Consulting and Clinical Psychology,* 1982, *50,* 950–971.
    This report reviews the literature on behavioral procedures that enhance compliance and influence outcomes. There

is a growing body of research that confirms the value of feedback of drug levels and the value of reinforcement for medication intake. Self-monitoring techniques for medications and symptomatology have not been as effective. The authors note the promise of self-regulation and tailoring techniques, even though further research is necessary. The authors also point to the need for more research to establish goals for compliant behavior and to measure the relation of adherence to treatment outcome.

Iwata, B. A., and Becksfort, C. M. "Behavioral Research in Preventative Dentistry: Educational and Contingency Management Approaches to the Problem of Patient Compliance." *Journal of Applied Behavior Analysis,* 1981, *4,* 111–120.

Patients enrolled in an ongoing program at a periodontal practice received three to five sessions of instruction in preventive dental care. Half the subjects also had a portion of their fees refunded if their dental plaque scores fell. Posttreatment results indicated that those in the latter group had plaque scores significantly below baseline and below the scores for subjects in the instruction only and control groups. These improvements were maintained at a 6-month follow-up. The authors conclude that instruction in preventive hygiene care does not strongly influence compliance. The introduction of monetary reinforcement, however, produced a durable change in compliance with a preventive dental regimen. Although it may not be economically feasible to institute such a regimen, other forms of reinforcement may be as effective, such as token reinforcements or systematic social praise.

Kaplan, N. M., Simmons, M., McPhee, C., Carnegie, A., Stefanu, C., and Cade, S. "Two Techniques to Improve Adherence to Dietary Sodium Restrictions in the Treatment of Hypertension." *Archives of Internal Medicine,* 1982, *142,* 1638–1641.

Two simple techniques were assessed for their ability to increase hypertensives' compliance with dietary restrictions of sodium: overnight urine collection and immediate analysis of urine sodium content. These techniques were applied to a sample of hypertensives who resisted adopting the dietary changes.

The results indicate that after 6 months, 68% of the patients had reduced their sodium content by one third or more. There was also an associated decrease in mean blood pressure (11 mm Hg) over the control group. The use of such rapid and accurate estimates of urinary content appears to enhance compliance. Such methods are consistent with issues raised by other authors in this chapter.

Shephard, R. J., Corey, P., and Kavanagh, T. "Exercise Compliance and the Prevention of a Recurrence of Myocardial Infarction." *Medicine and Science in Sports and Exercise*, 1981, *13*, 1-5.

This report examined the effect of compliance with an exercise regimen upon the prognosis of postcoronary patients. The exercise program focused on progressive, long, and slow distance running. Regimens were individually tailored to bring patients to a certain level of fitness. Other factors associated with prognosis were also observed, including smoking behavior and disease severity. The results indicate a strong relationship between compliance with the program and reduced risk of a recurring infarction. In evaluating their results, the authors note that it is difficult to ascertain whether the benefits of the program are due to the physical activity or to the effects of some indirect variables related to adherence to the exercise regimen. Their results suggest that health habits and disease severity are not the main factors in predicting prognosis.

Stunkard, A. J. "Adherence to Medical Treatment: Overview and Lessons from Behavioral Weight Control." *Journal of Psychological Research*, 1981, *25*, 187-197.

Rather than a personality trait, compliance is more properly viewed as a behavioral event. Compliance is greatly influenced by several factors. First, it is influenced by the complexity of the treatment regimen. The more complex, the greater the number of medications and their corresponding side effects, and the longer the duration of the regimen, the likelier that compliance will be poor. A second major influence is patient factors, such as the degree of understanding of the regimen instructions, family support, and satisfaction with the physician.

Third are the characteristics of the clinic. Continuity of care, short waiting periods, and mail or telephone reminders all favorably influence compliance. Finally, attributes of the clinician play an important role. Warmth, empathy, and interest toward the patient help motivate the patient to complete the treatment successfully.

Preparation
for Stressful
Procedures

Many medical encounters are sudden and do not allow for coping or anticipation. As a result, the medical treatment program must often deal with the anxieties produced. However, there are a number of diagnostic and therapeutic procedures in medicine and dentistry where the patient has a chance to prepare for unavoidable discomfort. An effective protocol for these procedures not only benefits the patient's psychological well-being but also reduces the anxiety of the primary health care team, thus enhancing the efficiency of their activities.

Increasing Tolerance
for a Painful Clinical EMG Examination

AUTHORS: Robert M. Kaplan, Gail Metzger, and Charles Jablecki

PRECIS: Description of the use of pretreatment cognitive and relaxation techniques to increase tolerance for a painful electromyographic examination.

INTRODUCTION: There is a growing interest in developing procedures that can prepare individuals for painful clinical examinations. Research has shown that cognitive and behavioral techniques can help patients tolerate pain. However, this research has focused on pain tolerance and the perception of pain in laboratory-induced conditions. Thus, it is only speculative that such results can be generalized to a clinical practice, since many factors operate in a clinical setting that are not found in the laboratory (for example, clinically induced pain may be exaggerated by anxiety).

The purpose of this study was to examine the effectiveness of cognitive and behavioral techniques in increasing tolerance to a painful EMG examination in a clinical setting. The EMG examination consists of two parts. The first is the stimulation of nerves and muscles using surface electrodes that carry electrical currents having a duration of from 0.01 to 1 millisecond with an output between 50 and 250 volts. The second phase consists of inserting needle electrodes into specific muscles to record action potentials during spontaneous or voluntary activity. The shocks and needle insertions produce considerable discomfort and anxiety, especially since this procedure is done without the use of tranquilizers or anesthetics.

METHOD: Subjects consisted of forty adult male patients who were scheduled to undergo a clinical EMG examination. They were randomly assigned to one of three experimental groups or an attention control group.

In the relaxation-training-only group, the subjects were

told of the effectiveness of relaxation in reducing pain and stress (natural childbirth methods were given as examples). They were then exposed to the tension release techniques of progressive relaxation training. Deep breathing techniques were then described as a way to achieve the desired state of relaxation. Finally, the subjects were instructed to close their eyes and visualize themselves being in the examination room. When they began to visualize the onset of the procedure, they were then instructed to rehearse the breathing technique in order to relax.

In the cognitive reappraisal group, subjects were told of the influence that positive or negative thinking can have on one's experience of a situation. These subjects received instructions to focus their attention on the positive aspects of the examination and to think in a positive, calming way. A tape recording of positive, coping self-statements was played to model the type of cognitive behaviors that they were to engage in while undergoing the exam. The subjects were told that the recording was of another patient who had gone through the procedure; the recording was thus narrative in style (for example, "When I felt some pain, I would say things like 'This does hurt, but I can handle it. One step at a time.' "). After hearing the tape, subjects were instructed to close their eyes and visualize being in the examination room. While imagining going through the procedure, they were to practice the type of positive self-statements they were to use. They were then given feedback from the experimenter and went through another rehearsal.

In the cognitive-behavioral modification group, subjects were given the same instructions that the cognitive reappraisal group received. Subjects in this combined condition received the relaxation training and allowed one rehearsal, followed by the cognitive modification instructions with one practice opportunity. Finally, they were instructed to rehearse both strategies by covertly engaging in the positive self-talk while breathing in the prescribed manner. Each of these treatment conditions lasted approximately 15 minutes.

In the attention control group, subjects did not receive any instructions regarding specific coping strategies. However, they were interviewed by the experimenter for 15 minutes in order to provide a control for exposure time and attention. Demographic and general health questions were asked in an attempt to convey interest and concern for the patient.

The EMG procedure always began within 15 minutes of the experimental training sessions. The dependent measures included heart rate, which was recorded prior to, during, and immediately after each electrical stimulation and needle insertion. These multiple physiological observations were averaged to obtain a single score. Following each stimulation or insertion, subjects were asked (by an observer blind to the experimental condition of the subject) to rate the degree of discomfort just experienced. These responses were given on an 11-point scale with "not painful" at one pole and "extremely painful" at the other (subjects were instructed about the use of the scale prior to the examination). Behavioral observations were also recorded during the procedure. These included gross body movements, facial grimaces, and distress vocalizations. These observations were recorded by the observer, whose accuracy was assessed at over 90%. After the EMG was completed, subjects filled out a postexamination questionnaire, which asked for self-ratings of anxiety and discomfort and about the perceived benefit of the intervention. Finally, the physician, who was also blind to the experimental condition of the subjects, rated the degree of discomfort displayed by each patient during the procedure on an 11-point scale, from "not distressed" to "extremely distressed."

The data analyses showed that the three experimental groups exhibited less distress than did the attention control group. Subjects in the control group also reported experiencing more pain during the examination than did patients in the other groups; experimental subjects reported receiving more benefit from the intervention than did the controls. Heart rates remained lower for the experimental subjects than for the controls. The two groups that received relaxation training had lower mean heart rates than the two groups not receiving such instructions. However, there were no significant differences in the effectiveness of the intervention among the three experimental groups.

Although there were no significant differences in the

effectiveness of the three experimental groups, the authors suggest that the cognitive-behavioral modification approach may be the most effective in increasing pain tolerance. They base their contention on other research, which divides responses to anxiety into two components, cognitive and somatic. Both of these components should be addressed by an intervention if it is to be truly effective. The results of this study appear to confirm this dual nature of anxiety. Subjects who received relaxation training showed greater decreases in heart rate than those in the cognitive group. Yet the cognitive group did show a greater change on the self-report measures. On a more pragmatic level, the cognitive-behavioral modification approach accommodates a wider variety of factors influencing pain perception and may appeal to a wider majority of patients.

COMMENTARY: This study highlights two important facts. First, behavioral and cognitive approaches to increasing tolerance to pain can be effective in a clinical setting. Second, the interventions used, because of their small time consumption, can be very practical and effective in a clinical practice and usually administered in the time a patient spends in the waiting room. In addition, this article is valuable in reminding us that behavioral treatments can be appropriate for many medical diagnostic procedures.

SOURCE: Kaplan, R. M., Metzger, G., and Jablecki, C. "Brief Cognitive and Relaxation Training Increases the Tolerance for a Painful Clinical Electromyographic Examination." *Psychosomatic Medicine*, 1983, *45*, 155–162.

Minimizing Anxiety in Hospitalized Children

AUTHORS: Lizette Peterson and Carol Shigetomi

PRECIS: A comparison of the effectiveness of three coping techniques in reducing anxiety in children awaiting elective tonsillectomies.

INTRODUCTION: Over the years, a variety of procedures have been developed for decreasing stress and anxiety in individuals preparing for painful medical procedures. These techniques are useful for assuring that such medical procedures are completed smoothly and without event for both patient and doctor. Although these techniques are successful, the authors contend that current techniques have limitations that restrict their effectiveness. Three major difficulties are as follows: (1) Viewing a model successfully undergoing the anticipated procedure does not by itself provide patients with specific techniques to effect such coping themselves; (2) modeling or information procedures do not by themselves provide parents with specific techniques for giving their child emotional support throughout the hospital stay; and (3) current procedures do not offer specific ways for the patient to reduce pain. The authors believe that the benefits of modeling and information techniques can be greatly enhanced by introducing cognitive coping procedures that give patients a greater sense of control over their hospitalization. Such increased perceived control would also lessen aversiveness to any pain experienced. They also contend that such coping procedures in tandem with a modeling technique would be more effective than either procedure alone.

METHOD: Sixty-six children, thirty-five girls and thirty-one boys aged 2.5 to 10.5 years, participated in this study. All were hospitalized for elective tonsillectomies. None of the children had experienced surgery previously, and none had been hospitalized within a year of this admission. All children were treated in the same hospital where the study took place.

The children were randomly assigned to one of four ex-

perimental conditions. The first was the preoperative information procedure. Approximately 4 days before surgery, children and parents were invited to a "Big Bird Ice Cream Party"
at the hospital. Here, the experimenter narrated a story of a
typical hospital stay from admission to discharge while Big
Bird pantomimed the activities. Emphasized were the blood
test, administration of preoperative medications, postoperative
discomfort, and the need to consume fluids.

In the second experimental condition, the children were
taught coping procedures. The goal of this technique, as was
explained to the children, was to make them feel as content
and happy in the hospital as they felt when they were at home.
Three techniques were taught to the children. The first was cue-
controlled deep muscle relaxation. This was done by having the
children alternately tense and relax their muscles. Eventually,
the cue word *calm* and slow deep breathing were introduced.
Children practiced the sequence of tensing, relaxing, and say-
ing the word *calm* to themselves as they exhaled. The second
coping technique taught was distracting mental imagery. Here
children were asked to imagine peaceful, calming scenes that
made them feel happy. Parents were encouraged to help their
children make this scene as positive and vivid as possible by
using very detailed, descriptive language. The third technique
was comforting self-talk. The children were given two specific
sentences to use: "I will be better in a little while" and "Everything is going to be all right." They were encouraged to say the
sentences out loud and then silently to themselves and to construct other calming self-instructions.

The third experimental condition was the filmed modeling procedure. Here children and their parents viewed a film
that was a detailed, realistic portrayal of the hospitalization,
preparation, surgery, and recovery of a 7-year-old boy with
a hernia. The fourth condition was the coping plus filmed modeling procedure. Children in this group first received the preoperative information (via Big Bird), learned the coping techniques, and then viewed the modeling movie. All children
received a tour of the hospital, which included the operating
room, playroom, and patient suites in the pediatric ward.

The dependent measures were: fluid and food consumption, latency to void (recorded by parents during the first 10 hours after surgery), and child observational ratings. The laboratory technician who drew blood from all the children rated them on three Lickert scales: how anxious they appeared, how cooperative they were in following the procedure, and how well they tolerated the procedure (drawing of blood). Parents, nurses, and the experimenter also completed observational ratings on two 5-point scales measuring anxiety and cooperativeness. These measures were completed the morning before, the morning after, and the afternoon after surgery. Parents also completed self-ratings measuring confidence and calmness before and after the surgery. Two weeks after the discharge of their child, parents completed another scale that assessed how favorable they found the hospital stay.

The results indicated that children in the cognitive plus modeling group consumed more food than children in any other group after surgery. Ratings made by the laboratory technician also indicated that children in this group received significantly better ratings than those in the modeling-only group. Better child ratings were obtained from parents with children in the coping conditions than from parents with children in the other two groups. Parents with children in the modeling-only group rated their children as more anxious and less cooperative on the afternoon of surgery than parents with children in the other conditions. In addition, parents with children in the coping conditions rated themselves as more competent and less anxious following surgery than parents with children in the modeling conditions. Also, parents with children in the coping conditions rated the hospital experience significantly more favorable than the other parents. It appears that the coping techniques, though primarily directed toward the child, were effective in reducing parental anxieties and increasing parental feelings of self-efficacy.

COMMENTARY: Cognitive coping strategies were effective in making both parent and child feel less anxiety and a greater sense of control within the medical setting. Since parents of hospitalized children often experience high levels of anxiety, the authors believe that helping the parent reduce anxiety may be important in reducing the child's level of anxiety. Equipped with such effective means of dealing with anxiety associated with aversive events, patients and parents may even have long-lasting, positive psychological benefits.

SOURCE: Peterson, L., and Shigetomi, C. "The Use of Coping Techniques to Minimize Anxiety in Hospitalized Children." *Behavior Therapy,* 1981, *12,* 1-14.

Anxiety Reduction as a Function of Stimulus Preexposure and Coping Style

AUTHORS: Robert H. Shipley, James H. Butt, Bruce Horwitz, and John E. Farbry

PRECIS: An example of the reduction of anxiety about a stressful medical procedure by manipulation of stimulus preexposure and coping style.

INTRODUCTION: Techniques for reducing anxiety associated with stressful medical procedures have generally been effective, and most are based on modeling or providing accurate information. Viewing a model who initially manifests anxiety and then overcomes this arousal (coping model) is more effective than viewing a model who exhibits no fear throughout the procedure. Having individuals develop accurate cognitive expectancies of a procedure also helps to alleviate stress. This study examines the effect of the amount of prior nonreinforced exposure to stimuli associated with a stressful procedure. It was hypothesized that the more preexposure, the greater the habituation, and consequently the less the anxiety about the novel situation. Imitation of the model's coping responses was minimized by having the model appear fearful throughout the procedure.

An important variable in reducing patients' anxiety may be their characteristic mode of coping with stress. Thus, patients were also classified according to their repression-sensitization coping style. It was believed that sensitizers would exhibit decreasing levels of anxiety with increasing exposure; repressors would initially be low in anxiety, but increasing exposure would increase their anxiety and then reduce it (that is, their level of anxiety would be an inverted U function).

METHOD: The subjects consisted of sixty patients, fifty males and ten females, preparing to undergo upper gastrointestinal endoscopy. None had any previous experience with this procedure. They ranged in age from 22 to 80 years (mean 53.0). Patients were randomly assigned to one of three experimental conditions.

Each patient, regardless of experimental condition, was informed about the procedure on three occasions by the nurse, doctor, and the experimenter. The information concerned procedural details, likely sensations, and possible complications. The three conditions consisted of seeing a control videotape (26-minute tape about the memoirs of a distinguished physician) or the experimental videotape. (In this 18-minute tape, a 35-year-old white male actually received an endoscopy. The subject showed an average amount of distress, gagging several times and requiring some reassurance from the nurse.) There were two experimental groups, one seeing the experimental tape once (E1) and the other three times (E3). The tapes were shown the night before the procedure.

There were several dependent measures of anxiety. A physiological measure (heart rate) was monitored during the endoscopy; a behavioral measure of anxiety was completed by the physician and nurse and was designed to assess patients' fear before, during, and after the procedure. It consisted of eight items rated on a 5-point scale, ranging from "not at all" to "very much." A second behavioral index of anxiety was whether a patient received Valium during the endoscopy.

Finally, two self-report measures were included. Subjects completed the Spielberger State-Trait Anxiety Scale (STAI) the night before, the morning of, and 2 to 4 hours after the procedure. The state anxiety dimension was expected to vary over the experimental manipulations and over the course of the procedure. No such differences were expected on the trait anxiety dimension. The second self-report measure was the Post-Endoscopy Interview Schedule, which is a structured inquiry into the patients' reactions to the procedure. This measure was administered during the preparation videotape and before and during the endoscopy. A Modified Repression-Sensitization (R-S) Scale was also given to classify patients according to their style of coping with anxiety-provoking situations.

The results conformed to expectations. Subjects in group E3 were rated by the nurse and physician as being significantly less anxious both before and during the endoscopy than the controls. Those in E1 were rated significantly less anxious than controls during scoping. Results of the STAI scales showed no significant differences between the groups on the trait anxiety dimension. Following endoscopy, differences emerged on the state anxiety dimension, groups E3 and E1 showing significantly lower anxiety scores. The postendoscopy interview showed that the number of patients in E3 complaining about the procedure was significantly lower than the number of subjects in the other two groups. Subjects in the control group were significantly more annoyed during the procedure than subjects in the other two groups.

The results on the R-S classification scale also conformed with expectations. With increasing exposure to the videotape model, sensitizers exhibited lower mean heart rate increases during the endoscopy. Since sensitizers characteristically handle stress by being vigilant, overanxious, and alert to threatening cues, use intellectualization as a defense, and actively seek information about a stressor to prepare for experiencing it, they are initially high in anxiety; however, such arousal decreases as a linear function of exposure to the procedure. Repressors, on the other hand, had lower mean heart rate increases in the control and E3 conditions. Repressors in E1 showed a much higher level of anxiety than repressors in the other two groups (thus creating an inverted U function). The authors contend that repressors are characteristically not overtly anxious and handle impending stress by repressing it or denying it. Consequently, they would be initially low in anxiety, but one exposure to an explicit videotape of the endoscopy would impair their repressing defenses and increase their arousal. However, repeated exposures to such a tape decrease anxiety as in sensitizers.

Overall, the results were consistent with predictions in that group E3 subjects evidenced the least anxiety about the endoscopy, followed by subjects in group E1 and then the controls. The authors suggest that this study supports the extinction/habituation hypothesis. Three exposures to the taped model produced greater habituation or extinction of emotion than one exposure. Even one viewing produced greater habituation than no exposure.

COMMENTARY: As the authors note, sensitizers and repressors may benefit from different preparation procedures for stress. Sensitizers might benefit from extensive preparation for the stressful procedure. Repressors could be exposed to messages that support their defenses by minimizing the stressfulness or encouraging avoidance by selective attention and calming self-talk. Regardless of the theoretical interpretation of the results, the effectiveness of repeated preexposure to a stressful medical procedure in reducing patient anxiety is of high practical importance.

SOURCE: Shipley, R. H., Butt, J. H., Horwitz, B., and Farbry, J. E. "Preparation for a Stressful Medical Procedure: Effect of Amount of Stimulus Preexposure and Coping Style." *Journal of Consulting and Clinical Psychology,* 1978, *46,* 499-507.

Reducing Stress in Children's Responses
to Repeated Dental Procedures

AUTHORS: Lawrence J. Siegel and Lizette Peterson

PRECIS: A report assessing the effects of sensory information and training in coping skills on preschool children's responses to repeated, stressful dental procedures.

INTRODUCTION: Reducing children's distress over dental procedures is an important issue. Systematic desensitization and filmed modeling techniques have had some effect in reducing anxiety, but their success usually depends on the subjects' age and previous dental experience. The techniques proposed in this report—sensory information and coping skills—may be more effective in reducing anxiety that may be generalizable to a larger subject population. It may also be more cost-effective, since it requires little investment of time and little need for specialized equipment. Although previous research has clearly shown the efficacy of these methods, this report examines the utility of these techniques in reducing anxiety and facilitating cooperation over a repeated number of exposures to dental procedures.

METHOD: The subjects consisted of twenty-six preschool children ranging in age from 42 to 71 months (mean 59.8). The majority of these children had no previous contact with a dentist.

Subjects were randomly assigned to one of three experimental conditions. The first was the coping skills condition, where children were taught general relaxation and deep and regular breathing with the pairing of relaxing cue words (*calm* and *nice*). Guided imagery techniques were used to help the children think about pleasant scenes and activities. Finally, subjects were instructed in the use of calming self-talk by repeating the sentences: "I will be all right in just a little while. Everything is going to be all right." In the sensory information group, children were presented with a description of the procedures to be encountered, typical sensations, and sights and sounds they would experience. A brief tape recording of some of these sounds, in particular that of the dental drill, was played for the children. The subjects were then told how they would feel at various points during the treatment (for instance, "After the dentist finishes, your mouth will feel tingly and heavy"). Finally, there was the experimenter contact control group. Here children were read a chapter from *Winnie the Pooh*.

A variety of anxiety measures, rated by independent observers, were used: (1) the Behavior Profile Rating Scale to measure maladaptive behavior, (2) a 7-point scale to measure cooperation and anxiety, and (3) responses to the injection of the anesthetic. Arousal levels were also determined by recording radial pulse for 30 seconds just before and immediately after the dental treatment.

Each child visited the dentist three or more times. These visits were scheduled 6 to 10 days apart. During the first session, baseline measures were obtained. This appointment consisted of an examination and standard cleaning. In the remaining sessions, behavior was measured during the placement of amalgam restoration fillings. Involved in these sessions was the use of topical anesthetic and the injection of a local anesthetic. These sessions lasted approximately 30 minutes. The dentist, oral hygienist, and observers were blind to the experimental condition of the children. About one half hour before the second visit, children received their respective experimental treatment procedure, which lasted approximately 10 minutes.

The results indicated no significant differences between the groups on any of the measures at pretreatment. However, significant differences emerged at the first and second posttreatments. Subjects in the two experimental conditions exhibited significantly less maladaptive behaviors, were more cooperative, appeared less anxious, and were less distressed during the injection of the anesthetic than were subjects in the control group. There were no significant differences between the sensory information and coping skills conditions on any of these measures. However, the sensory information group had significantly lower pulse rates than the other two groups after the two posttreatment dental sessions.

The authors conclude that one treatment presentation was sufficient to reduce significantly anxiety, disruptive responding, and physiological arousal and to increase cooperativeness during the dental procedure immediately following the presentation. In addition, these gains were maintained during a second dental procedure administered 1 week later. Some of these children experienced more than two sessions, and an evaluation of these single-subject data indicates that these benefits are effective and maintained over several such visits.

COMMENTARY: The two procedures outlined appear to be useful strategies in reducing emotional arousal in children preparing for a dental procedure. These protocols involve a small cost and yet their benefits are immediately evidenced and maintained over a period of time. Although subjects were mostly blacks from a lower socioeconomic level, the authors contend that these procedures could be productively used with children from other economic backgrounds.

SOURCE: Siegel, L. J., and Peterson, L. "Maintenance Effects of Coping Skills and Sensory Information on Young Children's Responses to Repeated Dental Procedures." *Behavior Therapy*, 1981, *12*, 530–535.

Additional Readings

Kaplan, R. M., Akins, C. J., and Lenhard, L. "Coping with a Stressful Sigmoidoscopy: Evaluation of Cognitive and Relaxation Preparations." *Journal of Behavioral Medicine*, 1982, *5*, 67–82.

These authors examined the effectiveness of two brief interventions designed to facilitate coping with a stressful sigmoidoscopy—self-instructional training and relaxation. In the former condition, subjects were told to focus their attention on either their own (internal) or the physician's (external) ability to regulate the situation. A no-treatment control group was also included. Half of all subjects received relaxation training (including those in the control group). Those receiving the self-instructional strategies rated themselves as less anxious, had fewer body movements during the exam, and made fewer verbalizations than the controls. Those receiving external instructions felt the exam took less time but had an elevated heart rate during the procedure. Those receiving relaxation training tended to overestimate the length of the exam but rated themselves less anxious and made fewer requests to stop the exam than those not receiving such training.

Kobasa, S. C., Maddi, S. R., and Puccetti, M. C. "Personality and Exercise as Buffers in the Stress-Illness Relationship." *Journal of Behavioral Medicine,* 1982, *5,* 291–404.

This study examines the influence of exercise and personality-based hardiness (a measure assessing alienation and commitment) in moderating stressful events and the association of these measures with an increased risk of illness. Self-report measures were collected from 137 male business executives. The results indicated that both hardiness and exercise interact with stressful events in reducing the likelihood of illness. These two factors also have an additive effect in that people who are active exercisers and high in measures of hardiness remain healthier than those high in only one of these measures. The authors contend that hardiness serves as a buffer that transforms events so as to reduce their stressfulness, while exercise moderates stress by reducing the organismic strain of the stressful event.

Wilson, J. F., Moore, R. W., Randolph, S., and Hanson, B. J. "Behavioral Preparation of Patients for Gastrointestinal Endoscopy: Information, Relaxation, and Coping Style." *Journal of Human Stress,* 1982, *8,* 13–23.

These researchers compared the effectiveness of (1) informing patients of expected sensations, (2) training patients in systematic muscle relaxation, and (3) receiving normal hospital procedures as strategies for reducing fear, anxiety, arousability, and avoidance in patients undergoing gastrointestinal endoscopy. The results indicated that the information and relaxation groups had reduced heart rate increases during the procedure and lowered ratings of distress. The relaxation group experienced greater positive mood changes following the procedure. It was also found that patients benefited most from preparations that matched their preferred style of coping, although they were not harmed by a preparation that did not. The authors suggest that using coping styles as a criterion for excluding patients from certain preparation techniques is inappropriate.

Zelter, L., and Le Baron, S. "Hypnosis and Nonhypnotic Techniques for Reduction of Pain and Anxiety During Painful Procedures in Children and Adolescents with Cancer." *Journal of Pediatrics,* 1982, *101,* 1032-1035.

This study compared the effectiveness of hypnosis and behavioral techniques in reducing pain and anxiety in children and adolescents receiving bone marrow aspiration or lumbar puncture. Measures of pain and anxiety were determined by self-report and observer ratings. Hypnosis was found to significantly reduce pain as effectively as the nonhypnotic techniques. During marrow aspiration, the effect was not as pronounced. Anxiety was only reduced by hypnosis. During lumbar puncture, only hypnosis reduced pain, and hypnosis was more effective in reducing anxiety than the behavioral techniques. These results argue for hypnosis as a viable intervention for reducing the anxiety and pain associated with a painful medical procedure.

4

Therapies
for Recurrent
Physical Distress

The high regard for traditional medical practice does not usually extend to those disorders that never seem to go away. The patient who is told "to learn to live with it" often seeks other sources for relief. With increasing frequency, physicians themselves enlist the services of other therapists who are likely to improve a patient's health status when neither more drugs nor surgery seems appropriate. This chapter focuses on health disorders that constitute the bulk of such complaints. These reports examine a variety of somatic dysfunctions in which various therapeutic styles are used. Taken together, these reports demonstrate the remarkable clinical utility that established behavior therapy procedures hold for the general practice of medicine.

137

Menstrual Problems

The menstrual cycle is accompanied by changes in hormonal and muscular levels. For many women, the monthly period is accompanied by much somatic distress and often considerable debilitation. Medication by itself does not always provide the desired relief. Behavioral techniques that offer patients a measure of control by inducing a generalized relaxation effect or reducing EMG levels of specific muscle groups have been shown to be effective treatments. Beneficial results have been reported for procedures that rely heavily on biofeedback as well as cognitive and self-control strategies. This class of discomfort presents many challenges to the specialty of behavioral medicine, including not only therapeutic aspects but psychometric, psychogenic, and other psychological issues as well.

Treating Dysmenorrhea with Biofeedback and Relaxation Training

AUTHORS: Carl D. Bennink, Linda L. Hulst, and James A. Benthem

PRECIS: An examination of the effects of EMG biofeedback and relaxation training in controlling primary dysmenorrhea.

INTRODUCTION: The use of biofeedback training to provide relief from primary dysmenorrhea has previously been studied and has included modalities involving alpha brain waves, the frontalis muscle, hand temperature, and vaginal temperature. Recent reviews of these studies indicate that biofeedback training is either not successful or not superior to other behavioral interventions. The authors partly attribute this result to the types of feedback used. It is hard to postulate a relationship between increased control of the frontalis muscle, alpha waves, or hand temperature and reduced symptoms of dysmenorrhea, especially since it is the increased tonus of the uterine muscles that is implicated in this disorder. Attempts to promote greater control over the uterine muscles or associated areas may greatly enhance a biofeedback training intervention. This study investigated such attempts, as well as investigating whether biofeedback is superior to other types of behavioral interventions.

To evaluate the effectiveness of treatments, clear criteria of success must be developed. Two important criteria include (1) reduction in a patient's experience of pain during menstruation and (2) the patient's ability to consciously reduce or control the level of myometrial tension during menstruation. This study compares the effectiveness of EMG training with general relaxation training in terms of these criteria. The authors hypothesized that biofeedback may not be superior in reducing patients' experience of pain but is more useful than relaxation training in increasing patients' ability to consciously reduce myometrial tonus during menstruation.

METHOD: Fifteen females, mean age of 19.2 years, participated in this study. They were selected on the following bases: (1) All experienced spasmodic dysmenorrhea as determined by the Menstrual Symptom Questionnaire; (2) all experienced "moderate" to "very severe" menstrual cramping as determined by the Symptom Severity Scale (SSS); (3) none had a history of pregnancy; (4) none were using oral contraceptives; (5) all appeared highly motivated to complete this study, which lasted for several months; (6) all expressed a willingness not to take any medications for menstrual pain relief during the course of the study; and (7) all had been previously diagnosed as not having an organic disease underlying their condition.

Subjects were randomly assigned to one of three conditions: EMG biofeedback plus relaxation training, relaxation training alone, and no treatment (control). Five subjects were in each group. After the completion of the menstrual cycle following their initial interview, individuals recorded the subjective severity of abdominal cramping on a rating scale every 5 days until 5 days before their next menstrual period and then every day until 5 days after its termination. The scale ranged from 1 ("very low level abdominal cramping barely entering awareness") to 5 ("intense, incapacitating abdominal cramping") and was marked off for each of the 24 hours in a day. For each menstrual cycle, several baseline ratings as well as ratings of discomfort during and immediately after menstruation were obtained.

Approximately one month after the initial interview, subjects returned to complete another SSS and were given exposure to the EMG procedure (subjects in the control group did not receive this exposure). Electrodes were then attached to the lower abdomen. Subjects were instructed to relax for several minutes while baseline EMG recordings were taken. During the third or fourth cycle, subjects received the treatment appropriate to their assigned group. Subjects in the feedback and relaxation condition received five 30-minute training sessions, three sessions prior to menstruation and one for each of the initial 2 days of menstrual flow. After a 5-minute baseline period was established, a 15-minute tape recording of general relaxation instructions was played. After hearing the tape, subjects were instructed to tense their abdominal muscles for 30 seconds and then to relax them for 2 minutes. This tense/relax sequence was repeated three times. Feedback consisted of an auditory signal that rose or fell in pitch with the level of tension in these muscles. The goal of the session was for the subject to terminate the auditory signal by reaching a predetermined criterion. The level when the tone would cease while tensing remained constant over all sessions. However, the level at which the signal was terminated for relaxation was decreased (that is, the subject had to become more relaxed) during each relaxation period in order to maintain a 75% success rate.

In the relaxation only condition, the same procedures were followed as in the previous group except that no biofeedback was provided. Subjects in the control group were contacted during this period and informed that training sessions would be scheduled for them during their next cycle. One week following the last treatment session and before their next menstrual period, all subjects (including controls) returned to the laboratory and completed another SSS. Each subject received one score for each SSS completed (there was a total of three) by summing the values for each of the fifteen scales contained in this measure. A second score was obtained for each subject by summing values for only three symptoms: cramps, backache, and abdominal pain. A third score was based only on the value for the cramps symptom.

No significant differences were found between pre- and posttreatment SSS scores when all symptoms were taken into account. On the second SSS-derived value, all subjects showed a reduction in these three symptoms from pre- to posttreatment intervals, but this trend was significant only for the EMG biofeedback and relaxation training condition. The intensity rating scales showed no significant differential effects upon intensity ratings between the two treatment groups.

From the EMG data, two important results emerged. First, during the first day of menstruation, EMG activity levels in the lower abdomen increased significantly over EMG levels recorded on day 2 of the period and during premenstrual training. Second, subjects in the biofeedback and relaxation condition were able to maintain significantly lower levels of abdominal muscle tension on the first day of menstruation than subjects in the relaxation only group. This latter finding provides additional support to research suggesting that the utility of biofeedback over other forms of relaxation interventions may be evidenced only during stress-induced situations. The authors reason that on the first day of menstrual flow, when physical discomfort is highest, levels of experienced stress are also elevated. It was during this period that the biofeedback was clearly shown to be more effective than the relaxation only condition.

The authors report that only those subjects in the feedback condition reported a reduction in menstruation-related symptoms. Yet the biofeedback had an effect on only a limited group of symptoms as determined by the SSS (backaches, cramping, and abdominal pain).

According to the criteria listed (reducing the subjective experience of pain and increasing conscious control over myometrial tension), EMG feedback in conjunction with relaxation training is superior to relaxation training alone in the treatment of primary dysmenorrhea.

COMMENTARY: An important aspect of this study is the authors' use of EMG feedback of the lower abdominal muscles. Although it is an indirect measure of uterine activity, the change in tension levels within this muscle group during menstruation indicates that such feedback can serve as a useful index of uterine tension. This muscle group can also be an important physical parameter for biofeedback in the treatment of dysmenorrhea.

SOURCE: Bennick, C. D., Hulst, L. L., and Benthem, J. A. "The Effects of EMG Biofeedback and Relaxation Training on Primary Dysmenorrhea." *Journal of Behavioral Medicine,* 1982, 5, 329–341.

Systematic Desensitization
for Primary Dysmenorrhea

AUTHORS: Daniel J. Cox and Robert G. Meyer

PRECIS: A study attempting to predict differential responsiveness to behavioral treatment for primary dysmenorrhea.

INTRODUCTION: Menstrual distress is a common problem among women. Although no single factor has been demonstrated to be entirely responsible for its severity, both physical (the action of progesterone on the uterus) and psychological (reaction to pain associated with menstruation) components are believed to be involved. Hormonal therapy is the most frequent and effective treatment, although behavioral methods have been successfully used, such as hypnosis and systematic desensitization (SD).

This study was planned to assess (1) the effectiveness of SD in reducing symptomology, (2) the differential response of spasmodic and congestive types, and (3) the effect of a male versus female therapist. Two symptom scales were used, the Daily Symptom Scale (DSS) and the Retrospective Symptom Scale (RSS). Also evaluated were how these instruments assess women reporting menstrual distress and those who do not and how sensitive the instruments are to treatment impact.

METHOD: Three subject groups were evaluated: a distressed group (DG), comprising eighteen women who experienced dysmenorrhea; a nondistressed group (NG), fourteen women who explicitly reported no menstrual distress; and a normative control group (NCG), fifty-five women believed to constitute a random sample of females so that an average distribution of the dependent variables could be determined.

The Taylor Manifest Anxiety Scale (MAS) was used as a measure of trait anxiety, and the Menstrual Symptom Questionnaire (MSQ) was used to distinguish congestive and spasmodic dysmenorrheic women. The dependent measures included the DSS, RSS, a menstrual semantic differential, and frontalis EMG measurements. Seven graduate students (four male and three female) were used as therapists. All were previously inexperienced in relaxation training and all received the same training procedures. All therapists were blind to the patients' pretreatment variables.

NCG subjects completed the RSS and semantic differential on three occasions after menstrual cycles 1, 2, and 3. Each administration was separated by 30 days and paralleled temporally DG and NG administrations. Subjects in the DG and NG groups completed the RSS, semantic differential, MAS, Locus of Control Scale, and MSQ. Subsequently, pain threshold, EMG level, and thermal readings were recorded. Subjects then returned home and kept DSS records daily during their next period.

After pretreatment evaluation, subjects in the DG were assigned a therapist and received four SD treatment sessions. Sessions were held on days 1, 7, 12, and 17 following cycle 2. The first session taught relaxation training and cued breathing. A relaxation audiocassette (with either a male or a female voice) was provided for practice at home twice daily. The second session included practicing exercises of seven muscle groups, cued breathing, and the presentation of SD images. Subjects were instructed to imagine scenes that produced anxiety associated with menstrual flow and then to attempt to reduce the anxiety by cued breathing. The purpose was to facilitate the use of the relaxation response in coping with experienced tension. The final two treatment sessions continued to use the relaxation training, cued breathing, SD imagery, and home practice. Posttreatment assessments were conducted 2 weeks after the end of the 6-month follow-up evaluation, at which time the DSS and the menstrual semantic differential were completed.

It was found that the RSS was able to discriminate among DG, NG, and DCG subjects and to be sensitive to treatment effects. At posttreatment it was found that DG and NCG subjects were not significantly different in their responses to the RSS, while NG subjects were still significantly less distressed than either of the other groups.

With regard to treatment effectiveness, DSS scores were

significantly reduced for the DG subjects at postassessment but still significantly higher than those for the NG subjects. Post-treatment attitude scores were significantly reduced for the DG and were not different from the NG at either pre- or postassessment. Overall improvement for the DG was also noted in medication usage, pain threshold, and subjective ratings of the treatment. These improvements were maintained at the 6-month follow-up evaluation, where it was also noted that symptom relief had continued to improve and that menstrual attitude scores had regressed to baseline.

Dividing DG subjects into spasmodic and congestive groups, high and low anxiety groups, and male and female therapist groups revealed no significant differences in performance. The authors conclude that type of dysmenorrhea, level of anxiety, and therapist gender are irrelevant variables in treatment and exert no differential effects.

COMMENTARY: The effectiveness of systematic desensitization in treating dysmenorrhea is documented. The authors contend that the effectiveness of this technique lies in its ability to reduce anticipatory anxieties relating to menstruation. Two other important findings emerge from this study. First, the null findings concerning type of therapist, type of dysmenorrhea, and levels of anxiety suggests that dysmenorrheic women can be considered a homogenous group for behavioral treatment. Second, the use of the RSS is valid and reliable for measuring menstrual distress. The authors suggest that this measure can provide important quantitative and qualitative information and should be used in research in this area.

SOURCE: Cox, D. J., and Meyer, R. G. "Behavioral Treatment Parameters with Primary Dysmenorrhea." *Journal of Behavioral Medicine*, 1978, *1*, 297–310.

Biofeedback in the Treatment
of Primary Dysmenorrhea

AUTHORS: Thomas F. Dietvorst and David Osborne

PRECIS: Description of the use of biofeedback and autogenic training for the treatment of primary spasmodic dysmenorrhea.

INTRODUCTION: Research on menstrual discomfort has indicated that there are two distinct, homogenous groups of dysmenorrhea sufferers who present different symptoms and may require separate treatment interventions. The first type of dysmenorrhea is spasmodic. This is described as spasms of acute pain that begin on the first day of menstruation and may be of such severity as to cause vomiting and fainting. The pain is localized in the areas of the body controlled by the uterine or ovarian nerves (such as the back, the lower abdomen, and the inner thighs). The second type of dysmenorrhea is congestive. It is a variation of the premenstrual syndrome. Women in this group notice the onset of menstruation several days in advance and during this period may experience increasing heaviness and dull aching pains in various bodily locations (such as the breasts, the lower abdomen, and the ankles). The pain may be accompanied by such premenstrual symptoms as lethargy, irritability, and depression. Research has indicated that progressive relaxation and imagery are effective in treating spasmodic dysmenorrhea but not congestive dysmenorrhea. This study examines the use of biofeedback-assisted autogenic training with a case of primary spasmodic dysmenorrhea.

CASE HISTORY: The patient was a single, 29-year-old, white female. She had no medical complaints other than dysmenorrhea. This condition was present from menarche at age 11 years. Her menstrual periods lasted an average of 7 days, with spotting on the first 2 days and a heavy flow on days 3 and 4. Her periods were regular in length and occurrence. Her MMPI profile suggested that she was a reserved individual and mildly depressed at the time of testing. There were no gynecological pathologies to account for her condition, and she was diagnosed as having primary dysmenorrhea. Hormone therapy and analgesics were ineffective in alleviating her complaints.

TREATMENT: Behavioral assessment included the Menstrual Symptom Questionnaire (MSQ), which contains twenty-five descriptors of reactions and discomforts that may accompany spasmodic or congestive dysmenorrhea. The patient rates each statement on a 5-point scale as being either characteristic or not characteristic of herself. The patient's score on the MSQ was 84. Scores greater than 77 (the midpoint) suggest that the patient has spasmodic dysmenorrhea, while scores under 77 indicate congestive dysmenorrhea.

The Symptom Severity Scale (SSS) was also used. This instrument measures fifteen symptoms on a 5-point scale of intensity. The SSS was completed after each of the two menstrual periods to provide a baseline. It was also completed at the end of each menstrual period for 2 months after treatment. The mean for the two pretreatment scores on the SSS was 38.5. The scores on the 2-month follow-up were 25 and 24 points, respectively, which reflect a decrease in menstrual discomfort. The patient provided additional evidence of relief when she indicated that she had not taken a day of sick leave from work during her menstrual period as she had been doing routinely before her treatment.

Two biofeedback evaluations were also performed, one in midcycle and the other during the period when she was experiencing discomfort. Each of these sessions lasted 50 minutes. The first biofeedback evaluation, before the treatment and in midcycle, revealed frontalis muscle activity between 1.2 and 3.3 microvolts and a hand temperature range between 89°F and 94°F. The second evaluation, conducted while the patient was experiencing discomfort, indicated low frontalis activity (between 1.2 and 1.5 microvolts), but dermal temperature indicated mild sympathetic arousal (88°F to 92°F).

At the end of the second baseline menstrual period, a series of eight 50-minute hand biofeedback treatment sessions was begun. The goal was to have the patient maintain a hand temperature above 95.5°F with her eyes open and without any mechanical feedback. This criterion was adopted on the basis of research indicating that warming hands between 95°F and 96°F is usually associated with a pleasant state of relaxation. This form of biofeedback, in conjunction with autogenic training, results in a very effective treatment tool for reducing sympathetic activity. The patient reached this criteria at the end of the eight treatment sessions. Also, during this phase of treatment, the patient practiced the autogenic phrases at home twice daily. The authors contend that such practice facilitates the acquisition of the hand-warming skills.

COMMENTARY: The results of this study indicate that biofeedback-assisted relaxation can provide an effective alternative to behavior modification in treating primary spasmodic dysmenorrhea. Its utility in treating congestive dysmenorrhea still needs to be established. This study provides a short, simple, and direct approach to providing relief from menstrual discomfort. The reduction of discomfort was obtained without relying upon desensitization techniques that use visual imagery of the stimuli surrounding menstrual onset, a method that has been a major component of previous treatment approaches. The authors also note that muscle tension reduction may not be essential to the treatment of spasmodic dysmenorrhea. However, the authors recommend that practitioners fully examine the behavioral parameters of an individual's complaint and on the basis of the findings determine which technique is preferable.

SOURCE: Dietvorst, T. F., and Osborne, D. "Biofeedback-Assisted Relaxation Training for Primary Dysmenorrhea: A Case Study." *Biofeedback and Self-Regulation*, 1978, *3*, 301–305.

Treating Dysmenorrhea
with Pain Management Techniques

AUTHORS: Marc A. Quillen and Douglas R. Denney

PRECIS: A description of the use of pain management training to foster increased self-control of primary dysmenorrheic symptoms.

INTRODUCTION: Most research on primary dysmenorrhea has focused on alleviating anxiety and distress, which exacerbate menstrual pain. This report assesses the efficacy of pain management techniques directed toward managing menstrual pain itself. Such an intervention program consists of four components: (1) a treatment rationale emphasizing active, voluntary self-control; (2) training in relaxation and related coping strategies; (3) guided rehearsal of the self-control procedure with imagined settings of symptoms evoked in the treatment setting; and (4) application training to extend these procedures beyond the treatment setting. This study examines the effectiveness of these techniques in controlling pain associated with both the spasmodic and congestive forms of primary dysmenorrhea.

METHOD: Twenty-four females volunteered for this study. All subjects completed the Menstrual Symptom Questionnaire (MSQ) and the Menstrual Distress Questionnaire (MDQ) before treatment. Baseline was established over two menstrual cycles, during which all subjects maintained daily records of menstrual complaints. After the second cycle, subjects were assigned to either the control or management training groups. There were no significant differences between the groups on any of these outcome measures.

Subjects in the treatment condition received four 2-hour, individually administered sessions scheduled 1 week apart between their second and third periods. Throughout all sessions, an active self-control rationale was maintained and emphasized. During the first session, subjects were taught progressive relaxation with alternate tensing and relaxing of opposing muscle groups. Subjects were provided with a tape of these instructions to practice each day until the next session. In the second session, subjects were taught a briefer relaxation procedure that eliminated the tensing exercises. They were also taught a technique for "turning off" sensations of pain and discomfort in the pelvic area by visualizing a warm, soothing liquid flowing from the abdomen to the knees. These sensations were to induce feelings of heaviness and relaxation in the pelvic and lower back areas. New tapes were provided with these revised relaxation instructions, which were to be practiced daily until the next session.

The third session began with subjects placing themselves in a deep state of relaxation without assistance from the therapist. They were then asked to imagine scenes involving the beginning of menstrual discomfort and to practice turning off the discomfort using the learned techniques. Scenes were repeated three times; five different settings where menstrual distress might occur were employed. The fourth session included additional practice designed to reduce pelvic discomfort. The session concluded with explicit instructions about employing these techniques beyond the treatment setting. These instructions included early identification and prediction of symptoms and early application of the learned techniques to these symptoms. Subjects in the control group received no treatment at all and were not contacted between their second and third periods.

Daily records of menstrual discomfort were collected from all subjects during their third period; these records were obtained and the MSQ administered 18 months later at the follow-up investigation. The results indicated that whether a subject had spasmodic or congestive dysmenorrhea had no effect upon the outcome measures derived from the daily records. These techniques were equally effective in treating both types of dysmenorrhea. Immediately following treatment, those receiving the self-management techniques scored significantly lower on each of the four outcome measures than did the controls.

On the MDQ, there were no differences between the two groups at pretest. At posttest, however, subjects in the treat-

ment condition reported significantly less general pain and autonomic symptoms associated with their menstruation than did
the controls. The therapeutic gains were maintained at the follow-up investigation 18 months later.

COMMENTARY: From posttest to follow-up, eight subjects
dropped out of the study for a variety of reasons (such as illness, loss of interest, and pregnancy). The outcome measures at
posttest indicated no differences between subjects who dropped
out and those who remained, thereby maintaining the integrity
of the follow-up results. This study presents two major findings.
First, self-management techniques that focus on controlling
pain directly associated with menstruation offer effective intervention for managing primary dysmenorrhea. Second, there was
no clinically significant difference in treatment between congestive and spasmodic dysmenorrheic subjects; they both responded equally well to this intervention.

SOURCE: Quillen, M. A., and Denney, D. R. "Self-Control of
    Dysmenorrheic Symptoms Through Pain Management Train-
    ing." *Journal of Behavior Therapy and Experimental Psychi-
    atry*, 1982, *13*, 123-130.

Additional Readings

Aberger, E. W., Denney, D.R., and Hutchings, D. F. "Pain Sensi-
    tivity and Coping Strategies Among Dysmenorrheic Women:
    Much Ado About Nothing." *Behaviour Research and Ther-
    apy*, 1983, *21*, 119-127.
        These authors measured pain thresholds, pain tolerance,
and self-reported pain in samples of spasmodic, congestive, and
combined dysmenorrheic and nondysmenorrheic women. No
differences in pain sensitivity were found among these groups of
women. The claim of hypersensitivity to pain in dysmenorrheic

women was not substantiated. In comparing the cognitive and behavioral coping strategies used by the subjects during the ischemic pain procedure, a few differences were found. However, the hypothesis that dysmenorrheic women are somehow impaired in their ability to employ effective strategies in coping with pain was not supported.

Hargrove, J. T., and Abraham, G. E. "The Incidence of Premenstrual Tension in a Gynecologic Clinic." *Journal of Reproductive Medicine,* 1982, *27,* 721–725.

The incidence of premenstrual tension (PMT) in over 1,300 patients who were not taking any hormonal contraceptives or therapy was studied. Nineteen symptoms were divided into four categories: PMT-A (anxiety, mood swings, and irritability), PMT-H (weight gain, abdominal bloating, and breast tenderness), PMT-C (headache, increased appetite, and heart pounding), and PMT-D (depression, crying, and insomnia). It was found that 50% of these women scored positive for at least one subgroup of PMT. When patients were classed into 5-year age groups, a peak incidence of 60% was found for women in their thirties. The most common subgroups were PMT-A and PMT-H, occurring alone and in combination. The least common subgroup was PMT-D, which included only twelve women. The mean duration of cycle length for these patients was significantly shorter than for patients without PMT.

Khuri, R., and Gehi, M. "Psychogenic Amenorrhea: An Integrative Review." *Psychosomatics,* 1981, *22,* 883–893.

These authors contend that amenorrhea results from the interaction of intrapsychic vulnerabilities, external stress, and neuroendocrine disturbances. Exposure to a known stressor may precipitate amenorrhea, or the condition may be associated with a psychiatric disorder. Although psychogenic amenorrhea often remits spontaneously, particularly when the patient has successfully adapted to the external stresses, psychotherapy can be a useful intervention for more persistent cases. Supportive psychotherapy, psychoanalytic therapy, group therapy, and hypnotherapy have all been used successfully in treating this condition. The authors suggest that such therapies should focus on the psychological etiology (such as external stress and psychiatric disorders) rather than on modifying hormonal functioning.

Scott-Palmer, J., and Skevington, S. M. "Pain During Childbirth and Menstruation: A Study of Locus of Control." *Journal of Psychosomatic Research*, 1981, *25*, 151–155.

This study investigated the relationships among reported pain, locus of control, and personality variables in women in labor and a matched control group of normal fertile women. The results indicated that women with greater internal locus of control experienced shorter labors with more intense pain per hour than women with an external locus. Length of menstrual period was also correlated with locus-of-control scores. These authors contend that the duration of acutely painful bodily experiences may be mediated by cognitive beliefs about one's perceived control over life events. These results have important implications for the treatment of disorders such as premenstrual tension and dysmenorrhea.

Slade, P. "Menstrual Cycle Symptoms in Infertile and Control Subjects: A Re-Evaluation of the Evidence for Psychological Changes." *Journal of Psychosomatic Research*, 1981, *25*, 175–181.

It is believed that negative cultural values surrounding menstruation may influence the occurrence of premenstrual and menstrual symptoms. If this premise is true, involuntarily infertile women should experience more severe changes in menstrual symptoms because of the additional negative significance of their bleeding phases. A group of infertile women and a control group were compared on symptom levels and timing. No significant differences were found on these dimensions between the two groups. Significant cycles for physical symptoms tended to peak perimenstrually. Peaks for psychological symptoms appeared almost randomly distributed throughout the cycle for both groups of women. The author contends that the 30% to 40% of women who are reported to suffer cyclic emotional changes that peak around menstruation may manifest maximal symptoms at this time due to only chance fluctuations.

Arthritis

Although arthritis is too commonly regarded as a disabling complication of old age for which nothing can be done, this erroneous view is slowly being corrected. Considerable numbers of case reports have suggested that personality and other psychological variables contribute to and modulate the symptom pattern of this disorder. Arthritics of all ages have been studied both by the traditional psychiatric culture as well as the behavioral one. Applications of behavioral therapies, either alone or in combination with larger, multidisciplinary treatment efforts, have been able to help arthritics improve their quality of life, reduce their pain, and enhance their compliance with health behaviors.

Treating Rheumatoid Arthritis
with Relaxation and Biofeedback

AUTHORS: Jeanne Achterberg, Phillip McGraw, and G. Frank Lawlis

PRECIS: An examination of the therapeutic effects of temperature biofeedback and relaxation training on rheumatoid arthritis (RA) sufferers.

INTRODUCTION: This research presents two studies that attempt (1) to determine if there are any differential effects between temperature elevation and reduction biofeedback and (2) to compare a combined program of biofeedback and relaxation training with traditional physiotherapy on psychological and physical variables. Temperature biofeedback has been shown to be effective in dealing with stress-related disorders. Temperature elevations in the affected joints produce a similar effect to that of heat applications and aspirin, two commonly used treatments for RA. Such vasodilation helps to counter the atrophication of the muscles in the area due to vasculitis. Temperature reduction training was also expected to have beneficial results since it would decrease hypermetabolic lysosomal enzyme activity, which is implicated in cartilage destruction.

METHOD: The first study employed twenty-four female RA patients. They were selected on the criteria of (1) a diagnosis of stage II or III rheumatoid arthritis, (2) current arthritic involvement in at least two joints, (3) stable levels of medication, (4) a minimum of a 1-year history of the disease, and (5) positive RA Latex. Subjects were randomly assigned to either the reduction or elevation condition for peripheral skin temperature.

   All subjects received a structured social history interview, two measures for locus of control (one for health and one for responsibility for life events) and a Profile of Mood States (POMS). Physical and functional abilities were measured pre- and posttreatment by a physical therapist (variables included range of motion, timed 50-foot walk, and an Activities of Daily

Living checklist). At pre-, mid-, and posttreatment, a psychologist recorded hours of sleep, times awakened, mood changes, percentage of body hurting, and amount of experienced pain. A physician also conducted a pre- and posttreatment joint count.

Subjects were treated individually for twelve 30-minute sessions over a period of 6 weeks. Except for differences in the biofeedback conditions, all subjects received the same instructions and training. Immediately after entering the treatment room, all participants rated the severity of their pain on a 10-point scale (1 meaning "hardly noticeable pain" and 10 meaning "debilitating pain"). A thermistor probe was then attached to each subject's index finger. A 5-minute baseline period was established during which skin temperature and muscle tension (measured via an EMG) were recorded. Next, taped pretreatment relaxation instructions were played, after which a second EMG and dermal temperature recording was made. The remainder of the session was devoted to temperature regulation (increase or decrease) using auditory feedback. All subjects were given standardized instructions for temperature change including some direction and suggestions for accomplishing the task. Finally, a rationale was provided for accomplishing these temperature changes that were based on medical information.

After 20 minutes, final dermal temperatures and a posttreatment EMG level were recorded. Patients were again asked to rate the severity of their pain on the 10-point scale. All subjects were instructed to practice the relaxation responses twice daily at home. After six sessions, the psychodiagnostic and criterion questions were given, and at the end of twelve sessions an evaluation (identical to the pretreatment session) was completed.

The results indicated that both biofeedback groups learned how to relax muscularly. The subjective pain ratings indicated no significant differences between these two groups but significant decreases for both in experienced pain after treatment. The psychological scales indicated no significant changes in locus of control. There were no significant differences between these two conditions on the POMS; however, the tension scale did show a significant decrease from pre- to posttreatment for the combined groups.

There also were no differential treatment effects on the physical/functional measures. There were significant increases in the number of hours slept each night, and the patients awakened fewer times. There was a general decline in the amount of body hurting and percentage of time hurting over the course of the treatment. Again, no differential biofeedback effects were found. A functional evaluation of Activities of Daily Living also showed significant changes in performance over the duration of the treatment. Because the other psychological measures did not change, the authors concluded that the effectiveness of the treatment was specific to physical functioning rather than to a psychological enhancement of well-being.

The second study compared the efficacy of biofeedback and relaxation training with that of traditional physiotherapy approaches. Subjects consisted of twenty-three individuals. Fifteen received thermal biofeedback (most of whom participated in the dermal regulation conditions of the previous study) and eight received physiotherapy. The thermal regulation procedures were identical to those previously reported as were the psychosocial interview and the physical/functional and evaluation assessment materials.

The physiotherapy was given in twelve sessions lasting 30 to 40 minutes. The approaches used were heat (hot pack or paraffin), cold (ice water or cryotherapy), exercise, and instructions on Activities of Daily Living. Subjects were not randomly assigned to these groups since most were in the process of using either a particular modality or several different ones at once. The authors contend that this group reflects the clinical situation that most patients experience; therefore, these subjects did not serve as experimental trials for a given modality. They were only being used as a comparison group. All subjects in this group were given an exercise program to practice at home twice daily. All exercises were active and extended throughout the ranges of patients' tolerance; no passive stretching was used.

The results for the psychological measures indicated that overall scores did not significantly change from pre- to posttesting for either group. The authors question the relevance and importance of such measures to physical change. Regression analyses of the biofeedback group showed that mood profiles were not predictive of outcome. The only scale that showed significant change was the Powerful Others scale on the Locus of Control test: subjects in the feedback group increased on this dimension and those in the physiotherapy condition decreased between the pre- and posttest measures.

Both groups improved significantly on the physical/functional measures (50-foot walking time and Activities of Daily Living scale). The biofeedback and relaxation group improved significantly more on times awakened during sleep and reported fewer disability-related work changes. All the significant interactions on the physical/functional measures favored the feedback and relaxation condition. This was true for the number of joints afflicted with arthritis, the self-report measure of physical activities, and measures of pain severity. The temperature and relaxation modality resulted in a consistently positive outcome or in no change over these dimensions. The physiotherapy group experienced negative changes on measures relating to physical and work activities, joint count, and pain severity.

The authors contend that the effectiveness of the thermal feedback and relaxation group may be due in part to the greater awareness of physiological functioning that subjects develop as a result of this training. Such an awareness may provide RA sufferers with the ability to identify and counter events or activities that may aggravate their symptoms.

COMMENTARY: This study illustrates the utility of thermal biofeedback and relaxation training in the management of RA. The type of temperature regulation procedure used (elevation or reduction) appears to be of little importance. The biofeedback approach appears superior to other, more traditional physiotherapeutic interventions as measured by the authors' physical/functional criteria. Of particular interest is the result that there were no pre- to posttreatment changes on the psychological measures for the feedback group (this was also true for the physiotherapy group). This indicates, as the authors point out, that the dynamics and effectiveness of this treatment protocol are not due to changes in intrapsychic processes but rather to changes brought about on the somatic variables relating to rheumatoid arthritis. The improvement observed in the feedback patients cannot be attributed to a placebo effect but results instead from real changes in physiological functioning.

SOURCE: Achterberg, J., McGraw, P., and Lawlis, G. F. "Rheumatoid Arthritis: A Study of Relaxation and Temperature Biofeedback Training as an Adjunctive Therapy." *Biofeedback and Self-Regulation,* 1981, *6,* 207–223.

Group Therapy in Use with Rheumatoid Arthritics

AUTHORS: Leslie H. Schwartz, Robert Marcus, and Robert Condon

PRECIS: Description of the use of a multidisciplinary team approach to group therapy that centers on the salient psychosocial issues for rheumatoid arthritics.

INTRODUCTION: Group therapy has established itself as a useful service to help patients adapt and function in new social environments resulting from a medical illness. It has been particularly beneficial with disorders of peptic ulcers, asthma, and migraine headaches. This report describes an attempt to apply this technique to the treatment of arthritis sufferers. Group leaders consisted of individuals from the fields of psychiatry, internal medicine, and physical medicine. Their goals were fourfold: (1) to facilitate communication among the patients, their families, and their physicians; (2) to help educate physicians to the emotional repercussions of chronic diseases; (3) to present factual material relevant to rheumatoid arthritis; and (4) to help patients live more realistically and comfortably with their disease.

METHOD: The group consisted of fourteen frank or classic rheumatoid arthritis sufferers, with both severe and minimal disability. They ranged in age from 23 to 65 years (mean 47). Twelve were female, two male; ten were white, four black; ten were married, two separated, one widowed, and one single. Sessions were held weekly for 90 minutes over a period of 8 months. Not all patients and physicians attended all the sessions.

The structure of the group was leader oriented in that the cotherapists often introduced new topics for discussion rather than wait for issues to emerge. Frequently, specific questions would arise about different aspects of rheumatoid arthritis and its management. In order to avoid a question-and-answer type forum, part of the session was reserved for detailed answers to these questions. The techniques employed in the sessions were very flexible. On two occasions role playing was introduced to help patients learn more effective ways to cope with anger. On several sessions spouses or children of the patients attended so as to provide the patients with other perspectives on the effects of rheumatoid arthritis on family dynamics and processes.

Many group members found the group experience to be an important part of the total management of their arthritis. They felt that their attendance in the group was as important as taking their prescribed medications. Other patients valued the group as a place where they could talk about the pain and frustration caused by the disease with people who could fully understand what they were experiencing. People who were unmotivated to attend the group on a regular basis either did not accept their arthritis as a chronic disease and had not yet experienced enough treatment failures to see the group as a viable therapeutic tool or felt that no type of treatment could be effective. However, the large majority of the patients found the group to be an important, rewarding, and beneficial part of their treatment.

The rheumatologist served as the leader of the group. He was also the primary arthritis care physician for each patient. He knew each patient's medical history and was thus instrumental in interpreting significant details of their behavior for the other therapists. He could also identify any discrepancies between patients' self-reports of arthritic disability and objective medical information, could determine the cause of flare-ups of disease activity after hearing patients discuss personal information in the group (such as the misuse of medications, personal stress, or abuse of joints). Such information is usually kept secret from the physician during routine visits.

The psychiatrist's role was to form an overview of the group's dynamics and to comment on issues of concern. He also instructed the other therapists in how to enhance the therapeutic effect of the group by making the therapists aware of specific group techniques (such as dealing with periods of silence and optimum seating and room arrangements). The third physician provided information about physical medicine and rehabilitative aspects of the treatment of rheumatoid arthritis. Through contact with patients in the group, he could evaluate their actual degree of functioning.

The group was successful in facilitating communication in three areas for the arthritic patients. First, the increased patient-physician interaction in the group allowed a deeper relationship to develop. The authors believe that this stronger, more personal relationship was critical in improving clinic attendance and compliance with medical regimens, which occurred during and following the group meetings. Second, by having family members attend various sessions, all concerned developed a better understanding of each other and a sensitivity to each other's needs. Exposure to other arthritic sufferers permitted these family members to put problems that they encountered in dealing with the patient in a better perspective. Finally, the group provided effective communication among patients with chronic diseases. Group members were able to discuss problems and frustrations in a social context with others who had similar experiences and were sympathetic. They were also able to learn from each other how to function in their environment more efficiently (for example, how to get out of a bathtub or how to tell off one's spouse). The group was seen as useful in providing the therapists with new insights into the personal experience of arthritis, which is only infrequently revealed in clinical practice.

Some of the major issues relevant to this group centered

on physical appearance, that is, not wishing to appear disabled and less attractive. Another major issue was the fear of becoming dependent on others. These dependency fears were evidenced in two maladaptive coping strategies: completely giving up and overcompensating for the disability. Frequently this issue was at the core of family and marital problems where patients felt they had to choose between satisfying personal or family needs. Other themes that emerged were the relationship between the affect and physical symptoms and concern over the termination of the group. The authors note how three patients exhibited an exacerbation of their condition within three weeks of the group's termination.

COMMENTARY: The authors conclude that the group approach was effective in helping patients modify their life-styles, improve communication with important social agencies (family, friends, and physicians), increase their compliance with physical therapy and medical regimens, and, in general, improve their quality of life. They also note that patients who regularly attended the group experienced fewer flare-ups of their arthritis during this treatment than in the year before attending the group. It appears that such a multidisciplinary group approach can be important not only in helping an arthritis sufferer understand his or her disease process and experience but also in providing a therapeutic forum where the many psychosocial issues relating to the disease can be advanced and addressed from a variety of perspectives. These findings warrant an enlarged and controlled study to establish the value of this approach.

SOURCE: Schwartz, L. H., Marcus, R., and Condon, R. "Multidisciplinary Group Therapy for Rheumatoid Arthritis." *Psychosomatics*, 1978, *19*, 5-9.

Managing Arthritic Pain in Hemophiliacs

AUTHOR: James W. Varni

PRECIS: A description of the use of self-regulation techniques in managing arthritic pain in hemophiliacs.

INTRODUCTION: It is estimated that 75% of hemophiliac adults are afflicted by arthritis, a condition that frequently presents a problem in their treatment. Anti-inflammatory medications are limited in their usefulness, and physical dependence is a constant concern. A unique problem confronts health care practitioners in treating a hemophiliac with arthritis: how to reduce the experience of arthritic pain while not interfering with the perception of the vital acute pain signal associated with internal bleeding. This report describes a technique that resolves this dilemma by using warming techniques to reduce joint irritation.

METHOD: Three hemophiliac subjects participated in this study, all of whom had marked degenerative arthropathy. They were 19, 26, and 28 years of age, respectively.

A 3- to 5-week baseline of the amount of pain experienced per week was established, after which pain self-regulation training began. The initial treatment session consisted of three components: (1) a twenty-five-step progressive muscle relaxation procedure that involved the alternate tensing and relaxing of major muscle groups; (2) meditative breathing exercises whereby the individual inhaled through the nose and, while slowly exhaling through the mouth, subvocally repeated the word *relax*. Each subject would visualize the word *relax* in soothing colors as if written in colored chalk on a blackboard; and (3) guided imagery training, initiated after components 1 and 2 were completed.

During training, subjects were instructed to visualize themselves in a scene identified or associated with past experiences of warmth and arthritic pain relief and then subjectively reexperience it. This scene was invoked initially by the therapist using a detailed multisensory description. Once the scene was visualized, further suggestions were given, including imagining blood flow from the forehead down the body to the targeted arthritic joint. Although subjects had many arthritic joints, the one most painful was selected as the target joint and was the focus of treatment. It was believed that reduction of pain in this joint would generalize to other areas as well. Images of warm colors such as red or orange, sensations of warm sand and sun on the joint in a beach scene, and statements relating to a reduction in pain as the joint felt warmer and more comfortable were also used.

After the first treatment session, the progressive relaxation exercises and the visualization of the word *relax* were discontinued. Subsequent sessions consisted of five deep breaths as an induction aid immediately followed by the imagery techniques. Each subject was instructed to practice the self-regulation techniques at home at least twice a day for 15 minutes. This treatment protocol lasted 5 weeks.

All subjects were assessed on three dimensions both during treatment and at follow-up. The first was physiological, which used a thermal biofeedback device attached to the targeted joint. It was not used to provide feedback to the subjects or to serve as a training device. All subjects were asked to increase temperature in the joint area while they had their eyes closed. Subjective ratings were also used. Subjects rated the intensity of their arthritic and bleeding pain and their daily tension levels on a 10-point scale. Subjects also used a 7-point scale, ranging from +3 (much better) to −3 (much worse) to evaluate their pain, sleep, mobility, and overall improvement. Finally, each subject's medical chart was evaluated on the basis of bleeding episodes, number of hemorrhages, and amount of analgesics ordered.

The results were very encouraging. The subjective ratings indicated that the self-regulation techniques significantly reduced the number of days of perceived arthritic pain per week for all three subjects. Follow-up assessments (conducted from 7 to 14 months after treatment) showed that these gains were maintained. The author points out that this pain reduction was for all joints, not just the target joint. The self-rating scales showed positive changes for comparative arthritic pain, mobility, sleep, and overall improvement. There were, however, no changes in bleeding pain perception. Skin temperature recordings over the targeted joint rose from baseline to follow-up (average increase was 4.1°F). Although the number of bleeding episodes remained constant from pre- to postassessment, the number of analgesics taken decreased for all subjects.

COMMENTARY: Two important findings emerge from this study. The first was the effectiveness of the self-regulation techniques in managing chronic pain associated with arthritis. The imagery techniques were sufficient to initiate the necessary thermal warming of the afflicted joints to provide pain relief. Second, these pain-reducing procedures did not interfere with the person's perception of pain related to internal bleeding. The author contends that the consistency between the self-report pain ratings and the medical records validates their use in the differential assessment of arthritic and hemorrhaging pain perception.

SOURCE: Varni, J. W. "Self-Regulation Techniques in the Management of Chronic Arthritic Pain in Hemophilia." *Behavior Therapy*, 1981, *12*, 185–194.

Increasing Compliance in Rheumatoid Arthritis Patients

AUTHORS: Craig D. Waggoner and Robert B. LeLieuvre

PRECIS: The presentation of an effective technique to measure and increase compliance in rheumatoid arthritis patients.

INTRODUCTION: Compliance is an essential component to

any treatment intervention. Much research has been devoted to examining factors that affect compliance and how it can be enhanced. Although there are many variables that affect compliance, some of which are discussed elsewhere in this text, most noncomplying rheumatoid arthritis patients are relatively young, are taking medications, and are engaged in activities other than those of a housewife (who, quite to the contrary, are usually compliant).

The popular measurement of compliance with nonoral treatment regimens is the patient self-report. There are, however, weaknesses in this approach that can create artifacts in the results. What is needed is an objective measure of compliance. Research on compliance with oral medicine regimens has shown that some types of objective measures not only measure the degree of compliance accurately but also enhance it. The purpose of this study is to present such a measure.

METHOD: The subjects consisted of twelve persons, three males and nine females, who had either mild (less than four swollen joints per hand) or moderate (four to eight swollen joints per hand) arthritic conditions. Those with a more severe condition were not included since it would have impeded their performance on the measuring device.

The measuring apparatus was a Hand Helper (Meddev Corporation), modified with a concealed, resettable electric counter having a four-digit visual display connected to the exerciser. The counter and display were battery operated. The counter recorded the number of hand squeezes completed by the patient and served as the objective measure of compliance. Compliance was determined by the ratio between the number of squeezes performed (read from the digital display) and the number of squeezes prescribed to the patient, multiplied by 100. The patients in the mild group ($n = 7$) were required to do three sets of ten hand grips daily, a total of sixty squeezes per day. The patients in the moderate group ($n = 5$) were required to perform two sets of ten hand grips, or forty squeezes daily. The ratio obtained served as the objective, dependent measure of compliance.

The experiment was conducted over a 7-week period. During the first session, all patients were given the Hand Helper with the counter *not* visible. All were instructed in its use and prescribed the appropriate number of exercises. No mention was made of the electronic counter or its use. The patients were instructed to maintain daily logs of the number of exercises completed and subjective records of the amount of pain, the degree of morning stiffness, and the degree of evening fatigue experienced. These procedures were followed for 2 weeks.

At the end of this baseline period, patients were randomly assigned to one of three treatment groups. These groups were differentiated by the point in the treatment when the subjects were informed of the counter and shown how to use it. The first group was informed at the beginning of week 7, the second group at the start of week 5, and the third at the start of week 3. After the subjects were shown how to use the visual display, they could use it for the duration of the experiment.

The results clearly indicate the effect that knowledge of the counter's presence had on individuals initiating and maintaining compliant behaviors. During the first period, when there was no visual display of the number of completed exercises, six of the twelve patients showed noncompliance (compliance less than 100%), with an average of 83% compliance. During the period of visual display, only two patients were noncompliant. They nonetheless exhibited a 97% compliance rate, a substantial decrease in noncompliant behaviors. The compliance of the remaining ten individuals either equaled or exceeded 100%.

An interesting observation in this study was the variability in compliant behaviors exhibited by the subjects before they knew about the visual display. There were substantial differences in compliant behaviors both between and within individuals regardless of when they were given access to the visual counter. However, after access to the counter was given, the amount of variability was greatly reduced, and almost all patients' performance approached the 100% level. The authors concluded that the use of the visual display did produce patient compliance.

Further data analysis indicated large discrepancies between

the number of exercises the patients reported performing and the number actually completed (the error rate) as measured by the counter. During the no visual display period, six patients reported completing more exercises than they actually did and five reported performing fewer than the counter indicated. There was an average error rate of ±62.97 during this phase. During the second phase, with the visual display, this error rate decreased to ±6.44. Subjective reports on the efficacy of the visual counter indicated that the counter was useful in reminding subjects when they fell behind in their exercise schedule, thus prompting them to complete the necessary number of exercises to fill their quota.

This study demonstrated that (1) compliance to a nonoral treatment protocol can be objectively measured, (2) the objective instrument can be manipulated to increase compliance, and (3) the assessment of compliance through self-reports can be unreliable.

COMMENTARY: The multiple time series design (varying the point in treatment when subjects were made aware of the visual counter) is a useful way to control for extraneous factors that could influence compliance at the time the experimental manipulation is introduced (factors such as weather and injections of medicine). It can be concluded that the visual display enhances compliance behaviors in rheumatoid arthritis patients. As the authors pointed out, the response to the visual display counter by the subjects could be attributed to either of two facts: (1) They now had a more accurate record of the number of exercises performed, or (2) they became increasingly aware that the number of exercises they performed was being monitored by the experimenters, a demand characteristic that motivated participants to perform at the expected level. Another important fact noted by the authors is that the apparatus, technique, and design of this study can be adopted for general applications wherever compliance to exercises is critical to treatment.

SOURCE: Waggoner, C. D., and LeLieuvre, R. B. "A Method

to Increase Compliance to Exercise Regimen in Rheumatoid Arthritis Patients." *Journal of Behavioral Medicine,* 1981, *4,* 191–201.

Additional Readings

Meenan, R. F., Gertman, P. M., Mason, J. H., and Dunaif, R. "The Arthritis Impact Measurement Scales." *Arthritis and Rheumatism,* 1982, *25,* 1048–1053.

The AIMS is an instrument designed to assess the health status of arthritis patients. The AIMS is self-administered and has scales that measure the physical, psychological, and social aspects of health states. This instrument has been shown to be a reliable and valid measure. It can be used successfully with at least four major types of arthritis, with a wide range of socio-demographic groups, and across time. The authors contend that the AIMS is a powerful tool and will prove useful as a method to assess arthritic outcome in a variety of settings.

Mindham, R. H. S., Bugshaw, A., James, S. A., and Swannell, A. J. "Factors Associated with the Appearance of Psychiatric Symptoms in Rheumatoid Arthritis." *Journal of Psychosomatic Research,* 1981, *25,* 429–435.

These authors examined, at bimonthly intervals, twenty-eight patients suffering from rheumatoid arthritis. Over the 1-year course of the study, disease activity, impairment of daily activities, presence of psychiatric symptoms, and changes in pathological tests were monitored and assessed. The results of the analyses indicated that psychiatric symptoms appeared in patients having a severe, active disease process that interfered with their daily activities. No regular association was found between particular features of rheumatoid arthritis and psychiatric complications. The results of this investigation underscore the need to monitor both the physical *and* psychological statuses of such patients; severe physical diseases can cause unwanted psychological complications. Constant assessment of the patient can aid in correcting such problems before they become serious.

Pinals, R. S., Masi, A. T., and Larsen, R. A. "Preliminary Criteria for Clinical Remission in Rheumatoid Arthritis." *Arthritis and Rheumatism*, 1981, *24*, 1308-1315.

To develop criteria for the clinical remission of rheumatoid arthritis, data were collected for 175 arthritic patients considered to be in complete remission and for 169 patients in partial remission or with active disease. Analyses yielded six criteria for maximal discrimination: morning stiffness absent or not exceeding 15 minutes, no fatigue, no joint pain by history, no joint tenderness, no joint or tendon sheath swelling, and no elevation of erythrocyte sedimentation rate. The presence of five or more of these criteria provided a 72% sensitivity for clinical remission and a 100% sensitivity in discriminating patients with an active disease process. Based on the results obtained with this sample, the authors estimate that these criteria would identify more than 90% of the rheumatoid arthritis patients in a general population sample. This study may well provide a model for developing comparable criteria for determining clinical remission in other disorders.

Vollhardt, B. R., Ackerman, S. H., Grayzel, A. I., and Barland, P. "Psychologically Distinguishable Groups of Rheumatoid Arthritis Patients: A Controlled, Single Blind Study." *Psychosomatic Medicine*, 1982, *44*, 353-362.

These authors systematically collected measures of mood and psychological symptoms from sixty-eight arthritis patients on two standard questionnaires: the Brief Symptom Inventory and the Profile of Mood States. Two groups of arthritis patients were examined, one positive and the other negative with regard to the rheumatoid factor and erosive joint changes. A third group had other forms of arthritis. All patients were matched on chronicity and functional impairment as well as psychosocial background variables. The results of this investigation indicated distinct psychometric response profiles that allowed the patients to be accurately classified into three clinical groups. Accuracy ratings from 63% to 100% were obtained.

Chronic Pain,
Headache,
and Myofacial
Dysfunction

Pain is a matter involving neurophysiology, anatomy, and psychology. Chronic pain, however different from person to person, can be devastating to physical and mental health. Recent research has demonstrated that organic contributors to the pain sensation can be attenuated by behavioral interventions. Similarly, a number of behavioral strategies are available that guard against the learning of "sick behavior" that might otherwise maintain and aggravate pain symptoms among people who are predisposed to them. The proper evaluation and subsequent management of a chronic pain patient may involve approaches derived from psychosomatic medicine, psychotherapy, behavior therapy, and biofeedback and may utilize inpatient as well as outpatient settings. Because pain must be treated so often in medical practice, there is an extensive literature that offers the clinician ample information for planning health delivery services.

Treating Temporomandibular Joint Pain with Biofeedback

AUTHORS: Sven G. Carlsson and Elliot N. Gale

PRECIS: A description of the use of EMG biofeedback of the masseter muscle for the treatment of long-term temporomandibular joint (TMJ) pain.

INTRODUCTION: Biofeedback has been shown to be effective in treating TMJ pain. Since this condition is associated with increased tension in muscle groups surrounding the area, EMG feedback can provide useful information to subjects attempting to relax the masseter muscle. The purpose of this study was both to examine the effectiveness of biofeedback for intractable TMJ sufferers (those with whom other treatment interventions proved unsuccessful) and to increase their awareness of tension and their ability to decrease that tension. Feedback was given for the masseter muscle on the side most active in causing physical distress.

METHOD: Eleven subjects, six males and five females ranging in age from 21 to 61 years, participated in this study. All had a minimum of a 3-year history of TMJ pain. Selection for this study was based on the failure of other corrective treatments (such as bite guards and equilibration of dentition) to control the condition. Long-term sufferers were selected for this study on the authors' contention that such a group would be "placebo resistant." The authors believe that, generally, success with TMJ patients is often of a placebo nature. Whatever is done to these individuals at an early stage of the disorder appears to be successful. By using long-term sufferers it would be possible to test the effectiveness of biofeedback since any of the results would have to be attributable to the treatment and not to any psychological phenomenon.

　　　Masseter EMG responses were obtained by placing two surface electrodes over the main body of the masseter muscle on the side of maximal pain. The reference electrode was placed

on the dorsal surface of the nonpreferred hand. In order to ensure the identical location of the electrodes across training sessions, a template was made up for each subject. On each template a hole was cut marking the location of the electrodes
relative to the ear and nose.

Initially, all subjects were given explanations about the
role that muscular habits and tension play in TMJ pain. Situations in which muscular overactivity may occur were discussed,
and the subjects were encouraged to find instances of tension
increases in their daily lives. Misconceptions and misbeliefs surrounding the cause of TMJ pain were also discussed.

The subjects were then familiarized with the feedback
equipment, and they were shown recordings when the teeth are
clenched and when they are relaxed. This was repeated several
times to help the subject become aware of tension in the masseter muscle. During this phase the patients were asked to reach
a submaximal level of tension (individually determined) and to
maintain it (again, in an attempt to increase the subject's sensitivity to this level of tension). Periodically the visual feedback
monitor was covered and the subject was asked to estimate the
level of tension present. Feedback was then provided on the accuracy of the estimate. The goal was to increase sensitivity to
tension and awareness of its variations. This training continued
throughout the first few sessions.

During every session each subject received relaxation
training, where patients were instructed to reduce the amount
of muscle activity as much as possible. This was done in 1-min-
ute trials followed by a 30-second rest interval where the subjects could swallow and readjust their seating position. Verbal
reinforcing comments were given following a subject's successful performance. In later sessions, the subjects were instructed
to reduce masseter tension as quickly as possible from some
specified level. This procedure helped subjects to reduce muscle
tension as rapidly as possible.

Once a good awareness of muscle tension was reached,
subjects were requested to monitor their own levels of tension
for 2 days between sessions. They were to estimate muscle
tension every hour in terms of the multivoltmeter settings used

during the EMG feedback sessions. The purpose of this phase was to have subjects become aware of tension and to free them from any dependence on the feedback equipment.

Treatment was terminated based on clinical judgment. The criteria for this decision rested on the observation of no improvement in a subject's ability to relax as well as no reported declines in pain after six sessions. The number of sessions given ranged from six to eighteen. Most of the subjects improved within the six sessions allowed, most to a nonpain status. However, three of the eleven subjects required more than six sessions.

The effects of the treatment were further evaluated by an independent expert in oral diagnoses. The outcome judgment was based on the frequency, quality, duration, and severeness of the remaining pain, as well as remaining tenderness to palpation. These evaluations were completed 12 or more months after the termination of the treatment for eight subjects and 4 to 8 months after termination for three others. Outcome was measured on a 7-point scale: 1, significantly worse; 2, clearly worse; 3, slightly worse; 4, no change; 5, slightly better; 6, significantly better or symptom improved, possibly because of a related reduction in life stress; and 7, almost totally symptom free, unquestionably owing to the therapy. Of the eleven subjects, five were rated at 7. The abatement in their symptoms held constant for at least 1 year. Three other subjects were rated at 6, one patient was rated 5, and two were rated at 4 (no change).

There were no systematic relationships between outcome and performance during the treatment. The authors note that the two subjects rated as 4 were also the best relaxers—they rapidly learned to control masseter tension levels and obtained the lowest muscle potential of all subjects. The authors suggest that such a result may indicate a nonmuscular etiology of this disorder. A good ability to relax and an initial low level of muscle tension may serve as a diagnostic indicator of such an etiology and thereby signal the need for a different therapeutic approach.

Another explanation of these relative failures is these patients' nonacceptance of the authors' view that muscle tension was an important factor in the etiology of TMJ. Unlike the other eight patients, their belief of this view was described as superficial and temporary. The authors believe that this attitude decreased their motivation to monitor tension levels and to practice the learned relaxation techniques.

COMMENTARY: The authors conclude that the use of EMG biofeedback appears to be an effective approach to eliminating muscle overactivity in TMJ sufferers after other pain etiologies have been ruled out. The authors also suggest a possible sex difference linked to this disorder: Of the five completely cured subjects, four were female and both failures were males. Of the eleven subjects, five were women, of whom four were rated 7 and one was rated 6. However, the authors are aware of other, more global social dynamics that could explain this result (such as changes in sex roles within society).

SOURCE: Carlsson, S. G., and Gale, E. N. "Biofeedback in the Treatment of Long-Term Temporomandibular Joint Pain." *Biofeedback and Self-Regulation,* 1977, *2,* 161–171.

A Multimodal Approach
to Treating Tension Headaches

AUTHOR: Jorge Luis Figueroa

PRECIS: A description of the use of a multifaceted behavioral group treatment approach for managing chronic tension headaches.

INTRODUCTION: Tension headaches are most commonly described as bilateral, dull, constant pain usually centering in the forehead, frequently with occipital involvement leading to generalized pain. Typically accompanying such activity are complaints of cervical pain or tightness as well as trapezius tension. Such headaches often persist at varying intensities. Stressful events are frequently associated with the onset of such headaches. Psychological interventions, such as biofeedback, psychotherapy, or relaxation training, are usually introduced when traditional pharmacologic therapies (such as aspirin compounds) are ineffective. The psychological approach centers on techniques that reduce anxiety and tension or provide patients with more useful coping techniques for meeting their environmental demands. As the author points out, because of the wide range of etiological factors and the heterogeneity of tension headache sufferers, it is necessary to develop a treatment approach that can address a variety of problem areas. Such a wide-based approach will enable patients to emphasize the particular aspects of the treatment most appropriate to their needs. This study compares the effectiveness of a behavioral treatment program with traditional group psychotherapy and self-monitoring conditions.

METHOD: The subjects were fifteen chronic tension headache sufferers between the ages of 22 and 67 (mean of 33.9 years). None had any frank psychological or organic disturbances. The mean frequency of headaches per week was 4.2, the mean duration of each headache was 6.5 hours, and the average amount of medication taken per week was 16.5 pills. Subjects were randomly assigned to one of three treatment groups, each composed of five subjects.

During an initial interview, all subjects were given self-monitoring forms, which were to be filled out every night before retiring. Subjects in the treatment groups brought their responses to the therapy sessions weekly, while those in the self-monitoring group mailed their forms to the experimenter. Using this checklist, subjects were instructed to monitor level of relaxation, number of headaches, type and amount of medication, severity of headache, how long in advance they could detect the headache, and the extent to which the headache was disabling. Subjects engaged in this self-monitoring for 2 weeks before treatment (pretreatment measure), 2 weeks immediately after treatment (posttreatment measure), and 1 month after treatment was terminated for another 2 weeks (follow-up measure).

The behavioral group received a three-stage program over seven 90-minute sessions meeting twice weekly. The first stage consisted of helping subjects to identify stressful situations and to develop skills for dealing with them (problem-solving techniques). The second stage consisted of progressive relaxation training, anxiety management, and stress inoculation. Here subjects learned to identify and control tension responses and to reduce their reactivity to stressful events. In stage 3, subjects were taught direct pain management techniques that could be used in dealing with unavoided pain.

The psychotherapy group also met twice weekly for seven 90-minute sessions. This group focused on conflicts that resulted in headaches rather than on particular environmental conditions. Individual members discussed situations that appeared to be related to their headaches, and the group attempted to identify the associated conflicts that the person was experiencing. Also discussed were the particular ways these individuals attempted to handle these conflicts. The self-monitoring control group completed the same daily headache materials as the other groups and mailed them back to the experimenter every week. The members of the different groups never met, nor were they aware of the treatment protocols for the other groups.

The results of this study were analyzed by a multivariate model. According to the self-reports, there were significant decreases from pretreatment to follow-up in the frequency and duration of headaches for the behavioral treatment group. There were also significant differences between the behavioral group and the other two groups at posttreatment and follow-up periods. There was no significant change over time for either the psychotherapy or control groups and no significant differences between the two on these dimensions. With regard to the degree of disability caused by the pain, medications taken, and level of relaxation, there were significant pretreatment to posttreatment differences, which were maintained at follow-up for the behavioral group only. There was a significant difference between the behavioral group and the psychotherapy and control groups on relaxation level at follow-up only. The analysis of pain severity showed a significant decrease in severity only in the behavioral group from pretreatment to posttreatment, which was also maintained at follow-up. The psychotherapy group manifested a similar trend that only approached significance.

These results indicate that a behavioral approach within a group format can be effective for alleviating tension headaches. This multimodality protocol appears to be superior to a traditional psychotherapeutic intervention; in addition, the results obtained by patients given this treatment also appear longer-lasting than those obtained in the psychotherapy or self-monitoring groups. Although the behavioral group was more effective, the author cannot specify which aspects of the treatment package affected specific components of the headache complex. It is also possible that not all of the modalities used in the behavioral group were necessary for all participants.

COMMENTARY: The author concludes that a therapeutic program for pain behavior should have three important objectives: (1) teaching skills to cope with stressful situations so as to lower the probability that pain behaviors will be manifested, (2) directing attempts to correct or modify the pain mechanism, and (3) helping patients manage pain when it arises. Which of these elements are necessary for change to take place is not known, although it is impressive that such a multifaceted approach was effective in providing significant and durable changes in pain behaviors.

SOURCE: Figueroa, J. L. "Group Treatment of Chronic Tension Headaches: A Comparative Treatment Study." *Behavior Modification*, 1982, *6*, 229-239.

Chronic Intractable Benign Pain

AUTHOR: Jack J. Pinsky

PRECIS: A paper identifying the chronic intractable benign pain syndrome (CIBPS), its epiphenomenal correlates, and the problems patients with this syndrome present to the health care system.

PSYCHOLOGICAL ASPECTS: CIBPS has been characterized as a continual problem with pain that is not a manifestation of any active pathoanatomic or pathophysiological process. Patients invariably have a history of ineffective medical interventions for their pain problem, with a concomitant deterioration in psychosocial functioning.

The author specifies ten phenomenological correlates that both define the syndrome and reflect its severity:

- multiple pharmacologic and surgical treatments, and their side effects;
- drug dependency or abuse problems;
- escalating physical incapacity secondary to disuse;
- mood and affect changes contributing to general dysphoria;
- escalating psychosocial withdrawal or malfunctioning with increased loss of gratifications from these human inputs;
- interpersonal conflict with significant others;
- increased hopelessness and helplessness as dysphoria does not improve in spite of mounting numbers of "newer" or different treatments;
- conflicts with all levels of medical care personnel with heightening of dissatisfaction, anger, and hostility;
- decrease in feelings of self-esteem, self-worth, and self-confidence;
- progressive demoralization with increasing anhedonia that may be part of a serious depression.

The author distinguishes between two subgroups within this categorization: those that manifest all of these correlates, thus presenting a disturbed level of psychosocial and affective functioning, and those who manifest the first two characteristics of the syndrome but do not seem to have any of the socio-affective components. However, there is often no clear demarcation between these two groups, and an individual can always move from one category to another.

Individuals in the former category almost always present evidence of interpersonal conflicts with significant others. There is a long history of poor object relations. The syndrome is seen as being a maladaptive attempt at dealing with these underlying dynamics. When the syndrome no longer fulfills these unconscious needs adequately, a breakdown in ego functioning results affecting self-esteem, self-worth, and self-confidence.

CIBPS is clearly psychological in origin. Continued intervention focusing on possible organic causes can only perpetuate this syndrome. The author emphasizes that any treatment is an intervention into a chronic process and therefore the practitioner should be sensitive to issues other than the overt behavioral dynamics of the patient. Such an approach can provide a greater opportunity for treatment of the syndrome itself.

TREATMENT: The author asserts that such patients would respond positively to an intensive, milieu-oriented, inpatient treatment program that has a strong focus on cognitive oriented group psychotherapy. Inherent in this approach is the encouragement of learning new coping techniques that will enable patients to deal more effectively with their emotions, feelings, and social behaviors, including pain behaviors.

The author also suggests that professionals in outpatient centers who are confronted by such patients should organize them into groups where any individual can be exposed to the problems and issues confronting other chronic pain sufferers. Such a therapeutic process can help individuals work through various psychological problems that may be the cause of their condition. The author contends that such reality oriented, peer group therapy can be helpful in fostering more realistic self-perceptions and a better self-understanding of the patient's predicament.

Regardless of whether intervention is on an inpatient or

outpatient basis, the goal of therapy is to address the unobservable behaviors of the individual and to provide new ideational and affective insights into the underlying etiological dynamics of the syndrome. Subsequently, patients are encouraged to learn new and more effective ways of coping with these dynamics.

COMMENTARY: This paper is very useful in presenting the many dynamics associated with any physical disorder. A physician must address both the physical and the psychological needs of a patient in order to manage a patient's problem comprehensively. Basically, there are three aspects to pain: the disease (the actual organic component), the illness (the patient's own perceptions of the disease), and the predicament (how the disease and the patient's perceptions of the disease affect his or her life situation).

Individuals with CIBPS are particularly vulnerable to the consequences of their predicament. Whether the chronicity of the pain is the result of an organic problem, the expression of an underlying psychological problem, or both, the cognitive and social aspects of pain must be addressed if it is to be treated successfully. The group therapy approach suggested by the author appears to be a sound strategy.

SOURCE: Pinsky, J. J. "The Behavioral Consequences of Chronic Intractable Benign Pain." *Behavioral Medicine,* 1980, 7, 12–20.

Psychophysiological Correlates of Migraine

AUTHOR: Neil H. Raskin

PRECIS: A report (1) examining the degree to which tension and migraine headaches are similar; (2) reviewing the mechanisms, symptoms, and pharmacologic interventions for chronic headaches; and (3) reassessing conceptualizations of tension and migraine headaches from the perspective of traditional medicine.

INTRODUCTION: It has been commonly assumed that psychological factors are the primary causes of recurring headaches. Although research has shown the important role of stress and anxiety in precipitating such conditions, the author emphasizes the other trigger mechanisms that are of equal importance, such as glare, hunger, menses, and certain foods. These agents are believed to be more centrally involved in causing migraines since they create a biological predisposition toward such reactions. The current line of research focusing on these variables results in part from the inability to substantiate the hypothesis that neck and scalp muscle contractions and the dilation of extracranial arteries are the major sources of head pain.

The author also argues that epidemiological studies of tension and migraine headaches have shown no biological differences between the two types. In fact, there are more similarities than differences (such as similarities in age at onset, natural history, psychological data, and cerebral circulatory alterations during headache attacks). The only clinically important difference between the two headache conditions is the differential pharmacologic responsiveness; that is, some drugs are more effective for migraine sufferers than for tension headache patients, and vice versa. Instead of referring to tension and migraine headaches as two separate nosological entities, it would appear preferable to regard these conditions as lying on opposite ends of a "benign recurring headache" continuum and to regard variations of these clinical conditions as differing only with respect to the type of medication that is effective in treatment.

MIGRAINE MECHANISMS: The mechanisms responsible for headaches are not clearly known. Some explanations assert that headaches arise from the peripheral activation of pain receptors. The pulsing and stretching of arterial vessels and/or the contraction of skeletal muscles surrounding the cranium are believed to be sufficient to activate the peripheral sensory receptors, eventually resulting in the perception of pain. However, as the author points out, of the many individuals who habitually clench their teeth or commonly become anxious, all with frank contractions of the muscles around the head and neck, only a few report headaches. In addition, activities that produce vasodilation (such as hot baths and rigorous exercise) are rarely accompanied by headaches. Rather, the vasoactive medications used in treating chronic headache sufferers mainly influence the central nervous system, having only minor effects on the peripheral system. These and other research data appear to support the hypothesis that chronic headaches may be a genetic disorder of the brainstem pain modulation system, in which the production or regulation of various neurotransmitters may be defective.

Although a variety of factors may precipitate a headache attack (such as anxiety, hunger, certain foods, high humidity, pungent odors, excessive vitamin A, and some drugs), these precipitants account for only a minority of a person's headaches; the withdrawal of these precipitants leads to only slight improvement for the individual sufferer. The author asserts that for most patients these antagonists only exacerbate an underlying tendency toward headaches. These variables serve as biological markers of a decreased threshold to certain stimuli that do not ordinarily cause headaches in nonmigraine sufferers.

The exact pathophysiology of migraines is not known. Research evidence suggests that circulating biochemical factors underlie the condition. Specifically, it is hypothesized that the release of serotonin from the serotonergic neural circuit within the brainstem is defective, resulting in low serotonin levels as well as increased neuronal firing rates. Further support for this theory is derived from the physiological action of the antimigrainous drugs, which suppress the firing rate of the serotonergic neurons located in the brainstem.

TREATMENTS: The author strongly recommends pharmacologic protocols for treating migraines. He claims that therapies that do not use medications (especially biofeedback) are effective for only a small number of patients.

The earlier an acute migraine attack is dealt with, the greater the chance of it being aborted. Aspirin, dextropropoxyphene, or codeine can be effective, as can isometheptene and ergotamine (the latter for prophylaxis). Given the low absorption rate of oral medications and the high incidence of vomiting during migraine attacks, it may be best to administer medications in the form of suppositories.

A prophylactic treatment approach should be considered for individuals who experience frequent attacks and for individuals for whom medication does not adequately suppress a migraine onset. This is accomplished by having the individual continually ingest a medication until it accumulates to a therapeutically useful level in the bloodstream. Until this level is reached, patients should be provided with ergotomine to handle any intermediary attacks. Once an effective prophylaxis is found, it should continue to be ingested for up to 6 months and then gradually decreased in order to determine its continued need. Although there is no evidence that these drugs alter the mechanisms associated with migraines, patients can often discontinue medication after 6 months, and they usually report fewer and less severe migraine attacks. The most effective medication in this treatment is methysergide, which offers the greatest probability of making a program symptom free. Since it does have potentially dangerous side effects (such as compromising renal, cardiac, and pulmonary functioning), it may be better to begin with a less powerful analgesic, such as amitriptyline, propranolol, cyproheptadine, or phenelzine.

The author is aware that there are emotional reactions to any chronic pain experience and that such affect can aggravate or maintain migraine attacks. Psychotherapy may benefit some patients by helping them to cope with the secondary emotional consequences associated with the chronic pain. Although there have been no adequately controlled studies assessing the effectiveness of this treatment modality, the author cites some commentaries contending that psychotherapy is not really justified as an intervention for migraine sufferers. Evaluations of large numbers of individuals who received psychotherapy yield unencouraging results. The author believes that a supportive patient-physician relationship that provides sufficient emotional support and gratification to the patient can be more than sufficient in handling the affect that can trigger or result from migraine attacks.

The author presents research evidence illustrating that migraine sufferers do not significantly differ from nonsufferers on certain personality variables (such as stress and ambition) and that there is no justification in referring to migraine as being psychogenic in origin. Stress can nonetheless exacerbate a migraine attack; thus, the use of various relaxation techniques to reduce its impact can be helpful. However, its effectiveness is evidenced as long as these techniques are being practiced. The author believes that relaxation may benefit some patients, but he doubts the long-term effectiveness of this approach.

COMMENTARY: Of major import to this article is the contention that all benign recurring headaches are a function of a common, underlying, genetically determined, biological predisposition. Secondary to this perspective is the belief that peripheral changes associated with migraines (such as vasodilation) are only secondary to other, more basic processes. The author calls for more direct and concrete treatment interventions, especially those that focus on these biological systems.

SOURCE: Raskin, N. H. "Migraine." *Psychosomatics,* 1982, *23,* 897–907.

The Chronic Pain Syndrome

AUTHORS: James B. Reuler, Donald E. Girard, and David A. Nardone

PRECIS: An examination of the theoretical and practical approaches to the chronic pain syndrome.

INTRODUCTION: Chronic pain is a complex neurophysiological condition that, when not fully understood, can cause frustrations for and mismanagement by health care professionals. This paper highlights common misconceptions of this syndrome as well as its treatment. The authors contend that the tendency to apply a disease model in interpreting pain that assumes an underlying pathogenic factor is simplistic and not profitable. By categorizing the pain as being either organic or psychogenic in origin, the learned behaviors that may be maintaining a person's pain experience are ignored.

From this learning model perspective, the authors contend that the longer pain is experienced, the more psychological variables contribute to the neurophysiological mechanisms underlying the pain behavior. Thus, pain produced from organic lesions facilitates emotional change. Research of premorbid personality traits has shown that neurotic tendencies of chronic pain patients are a result, not a cause, of the chronic pain. This may explain why patients with organic or psychogenic pain cannot be discriminated by psychological tests such as the MMPI. Therefore, it is important to identify the variables that are maintaining the pain rather than determining whether the pain is real or not. This learning perspective may clarify issues surrounding the pain syndrome that are not fully understood (such as the placebo effect and the misuse of narcotic analgesics by the patients). This framework also argues for a variety of therapeutic approaches that address the main issues related to an individual's pain predicament.

MANAGEMENT: A general approach to managing the chronic pain syndrome requires the development of an overall therapeutic goal. The goal is determined by considering the psychological, social, and economic impact of the condition on both the patient and the patient's family. The authors recommend a multidisciplinary approach, integrating the professional expertise of the primary physician, social worker, psychologist, nurse, and physical therapist. The therapy should be tailored to the specific needs of the patient and the type of pain process evidenced (that is, whether it is secondary to an organic disease, like cancer, or is a benign form of chronic pain, which must be approached differently).

The authors present and discuss the efficacy of a variety of treatment modalities. The most common intervention is the use of medications. For individuals with mild to moderate pain, aspirin may be the most effective. Research has shown that 650 milligrams of aspirin are more effective in managing pain from cancer than other light oral analgesics. For patients with malignancy, narcotics are often prescribed, sometimes with distressing side effects. These drugs (such as morphine or codeine) do not remove the perception of pain but rather alter its affective interpretation, thereby rendering the pain less distressing to the patient. In prescribing any narcotic, the effects of the agent on the patient's physical and psychological condition must be considered. Another group of drugs for managing pain are those with psychoactive properties. Although their action is not fully understood, they may block the pain-anxiety-depression-pain sequence by facilitating cortical inhibition of sensory activity, stimulating central nervous system endorphins, or blocking dopaminergic receptors or reuptake of brain seratonin.

Electrical stimulation is yet another treatment modality. It is believed that electrical stimulation inhibits the transmission of neuronal impulses at the substantia gelatinosa in accordance with the gate control theory. Although there are no established sites for electrode placement, stimulation usually occurs at trigger sites, which may be within areas of the pain, at a distance from them, or along major peripheral nerves. Transcutaneous nerve stimulation is the simplest form of this approach and has been used effectively for cervical and lower back pain, peripheral nerve injury, amputation stump pain, neuralgia, and phantom limb pain. Dorsal column stimulation and percutaneous epidural stimulation are more advanced techniques using this concept and involve more sophisticated technology, both mechanically and surgically. Acupuncture is a related method that has been shown effective in treating chronic lower back pain. The mechanisms involved are believed to be very similar to those of transcutaneous stimulation. Acupuncture also seems to involve the release of endorphins, since research has shown that acupuncture-induced analgesia can be reversed with naloxone.

Neurosurgical ablation is another approach to managing pain that is secondary to a malignancy and unresponsive to other modes of treatment. Although the specific mechanisms of pain relief are not fully understood, it may result from alterations in brain endorphin levels (this is in regard to a hypophysectomy). This technique is also effective for patients suffering from tic douloureux that is unresponsive to chemotherapy. It can be a safe technique for elderly and debilitated patients.

The use of injections that block nerve impulses can be useful in diagnosing the origin of pain, in predicting the effect of a permanent ablation, or in therapy (which requires long-acting neurolytic agents such as ethyl alcohol and phenol). Blockage of sympathetic pathways may relieve pain associated with causalgia, vasospasm after surgery, abdominal visceral disease, or reflex sympathetic dystrophy syndromes.

EMG biofeedback is becoming increasingly popular. It enables individuals to gain increased control of autonomic and somatic systems. The ability to reduce muscle tension in conjunction with relaxation techniques can be effective in maintaining pain relief. It has been successfully used in treating muscle tension headaches and neck pain, especially that of malignant origin, and most successfully in patients who use significant denial in handling impaired functioning abilities due to illness.

Finally, behavior modification is an intervention that can be used effectively with chronic pain patients whose pain is not associated with a malignancy. This approach requires commitment and motivation by the patient and family. The pain clinic concept, in which a multidisciplinary team provides in-depth assessment of pain and its associated behaviors in an individual patient, can facilitate changes in pain behavior. The goals of such a program are threefold: (1) to identify and eliminate positive reinforcers of pain behavior, (2) to increase a patient's physical activity, and (3) to decrease or eliminate drug use in controlling pain. These goals are achieved by behavioral strategies that provide patients with new ways of perceiving their pain and coping with it.

COMMENTARY: This report correctly emphasizes distinguishing chronic pain of benign origin from pain that is secondary to malignancy. Each etiology requires specific interventions with different treatment goals. The available therapeutic alternatives approach pain behavior differently, from organic systems to psychophysical processes. The authors contend that effective treatment should address not only the organic symptoms but also the impact of pain upon the individual. As such, treatments should address the unique needs of the patient, and professionals should be aware of both physical and psychological needs when formulating a treatment regimen.

SOURCE: Reuler, J. B., Girard, D. E., and Nardone, D. A. "The Chronic Pain Syndrome: Misconceptions and Management." *Annals of Internal Medicine*, 1980, *93*, 588–596.

Treatment of Myofacial Pain Dysfunction

AUTHOR: Barry J. Wepman

PRECIS: A description of the treatment of chronic myofacial pain dysfunction with EMG biofeedback and general relaxation training.

TREATMENT: Patients who presented themselves with temporomandibular pain were given a series of treatment sessions, both in the author's office and in their homes. The program was designed to increase patients' awareness and control over specific facial muscle groups (the frontalis and the masseter) as well as to provide general coping skills in dealing with stress.
    Throughout the treatment process, the author stresses the

need for patient-therapist rapport so that the patient can be open about his or her feelings throughout the course of therapy. A frank relationship is important in educating the patient about biofeedback, what it is and what it can do, as well as clarifying the patient's tasks during treatment. This education, or "cognitive restructuring," is useful in making the patient aware of secondary gains, coping techniques with stress, and etiological factors related to the syndrome.

During the biofeedback treatment, all patients were given general relaxation exercises (presented on audiotape), which they were to practice in their homes twice a day. This was done to help the patients improve their response behaviors in stressful situations.

The first therapy session was devoted to a personal history of the presenting complaints and to introduce the patient to the procedures to be used. The patient's responsibilities were outlined, and he or she was given the necessary recording sheets. During this session, the therapist assessed whether the patient was appropriate for treatment and provided preliminary information on the treatment process. Also, any questions that the patient had were answered.

During the second session, patients were introduced to the equipment, and a series of baseline recordings were taken. These readings measured how much the patient could constrict and relax the masseter and frontalis muscles. Patients were also given the relaxation tape that they were to use at home. Any questions or reservations that the patient had about the treatment were addressed.

The third and subsequent sessions were devoted to the treatment procedures. These sessions were approximately 40 minutes in length. Specific training was given for relaxation in 1-minute segments followed by 30-second rest periods. The author maintained that the best results were obtained within eight sessions. The author also suggested that the feedback electrodes provide the patient with bilateral information; an active electrode placed over each masseter and the reference electrode placed over the frontalis muscle. In this manner, one reduces the risk, however slight, of jaw dislocation during treatment.

Of the eight patients treated in this study, two obtained complete relief of symptoms, four obtained partial relief, and two obtained no relief. The author properly concludes that biofeedback can be a useful approach to the treatment of myofacial pain, yet it is a treatment modality that has limitations.

However, the author does present two brief case studies from his sample (one who was successfully treated and one who was not), and it is interesting to note the differences in personality type. The patient whose outcome was successful was described as being a professional who was very intelligent, ambitious, and anxious to overcome this difficulty. The patient for whom the procedure was unsuccessful was described as passive and having a long history of somatic complaints believed to be psychogenic. These differences (which are based on only two cases drawn from a small sample) raise some interesting questions about the utility of biofeedback with different personality types. Practitioners should remain sensitive to issues such as secondary gain and the behavioral predicament of their patients throughout the course of treatment.

COMMENTARY: This study is useful in presenting a relatively simple treatment procedure that requires only a small amount of treatment time. This procedure also employs many interesting techniques in addition to EMG biofeedback, such as having the patient keep a record of the amount of pain experienced, practice daily what was learned during treatment, and listen to relaxation tape recordings. These techniques were useful in encouraging patient compliance and in measuring the effectiveness of the treatment process.

Also important in this study was the recommendation that practitioners screen prospective patients, barring any patient who would be unlikely to benefit from biofeedback. The author describes three types of individuals for whom biofeedback is contraindicated: (1) psychotic patients, (2) patients prone to depression, and (3) patients who are passive and are unwilling to accept responsibility within a treatment procedure.

SOURCE: Wepman, B. J. "Biofeedback in the Treatment of

Chronic Myofacial Pain Dysfunction." *Psychosomatics*, 1980, *21*, 157–162.

Additional Readings

Hendler, N., Viernstein, M., Shallenberger, C., and Long, D. "Group Therapy with Chronic Pain Patients." *Psychosomatics*, 1981, *22*, 333–340.

This report evaluates the role of the psychologist in group therapy sessions for chronic pain patients. Outlined are some of the common themes encountered with such patients. The authors strongly support group therapy as an intervention for pain patients. Such sessions can provide an important mode of support for these individuals as they attempt to cope with their condition. Group therapy can also help foster increased self-reliance in these individuals. Finally, group therapy can be used effectively as an outpatient support group or as an intensive treatment method in place of hospitalization.

Malec, J., Cayner, J. J., Harvey, R. F., and Timming, R. C. "Pain Management: Long-Term Follow-Up of an In-patient Program." *Archives of Physical Medicine and Rehabilitation*, 1981, *62*, 369–372.

This report focused on the long-term impact of an in-patient behavioral program for managing pain. The program's goals were: (1) to increase physical activity (including social behaviors), (2) to decrease pain behaviors and encourage greater independence in activities, and (3) to maximize existing skills and develop new skills for coping with physical distress. Subjects were contacted an average of 18 months after discharge. Based upon the authors' multivariate criteria for determining success (which assessed medication usage, activity levels compared with employment status, recreational activities, and increases in pain), 37% of the patients were considered to have a successful outcome. Those behaviors that were maintained over the time of this follow-up were those most frequently practiced (such as exercises and the nonuse of medications). The authors suggest that increased behavioral practice of vocational and recreational activities enhances the long-term effectiveness of pain management programs.

Martin, M. J. "Muscle-Contraction (Tension) Headache." *Psychosomatics,* 1983, *24,* 319–324.

This review of the literature describes the etiologies, clinical manifestations, and therapeutic interventions for tension headaches. There appears to be great disagreement about the contributing factors as well as the most effective therapeutic approach. This author contends that tension headaches are a multifaceted illness, and no one intervention is totally effective. Greater consensus is needed in the field before better interventions can be developed. The controversies appearing in the literature argue for the need to establish uniform criteria of the illness.

Timming, R. C., Cayner, J. J., Malec, J. F., Harvey, R. F., Schwettman, R. S., and Chosey, J. "Inpatient Treatment Program for Chronic Pain." *Wisconsin Medical Journal,* 1980, *79,* 23–26.

This report describes the effectiveness of a multidisciplinary, inpatient treatment program for chronic pain patients. The pain management program focused on increasing activity levels, the withdrawal of nonessential pain medications, and behavior self-management (assisting patients in increasing their repertoire of "well behaviors" and decreasing "pain behaviors"). The authors contend that psychosocial counseling to facilitate healthy behaviors is crucial to any program treating chronic pain patients. Fostering self-control techniques to reduce anxiety, depression, and pain rather than the use of medications is an important therapeutic goal.

Webb, W. L. "Chronic Pain." *Psychosomatics,* 1983, *24,* 1053–1063.

There are many psychosocial consequences of chronic pain. In many instances, chronic pain helps a person to communicate to others or to maintain a particular role. Patients' families can reinforce the pain and retard patients' progress. Therapeutic interventions must address these issues and break the patterns that maintain the pain experience. The author contends that promoting the concept of wellness among the general public (in contrast to promoting disease treatment alone) could help to decrease reliance on pain for gaining attention, sympathy, or other psychological goals.

5

Therapies
for Selected
Adult Disorders

Many medical specialties are organized by the affected body system. Behavioral therapies and applications that are appropriate for these medical specialties are presented in this chapter. While not covering all medical specialties, the collection describes common problem areas where behavioral interventions have been successful. Many of these reports address serious medical health problems that have not been responsive to conventional medical protocols. Admittedly, several of the treatments described here are controversial and require replication and careful evaluation before their use can be recommended without reservation.

Fecal
and Urinary
Incontinence

Few medical problems have such highly charged social and psychological implications as incontinence. However, not only is incontinence embarrassing and discomforting for the patient, but the conventional corrective methods are often inadequate or pose other risks (such as infection). Not all cases of incontinence signal impending dementia. Indeed, a number of paraplegics, diabetics, and other nongeriatric patients suffer from this condition. Although some cases of incontinence probably result from psychological or cortical control problems, many incontinent adults lack adequate functioning of the musculature that controls voiding. In some cases, biofeedback procedures can reinstate appropriate behaviors quite dramatically. At other times, hypnosis or other behavior therapy can solve problems of retention or incontinence. Commonly a judicious blend of behavioral strategies designed by competent therapists can provide the primary care urologist or gastroenterologist with the most effective treatment options.

Hypnosis in the Treatment of Urinary Incontinence

AUTHORS: R. M. Freeman and K. Baxby

PRECIS: A description of the use of hypnotherapy in treating urinary incontinence caused by an unstable detrusor.

INTRODUCTION: Detrusor instability is a common cause of urinary incontinence. Because of this condition, an individual cannot inhibit detrusor contractions while the bladder is being filled. This condition is manifested by frequent voiding, urgency in voiding, and incontinence. The authors contend that since psychological factors are implicated in the etiology of this disorder, hypnosis may be an effective treatment by providing psychophysiological suggestions to alter detrusor functioning. This study also attempts to ascertain if women with detrusor instability are more susceptible to hypnotic suggestions than the general population.

METHOD: Data were collected on a sample of sixty-three females aged 17 to 74 years. Subjects were selected on the following criteria: (1) urodynamically established detrusor instability, (2) no evidence of stress incontinence, (3) no evidence of outflow obstructions, (4) normal appearances on cystoscopy, (5) normal neurological functioning, and (6) no ingestion of medications that could affect the detrusor. All subjects were unresponsive to previous therapeutic interventions. All had a long history of incontinence (mean of 7 years and range of 1 to 40 years).

All individuals underwent cystoscopy, a neurological examination, and an urodynamic examination before behavioral treatment. All subjects kept voiding charts indicating the frequency of micturition and incontinence. Since there was no control group (the authors believed that asking subjects to participate in the study but not to receive treatment for their disorder would be unethical), there was a 1-month waiting period between the baseline measures and the initiation of the treatment program. During this period one subject became symptom free

and declined further treatment, while eight improved sympto-
matically but requested further treatment. Two subjects dropped
out of the study. The remaining fifty-four subjects showed no
change.

Treatment consisted of twelve sessions of hypnotherapy.
In these sessions, suggestions to remove direct symptoms and
to increase ego strength were given over a period of 1 month.
Subjects were also provided with a cassette tape of instructions
and suggestions that they were to play at home. Hypnotic
depth was ascertained via the Stanford Hypnotic Clinical Scale.
Three months after the termination of treatment, all subjects
underwent another cystoscopy. Follow-up data were compiled
from 6 to 14 months after the completion of treatment.

Fifty patients completed the treatment; of these, twenty-
nine were symptom free, fourteen were considerably improved,
and seven showed no change. Six patients refused a repeat
cystoscopy after treatment. Of the remaining forty-four, twenty-
two exhibited detrusor stability as determined by the cysto-
metrogram. These forty-four subjects also received a posttreatment urodynamic evaluation, which indicated that the mean
maximal cystometric capacity had significantly increased over
baseline. In the sixteen patients for whom there was continued
instability, the height of the unstable contraction was significantly reduced after treatment. Finally, no differences were
found to support the hypothesis that women with unstable detrusor incontinence are more hypnotically suggestible than
normals. The distribution of susceptibility scores closely paralleled published norms.

Seven patients, five of whom had been symptom free, re-
lapsed, three at 1-year posttreatment and one each at 10, 8, 7,
and 2 months. Three of these relapses occurred after the death
of a close relative. Treatment was readministered to six of
these patients, and five were rendered symptom free. The other
forty-three symptom-free or improved patients exhibited no evidence of relapse at follow-up.

The authors contend that hypnosis focuses on increasing
bladder control at an unconscious level. It is a useful treatment
approach for this condition, since it is noninvasive and inexpensive, involves only a moderate amount of time and staff, and

does not require hospitalization. The success rate can be improved if there is a good patient-physician relationship. The hypnotic treatment provided very durable results, with only 14% of the sample showing a relapse. Three of these relapses were clearly associated with bereavement. This study also dispels the myth that the removal of a symptom through hypnosis results in the development of a more serious substitute symptom (such as suicidal tendencies) among nonhysterical neurotics. Such behaviors were not evidenced in this subject sample. Unstable detrusor functioning is not a hysterical condition, since there is abnormal functioning in the observed physiological system that can be verified objectively.

COMMENTARY: The authors assert that since hypnosis was effective in treatment detrusor instability, the hypothesis is strengthened that psychological variables play a crucial role in the etiology of this disorder. This hypothesis is further supported by the fact that there is a placebo response rate of approximately 25% for this condition. The authors believe that detrusor instability is a true psychosomatic disorder. As such, hypnosis can be very useful in altering intrapsychic processes that predispose an individual toward urinary incontinence.

SOURCE: Freeman, R. M., and Baxby, K. "Hypnotherapy for Incontinence Caused by the Unstable Detrusor." *British Medical Journal*, 1982, *284*, 1831–1834.

Biofeedback Therapy for Fecal Incontinence

AUTHORS: David A. Goldenberg, Kathie Hodges, Theodore Hersh, and Horacio Jinich

PRECIS: A description of the use of rectosphincteric manometry and visual biofeedback in the treatment of fecal incontinence.

INTRODUCTION: Fecal incontinence can result from a variety of surgical and medical conditions, including hemorrhoidectomy, rectal prolapse repair, multiple sclerosis, and cirrhosis. Although many interventions are available, operant conditioning in the form of biofeedback appears to be the most effective. The authors contend that since this type of conditioning is noninvasive and does not have undesirable side effects, it should be the treatment of choice.

METHOD: The subjects for this study consisted of six males and six females between the ages of 12 and 78 years. The duration of their condition ranged from 10 months to 24 years. Daily incontinence was present in eleven of the subjects.

The technique employed was the three-balloon system, which consists of a hollow cylinder carrying two balloons to measure internal and external anal sphincter pressures. A third balloon is placed through the tube into the rectum to simulate rectal distension. These balloons are connected to a polygraph that displays variations in pressures.

Initially, the sensory threshold level for perceiving rectal distension was determined for each subject (this is the smallest amount of distension necessary for the subject to perceive any change). Biofeedback training then began. Subjects were able to view their manometric tracings on the polygraph. While viewing their responses, subjects were instructed to elevate internal and external sphincter pressures whenever rectal distensions were perceived in an attempt to simulate a normal response on the tracing. Some patients had high sensory thresholds (30 cubic centimeters). In these cases, systematic sensitization procedures were used to enable the subject to sense rectal distension at more normal levels. This was accomplished by gradually decreasing the volume of the rectal balloon until the subject was able to sense the lower volumes consistently.

Correct responses were rewarded with praise and encouragement. As subjects' performance improved, the visual feedback was withheld intermittently to reduce their dependence on the devices for initiating appropriate sphincter responses. After the session was completed, subjects were instructed to practice prescribed sphincter exercises and to use their new training at the slightest perception of rectal fullness. Follow-up information was obtained between 12 weeks and 24 months after the termination of treatment.

Ten of the twelve subjects were found to have a good response to treatment. Six of these subjects were completely continent; three experienced less than one episode of incontinence per month (characterized by the slight seepage of liquid stool); one subject had slight seepage less than once per week. Nine of these responders required only one treatment session. The remaining two subjects showed no improvement. One of these subjects was an elderly man with organic brain syndrome who was unable to follow the treatment instructions. The other subject was a 12-year-old boy who had had a pull-through procedure for an imperforate anus. The authors believe that his ambivalence and complex family dynamics hindered his compliance with the requirements of the study.

Considering the variety of etiologies for incontinence in this subject population, the results strongly support the utility of biofeedback in treating this condition. The authors present two cases in detail. One subject, whose incontinence was secondary to multiple repairs for rectal prolapse, had a complete loss of internal sphincter tone as well as weak external sphincter contractions. Treatment was able to reduce incontinent episodes to infrequent seepage of liquid stool. The other case report described a subject who had no reflex contractions of the external sphincter as well as a sensory threshold for rectal distension above normal limits. Biofeedback was able to lower the threshold to 20 cubic centimeters. It also enabled the subject to make appropriate external sphincter contractions that were synchronized with internal sphincter relaxation. This subject was completely continent at follow-up.

COMMENTARY: This study is important for two reasons. First, it shows the effectiveness of manometric biofeedback in eliminating incontinence in individuals whose problem is secondary to a surgical procedure (such as excision of an anal fistula or proctoscopy). Second, this operant conditioning technique was useful in subjects who had abnormally high sensory threshold levels to rectal distension. It had been suggested that individuals with high thresholds would not be successful candidates for this treatment. Yet the five subjects in this study with this condition were able to decrease their thresholds to near normal or normal limits. It may be that the preliminary sensitization procedures removed this difficulty. The authors suggest four conditions that promote the success of a biofeedback protocol: (1) Subjects must be highly motivated to be rid of their condition; (2) individuals must be able to understand the procedure and follow directions; (3) the response used must be under the control of the nervous system and the end organ must be capable of responding; and (4) subjects must be able to sense a recognizable cue that will alert them to initiate the response (such as rectal distension).

SOURCE: Goldenberg, D. A., Hodges, K., Hersh, T., and Jinich, H. "Biofeedback Therapy for Fecal Incontinence." *American Journal of Gastroenterology,* 1980, *74,* 342–345.

Treating Incontinence in Psychogeriatric Patients

AUTHOR: Ezio Sanovio

PRECIS: A controlled case study of the behavioral treatment of fecal and urinary incontinence in two geriatric patients.

INTRODUCTION: The author reports that most cases of incontinence do not result from any organic dysfunction and that 80% of all geriatric patients who are incontinent are physically capable of controlling their bladders if motivated. The author contends that in chronically institutionalized patients, incontinence may be a learned behavioral pattern acquired through reinforcement within the institution. The author used a toilet training approach developed by Azrin and Foxx and modified to meet the particular needs of the aged incontinent residents of a psychiatric ward. Both patients studied were diagnosed as having senile mental diseases, and although incontinent, they were physically able to perform appropriate toileting behaviors independently.

METHOD: Two male psychogeriatric patients were studied. Subject 1 was a 60-year-old suffering from mental deterioration due to chronic alcoholism. He became enuretic 3 years before treatment and was incontinent at least four times a day. Subject 2 was a 77-year-old diagnosed as suffering from senile dementia and had been fecally incontinent for at least 2 years. A pocket-sized portable urine alarm was attached to the pants of subject 1 to signal daytime accidents.

Each patient was given large amounts of their favorite drinks and snacks in order to increase the frequency of bowel movements and urination. Every hour the subjects were taken to the bathroom by the trainer using minimal verbal or physical guidance. This assistance was removed as soon as possible; after the second day of training, no guidance was provided. A positive practice procedure was used to establish the habit of toileting and to negatively reinforce accidents. This procedure required the subject to walk to the toilet, remove his clothing, sit on the toilet for a few seconds, replace his clothing, and leave the toilet. This process was repeated for several trials without interruption for a maximum of 30 minutes. Every 20 minutes, the trainer would inspect the patient to see if an accident had occurred. If the patient voided during the 5 minutes he was on the toilet, he was strongly praised and rewarded by the trainer; otherwise, the subject was returned to the recreation room in the ward. Cigarettes, candy, snacks, and music were used as reinforcers. If an accident occurred while the subject was in the ward, the person was directed to the toilet and given cleanliness training; that is, he was required to change his soiled clothing and to clean the soiled area.

A baseline measurement of the frequency of incontinent behaviors was established over a 4-day period. Treatment was then given 10 hours a day for 5 days. On the sixth day a reversal phase was introduced, where positive and negative reinforcement was not contingent on the subject's behaviors. The same amount of positive and aversive activities were administered as during the treatment phase but at random intervals. This phase lasted 4 days and was followed by a second, 8-day treatment phase where the reinforcers were again made contingent. On the second day of this phase, the continuous reinforcement schedule was gradually withdrawn and an intermittent schedule was introduced.

Both subjects showed a substantial decrease in incontinent episodes during the first treatment phase and an increase in independent toileting behaviors over baseline. These improvements disappeared during the reversal phase but reappeared during the second treatment phase. The incidence of appropriate toileting behaviors was also more consistent during the second treatment phase. At an 8-week follow-up, the level of continent behaviors achieved during the second treatment period was maintained.

The author contends that contingent reinforcement plays a critical role in the treatment of incontinence. Negative reinforcers (such as cleanliness training and positive practice sequences) may be useful as secondary interventions when positive reinforcers are not effective.

COMMENTARY: This study, aside from presenting an effective treatment approach to incontinence, is important in that it assesses the generalizability of this therapeutic procedure to a sample of aged subjects with added diminished mental capacities. In individuals with no underlying organic lesion accounting for incontinence, the behavioral modification procedure can effectively provide the necessary motivation and reinforcement for relearning appropriate toileting behaviors.

SOURCE: Sanavio, E. "Toilet Retraining of Psychogeriatric Residents." *Behavior Modification,* 1981, *5,* 417–427.

Treating Fecal Incontinence with Biofeedback

AUTHOR: Arnold Wald

PRECIS: A description of the use of visual biofeedback for external sphincter contractions in the treatment of fecal incontinence.

INTRODUCTION: Fecal incontinence is a common problem that can have a traumatic effect on an individual's psychosocial functioning. Although biofeedback has been successfully employed in treating this condition, its success has not been universal. This suggests the need to develop more specific criteria for selecting patients likely to benefit from this type of treatment. These criteria should include both physiological and psychological factors. In this study, there were a variety of causal factors underlying the subjects' fecal incontinence, including irritable bowel syndrome, diabetes mellitus, Crohn's disease, and previous anal sphincter repair. Two subjects had no underlying cause that could be ascertained.

METHOD: Seventeen subjects participated in this study, ranging in age from 10 to 79 years. There were eleven females and six males. All had had gross fecal incontinence for at least 6 months. These subjects were selected on the basis of (1) being able to sense rectal distension of any volume, (2) appearing cooperative, and (3) being able to tolerate the manometric apparatus. All had thresholds of rectal sensation within normal parameters (less than or equal to 30 milliliters of rectal distension).

Diagnostic anorectal manometry was done using a three-balloon technique, which allowed pressure measurements from the proximal rectum and the internal and external sphincters. Measurements recorded were the threshold of rectal sensation (smallest volume of rectal distension sensed), the presence of internal sphincter relaxation and the threshold of relaxation (smallest volume of rectal distension needed to initiate relaxation), and the presence and strength of external sphincter contractions and threshold of contraction (smallest volume of rectal distension needed to produce external sphincter contraction). Five subjects had no reflexive contraction of the external sphincter, eight had diminished external sphincter contractions, and four had normal contractions.

At the beginning of treatment, the importance of the external anal sphincter in bowel control was explained to all subjects. Those subjects who had normal external sphincter responses were instructed to engage in the normal pattern of muscle contractions so that their responses could be graphed by the biofeedback apparatus. This provided a clear illustration of the various muscle responses in a bowel movement. Those subjects who had a weak or absent external sphincter response were shown a normal manometric tracing. They were then instructed to practice various maneuvers until they could consistently replicate the normal pattern (increasing external sphincter pressure in response to rectal distension). Visual feedback was used to help subjects determine the appropriate responses. When the subjects mastered this technique, it was then repeated without the use of visual feedback. In addition, the volume of rectal distension was decreased in 10-millimeter decrements until the threshold of sensation was reached.

After the biofeedback process was finished, the subjects were instructed to practice anal sphincter contractions several times daily and to employ the technique whenever they sensed any rectal distension. Follow-up sessions were scheduled for all subjects 6 to 8 weeks after this initial session. Subsequent sessions were scheduled only if there was a regression. Follow-up information was obtained after a 4-week period and then at 3-month intervals. Such information was gathered from telephone interviews and once by a written questionnaire.

Twelve of the seventeen patients had a good response to the biofeedback treatment; that is, either soiling disappeared or the frequency of soiling episodes was reduced at least 75%. Also, patients had to express satisfaction with the results. The follow-up results indicated that ten of these twelve patients were completely continent, while the other two had only occasional soiling after treatment. Of the four subjects with diabetes mellitus, three completely improved. The fourth, considered to have a poor response to treatment, did experience a 3-month improvement, which was followed by a relapse. Of the nine remaining subjects having a positive response to treatment, four had irritable bowel syndrome, and one each had Crohn's disease, anal sphincter repair, and childhood encopresis, and two had an unknown etiology of the disorder. Of the five subjects with a poor response, four had irritable bowel syndrome. Two of these subjects did not return for the reinforcement sessions, one experienced only transient improvement, and the fourth (although not incontinent of solid stool) was unhappy with the seepage of mucus.

In an attempt to identify physiological factors that could predict success or failure for this treatment, rectosphincteric responses between the good and poor responders were compared. No significant differences between these two groups were found in the threshold of internal sphincter relaxation or the threshold of rectal sensation. Other physiological comparisons also yielded no significant differences. The author concluded that external sphincteric variables are not useful predictors of outcome performance. This study suggests that psychological factors may be more influential in determining outcome. Of the five poor responders, one showed considerable anxiety during all biofeedback sessions and gave evidence of significant psychological dysfunctioning. As mentioned earlier, two patients failed to return for the reinforcement sessions despite some improvement after the initial biofeedback session.

The author concludes that the most important information to be gathered from diagnostic anorectal manometry of patients is their ability to sense rectal distension. Subjects who responded successfully to biofeedback treatment all had rectal sensation thresholds within normal limits (less than or equal to 30 milliliters of distension). Because of the time required for biofeedback training, diagnostic manometry can be an important screening tool in identifying candidates for this treatment.

Also of importance are psychological factors that may be related to the outcome of biofeedback therapy, such as the patient-therapist relationship. Although psychological profiles were not obtained from the subjects participating in this study, casual observation of the subjects with poor responses indicate that intrapsychic factors may influence the results. This contention seems supported by the absence of differences in anorectal muscle functioning between good and poor responders. Both groups improved on these dimensions as a result of the treatment, yet the only observable difference between them appeared to be psychological.

COMMENTARY: This study illustrates the efficacy of biofeedback therapy in treating fecal incontinence. A testament to its effectiveness is the dramatic improvement obtained in patients with a variety of etiological causes. The author suggests three guidelines for selecting patients for this treatment: (1) Patients should be highly motivated and cooperative, (2) subjects with neurological diseases should be capable of some ambulation and have no serious neuromotor deficits in the gluteal region, and (3) diagnostic anorectal manometry should be done to assure that the patient can sense rectal distension within normal limits. Biofeedback can then be the treatment of choice as well as a simple and rapid technique for treating this disorder.

SOURCE: Wald, A. "Biofeedback Therapy for Fecal Incontinence." *Annals of Internal Medicine*, 1981, *95*, 146-149.

Additional Readings

Blaivis, J. G., and Labib, K. B. "Acute Urinary Retention in Women: Complete Urodynamic Evaluation." *Urology*, 1977, *10*, 383-389.

There are many theories on the etiology of urine retention in women, but few with supporting empirical findings. Consequently, differential diagnosis plays a critical role in evaluation. Based on the authors' experience, micturition symptoms, simple gas cystometry, and the test of bethanechol denervation supersensitivity can all provide erroneous information and misdiagnosis. A preferred alternative is the simultaneous measurement of intraabdominal and intravesical pressures via an EMG of the external urethral sphincter and voiding cystourethrography. These authors present a comprehensive and detailed format for evaluating women with acute urinary retention. Central to this method are complete neurological assessments and psychiatric evaluations.

Figueroa, J. L., and Jacob, R. G. "Treatment of Urinary Urgency and Excessive Frequency: A Case Study." *Behaviour Research and Therapy*, 1981, *19*, 261–264.

These authors present a case study treatment for a 39-year-old male with a 5-year history of excessive urinary frequency and urgency. The first phase of treatment used relaxation procedures to overcome the subject's reported anxiety and stress, which were associated with his condition. The second phase (6 weeks) consisted of retention control training, namely, a bladder-loading technique where fluid consumption was gradually increased while episodes of micturition were held constant. The results showed a decrease in frequency from 14 to 6.5 episodes a day and in urgency from 35 to 9.3 urges per day. The gains were maintained at 3- and 5-month follow-ups. The relaxation procedures appeared necessary to alleviate the problem. The authors stress the need for therapists to rule out organic causes for the disorder before initiating a behavioral treatment.

MacLeod, J. H. "Biofeedback in the Management of Partial Anal Incontinence." *Diseases of the Colon and Rectum*, 1983, *26*, 244–246.

Biofeedback was used as an office procedure in treating fifty patients with anal incontinence. The instrument was an intraanal plug containing two electrodes that was connected to an electromyometer. In four or fewer sessions, subjects were instructed in sphincter contraction and extraneous muscle relaxation. Seventy-four percent of the patients reported satisfactory improvement in continence. The procedure was successful in postsurgical patients except for those with "keyhole deformity" after anal fistulectomy. In nonsurgical patients (idiopathic and postradiation patients), the results were excellent. Poor results were obtained in patients whose incontinence was due to rectal prolapse or neurogenic causes. All therapeutic gains were maintained at a 1-year follow-up. The strength of this system lies in its simplicity and portability, and the author believes that it can be an important tool for managing anal incontinence.

Schnelle, J. F., Traughber, B., Morgan, D. B., Embry, J. E., Binion, A. F., and Coleman, A. "Management of Geriatric Incontinence in Nursing Homes." *Journal of Applied Behavior Analyses,* 1983, *16,* 235–241.

These authors examined the effectiveness of a behavioral management system designed to reduce urinary incontinence in nursing home patients. The main components of the program were prompting and contingent approval/disapproval. The program only required 2.5 minutes per patient per hour to administer. This program increased appropriate toileting 45% over baseline. Because of the many practical constraints imposed by an institutional setting, the ease of application of this procedure, as well as its effectiveness, seems well suited to this type of clinical setting.

Stanton, H. E. "Short-Term Treatment of Enuresis." *American Journal of Clinical Hypnosis,* 1979, *22,* 103–107.

This article outlines a short-term approach to treating enuresis that involves hypnosis. Emphasis is placed on the first 1-hour treatment session, which consists of three phases: (1) establishing rapport with the patient, (2) inducing a hypnotic trance together with suggestions directed at overcoming the enuretic problem, and (3) repeating these suggestions while the patient's attention is focused on another task. The second session (which is usually shorter) focuses on the repetition of the latter two phases. From the author's experience, the approach is usually sufficient, and a third session is not required. The use of hypnotherapy offers a rapid intervention procedure for eliminating enuresis in adults.

Bruxism

Grinding of teeth—relentlessly, compulsively, and often without self-awareness—presents a number of dental and other problems. When this behavior occurs during sleep, the noise is often annoying and disruptive to the other bed partner. Major restorative dental work may be required as a consequence of bruxism, and not infrequently some myofacial pain problems develop. One can speculate about neuroticism and other underlying causes, but such analytic exercises are not likely to offer much in the way of help or rehabilitation. A number of treatment paradigms taken from the behavior therapies have been designed to abort and extinguish bruxism, and they hold the promise of offering a major treatment advance for dentistry.

Treatment of Bruxism
with Counseling and EMG Feedback

AUTHORS: Jesus M. Casas, Phyllis Beemsterboer, and Glen T. Clark

PRECIS: A comparison of the effectiveness of stress reduction behavioral counseling and nocturnal treatments employing contingent EMG feedback for reducing daytime and nighttime bruxism.

INTRODUCTION: Bruxism is defined as a nonfunctional clenching and grinding of the teeth, a problem that can occur either awake or asleep. Although there is no definite etiology of bruxism, research findings suggest that psychophysiological factors such as fear, anxiety, stress, and frustration may contribute. Daytime anxiety and stress appear to exacerbate nocturnal bruxism. Some physiological indexes of stress, such as urinary catecholamines, have been significantly correlated with nocturnal EMG levels in bruxism patients. Much of the research in this area has centered on the effectiveness of various relaxation techniques such as hypnosis, autogenic training, biofeedback, and progressive relaxation. The present authors contend that although research supports the promise of such methods, there is as yet no conclusive evidence that they are effective. In addition, it has not been established that skills acquired by a patient to reduce bruxism while the patient is awake will reduce bruxism while the patient is asleep.

The research reported here attempts to substantiate these treatment approaches quantitatively. Four experimental treatment groups were employed: (1) stress reduction behavioral counseling only, (2) contingent nocturnal EMG feedback only, (3) combined behavioral stress reduction counseling and nocturnal contingent EMG feedback, and (4) no treatment. Two major hypotheses were tested. According to the first, behavioral counseling alone would be more effective than EMG feedback alone, since the coping techniques inherent in the counseling are preventive in nature, while the feedback minimizes a behavior that is part of the individual's repertoire. According to the second, the combination of counseling and EMG feedback should be a very effective treatment for bruxism.

METHOD: Sixteen subjects were employed for this study, all of whom exhibited moderate to severe symptoms of bruxism. None of these individuals had any intracapsular temporomandibular joint pathology. Nine were women and seven were men; their mean age was 29 years. The subjects were assigned in sequence to one of the four treatment groups.

Two types of measures were used in this study. The first, a subjective symptom questionnaire, was used for both screening and follow-up purposes. It consisted of two types of questions: those relating to symptoms of daytime clenching, such as sore jaw muscles on chewing and daytime pain in the ear and temporomandibular joint regions; and those relating to nocturnal bruxism, such as spouse reports of nocturnal grinding noises and the clenching and popping of the temporomandibular joint upon arising. The other dependent measure was masseter muscle activity as recorded by a portable EMG machine. Activity levels were recorded for ten nights before and ten nights after treatment. Evaluation of tooth wear, muscle palpation, and subjective complaints determined the most active side of the mouth, which was then measured by the EMG. Before treatment, each subject was instructed in how to place the electrodes. The EMG device recorded cumulative totals of electrical activity above 20 volts. These totals along with amount of sleep time were recorded by the subject. The mean individual EMG levels and the standard error were calculated for each recording period.

The separate treatment groups differed in both format and organization. The stress reduction behavioral counseling was conducted over four weekly, 1-hour individual sessions. The goal of this treatment was to help the subjects develop more adaptive, stress-related cognitive responses that would alter the related physiological expressions of the experienced stress. Subjects were helped in identifying specific anxiety-provoking situations as well as their reactions to them and then in restructuring their cognitions into specific self-statements more suited to coping with their affect (such as "This is not as bad as I thought" and "I can handle this"). Subjects were also instructed to use internal speech to help them relax. In the second and following sessions, EMG feedback was used to facilitate learning and to confirm the value of using relaxation-related self-statements.

Subjects in the contingent nocturnal EMG feedback group received a response-oriented therapy. Each time a subject's masseter muscle activity exceeded the predetermined threshold, an auditory signal was emitted that awakened the individual and kept him awake for several minutes. The natural aversiveness associated with being awakened during the night was assumed to provide the necessary incentive to reduce or extinguish the bruxism. The electrode assembly was the same as the one used for the EMG recordings taken before treatment. The same masseter muscle was also used. The participants used the EMG instrument every night for a period of 2 weeks.

The combined counseling and EMG feedback group followed the same format used in the counseling only group, but during the last 2 weeks of treatment subjects used the EMG feedback unit at night. The control group was given no treatment, nor were they provided with information regarding the availability of other treatments. Each subject in this group was told that they were being placed on a waiting list until a treatment group could begin. Subjects in this group also had their nightly EMG activity recorded but did not receive any nocturnal EMG feedback. The interval between pre- and posttreatment data collection was the same for all groups.

The results indicated that the three treatment conditions were significantly more effective than no treatment. The authors contend that the use of stress reduction behavioral counseling seems more beneficial than EMG nocturnal feedback alone, but this difference was not significant. Also, the addition of EMG nocturnal feedback to the stress reduction counseling did not significantly enhance the effectiveness of the counseling. The authors concluded that stress reduction skills learned while an individual is awake *can* reduce nocturnal bruxism.

The results obtained on the posttreatment questionnaire at the 2-month follow-up were also very illuminating. With regard to the behavioral counseling alone group, 75% (three of four) reported a decrease in daytime clenching symptoms, but only 25% (one of four) reported a decrease in nocturnal bruxism. The contingent nocturnal EMG feedback alone group reported that 75% (three of four) had a decrease in nocturnal bruxism, but only one of the three subjects who had a history of daytime clenching before treatment reported a decrease in daytime clenching. In the combined treatment group, 75% reported a decrease in nocturnal bruxism and 50% reported a decrease in daytime clenching. Finally, the waiting list control group had one individual who reported a decrease in nocturnal bruxism. All others indicated no change in symptoms.

COMMENTARY: This study illustrates the effectiveness of two different types of treatment interventions for bruxism. Behavioral counseling in stress reduction has important therapeutic value in that it is less obtrusive and bothersome for the patient than the use of contingent nocturnal EMG feedback. It also has the added benefit of being a more preventive approach, since it helps patients to deal with stress and anxiety caused by a wide range of situations. In turn, this may help prevent the occurrence of nocturnal bruxing.

Although the authors concluded that the behavioral counseling was more effective than EMG feedback, over the long-term the different strengths of each type of treatment become more clearly visible. After 2 months, the behavioral counseling approach appears to have a greater effect on daytime clenching than on nocturnal. Just the oposite occurs for the contingent EMG feedback. As the authors point out, the follow-up results indicate that to obtain a more generalized and durable decrease in bruxism, both of these approaches should be incorporated into a single treatment.

SOURCE: Casas, J. M., Beemsterboer, P., and Clark, G. T. "A Comparison of Stress-Reduction Behavioral Counseling and Contingent Nocturnal EMG Feedback for the Treatment of Bruxism." *Behaviour Research and Therapy*, 1982, *20*, 9–15.

Therapeutic Approaches to Bruxism

AUTHORS: Alan G. Glaros and Stephen M. Rao

PRECIS: A report examining the strengths and weaknesses of several treatment interventions for bruxism.

INTRODUCTION: Bruxism is a psychophysiological disorder that has been largely unexplored. Psychologists frequently perceive it as mostly a dental problem, while dentists perceive it as a psychological one. The result has been a general neglect of the problem. This report presents some of the major treatments used for this disorder and assesses their efficacy.

TREATMENT APPROACHES: The dental treatment approach tries to eliminate those factors that trigger bruxism behavior or to prevent further damage to the teeth and supporting tissues. Occlusal adjustment is a common technique and has been shown to be very effective. However, proper adjustment is often difficult to attain. This is due to the high muscle tonus of bruxism patients, which makes proper occlusion difficult. Also, since bruxers are very sensitive to changes in occlusion, identifying and eliminating the trigger factors is difficult. Another widely used technique is the use of occlusal appliances (such as bite plates or occlusal splints). This approach has two advantages: (1) These appliances are easily made, and (2) they prevent further wear to the teeth and surrounding tissues. It has been postulated that the effectiveness of these appliances depends on the interruption of the feedback mechanisms that maintain the bruxism behaviors. Further research is needed to evaluate this hypothesis.

Another therapeutic approach focuses on psychotherapy and psychoanalysis; here bruxism is seen as the physical manifestation of emotional disturbance. Since bruxism is merely a symptom, treatment of the underlying emotional problem is expected to cure the condition. The authors point out that no empirical data support the value of psychotherapy for this disorder. They suggest that a more promising approach to the psychological treatment of bruxism is to conceptualize the problem in terms of learning theory.

Avoidance conditioning is one such approach. In this paradigm, when the rate of grinding exceeds a predetermined level, a noxious auditory signal is administered via earphones to the subject for a short time (such as 3 seconds). Research has shown this approach to be effective in reducing the frequency of bruxism behaviors. However, since only high-intensity grinding noises are used as the dependent variable, it is not known whether such conditioning affects low-intensity grinding. Bruxism associated with highly audible noises may be replaced with an equal or higher number of low-intensity grinds. The authors suggest that masticatory muscle activity may be a better dependent measure for this type of paradigm.

Massed practice is another treatment approach; here bruxism is elicited repeatedly until pain or discomfort arises. The cessation of the behavior is then associated with decreases in muscular fatigue and becomes positive reinforcement for not grinding. Typically, subjects are instructed to clench for 1 minute and then to relax for 1 minute. Five repetitions of this activity constitute one block of trials, and subjects perform six blocks per day for 2 weeks. Research has indicated that even shorter clenching intervals are as effective, and the results of this treatment are maintained over time. However, the authors point out two limitations to studies reporting success with this approach: (1) The data are based on self-reports, which may not be as reliable as other measures, and (2) no attempts are made to control for placebo, expectation, or other nonspecific treatment effects. Although an encouraging intervention, more detailed and controlled research is still needed to evaluate its effectiveness.

Another general approach relates to tension reduction techniques. One approach is based on the assumption that in bruxers, the elevator muscles of the mandible are overdeveloped relative to the depressor muscles. Thus, training subjects to develop the depressor muscles should provide a counteracting pull from the elevators. The use of specific massages and exercises for these muscles has been shown to be effective in controlling such functional disturbances. However, there is a lack of controlled research on this approach.

Hypnosis has also been claimed to be an effective intervention. A similar approach centers on developing a physiological rest position of the mandible through patient practice and repeating the phrase "Lips together, teeth apart" during the day. The authors note that both of these procedures have yet to be subjected to experimental evaluation. Another approach is the use of tranquilizers to control bruxism. However, research has shown that such pharmacological agents may be the least effective of the tension reduction techniques. Any improvements in condition are usually not maintained for as long as improvements obtained through other self-control techniques.

Finally, biofeedback is a frequently used modality in treatment. The underlying assumption here is that by increasing a person's ability to discriminate between high and low levels of muscle tension, the proper response (relaxation) can be initiated when increased arousal is perceived. In some studies, subjects wore a portable EMG feedback unit for a period of 2 to 7 days, during which they were able to increase their awareness of muscle tension as well as learn how to relax it. Eventually the need for the feedback apparatus decreases as control increases. It has been suggested that coupling the tension relaxation procedure with this technique greatly enhances the efficacy of EMG feedback, since the relaxation procedure provides subjects with a defined response to high tension.

COMMENTARY: The authors present the major therapeutic approaches to bruxism as well as noting some of the limitations to these approaches. In all likelihood, the most effective intervention will incorporate techniques from several modalities to form a single, comprehensive treatment. As with any developing approach, further refinements are necessary. The authors suggest a few that will greatly assist in improving treatment success: (1) the development of more objective criteria for improvement, (2) evaluating environmental stresses that may be closely related to the incidence of bruxism for a given individual, and (3) developing a theoretical conceptualization of the disorder that can explain the interaction of dental, psychological, and neurophysiological variables in the etiology and maintenance of bruxism.

SOURCE: Glaros, A. G., and Rao, S. M. "Bruxism: A Critical Review." *Psychological Bulletin,* 1977, *84,* 767–781.

The Habit Reversal Technique in Treating Bruxism

AUTHORS: Michael S. Rosenbaum and Teodoro Ayllon

PRECIS: A description of the treatment of bruxism using the habit reversal technique.

INTRODUCTION: Habit reversal is a behavioral procedure that has been found to be very effective in eliminating nervous habits, such as tics. This procedure was developed (1) to increase a person's awareness of the habit movement, (2) to interrupt the chain of behaviors that results in the habit behavior as early in the sequence as possible, (3) to teach the person a new, competing response opposite to the habit movement but involving the same muscle group, and (4) to remove any social reinforcement for the habit or make it contingent on appropriate behavior. This research attempts to apply habit reversal to the treatment of bruxism.

METHOD: The subjects consisted of four individuals, one female and three male, between the ages of 23 and 42 years. Individual histories of bruxism were 2, 3, 10, and 20 years. The particular behaviors to be eliminated were jaw popping, teeth clenching, facial pain (for only one patient), and teeth grinding.

Initially all subjects were required to self-record the frequencies of the habit behavior daily. The one patient who also complained of facial pain in conjunction with teeth clenching also recorded the intensity of her pain every 2 hours as well as any use of pain medication. A baseline interval was established, which was the time between the initial interview and the first treatment session (approximately 7 days). Daily recordings were maintained for 4 weeks after treatment, and then self-recordings were made periodically during the week.

During the first treatment session, individuals verbally described and physically demonstrated the particular behavior for which they sought treatment. The subjects were then taught to detect early signs of the target behavior (any behavioral or muscular sensations occurring before and involved in the target behaviors). The subjects then listed and described those situations in which the target behavior was most frequent. A "habit inconvenience review" was done, in which subjects described the negative consequences associated with the behavior in question in order to increase their motivation to eliminate the problem behavior. These individuals were then taught an isometric exercise that was incompatible with the target behavior and that had the following characteristics: (1) It was opposite to the bruxism behavior, (2) it could be maintained by the subject for at least 1 minute, (3) it involved isometric tensing of the muscles involved in the target response movement, (4) it could not be noticed by others, (5) it could be practiced while the person performed normal activities, and (6) it prevented the target response from being a routine part of the person's daily activities. All subjects were encouraged to elicit this response whenever they felt the urge to engage in the target behavior, noticed any antecedent of that behavior, or were actually exhibiting that behavior. Finally, each subject was to imagine a situation with which the target behavior was frequently associated and to perform the competing response when the target behavior was detected. This symbolic rehearsal procedure was used to help increase the generalization of the competing response outside of the treatment session.

Two weeks after this treatment, two patients received a

relaxation and stress management treatment. This session was directed at enabling the subjects to define stress-producing events, to maintain a greater degree of composure, and to develop alternate methods for managing these sources of stress. Also involved in this procedure was a cognitive restructuring framework aimed at enhancing the subjects' self-concept and developing more realistic self-attitude. A third session was held for one of these subjects 1 week later, which centered on relaxation techniques to be used in any extremely stressful situation. There were follow-up sessions 1 month and 6 months after treatment.

Each of these subjects showed substantial decreases in the problem behavior after treatment, and this improvement was maintained over the 6-month follow-up period. Decreases in the target responses ranged from 77% to 99% over baseline frequencies. The one patient who also complained of associated facial pain did not report any significant decreases in perceived pain level throughout the course of this study. The authors suggest that pain, especially of long duration (this patient had pain for over 10 years), may be maintained by various environmental conditions and may exist as a behavior independent of the bruxism. However, this patient also received the relaxation and stress management treatment. During this phase of treatment, the level of pain experienced did decrease below that experienced with muscle-relaxing medications.

The authors suggest that the use of self-recordings may limit this procedure, since individuals may be unaware of occurrences of bruxism. It may be preferable to employ some portable feedback device, such as an EMG, that can indicate to the subject when bruxism occurs, and thus when to initiate the learned response that interrupts the behavior.

COMMENTARY: The habit reversal technique was useful in decreasing bruxism and maintaining this improvement over a period of time. This technique is useful because it (1) provides individuals with a functional analysis of their bruxism; (2) increases their sensitivity to behavioral and muscular activity in the facial area, including antecedent activity; and (3) provides subjects with a response that interrupts this chain of behaviors and can be easily incorporated into their normal routine.

SOURCE: Rosenbaum, M. S., and Ayllon, T. "Treating Bruxism with the Habit-Reversal Technique." *Behaviour Research and Therapy*, 1981, *19*, 87–96.

***

Additional Readings

Clark, G. T., Beemsterboer, P., and Rugh, J. D. "The Treatment of Nocturnal Bruxing Using Contingent EMG Feedback with an Arousal Task." *Behaviour Research and Therapy*, 1981, *19*, 451–455.

EMG auditory feedback was provided to ten heavy bruxers while they slept. When clenching occurred with moderate force, a signal sounded that awakened the subject. The person was then required to cross the room and record on a data card the time of night and the quality of sleep when awakened (arousal task). The results indicated that after 10 days, nine of the ten subjects had significant decreases in EMG activity in the masseter. A 3-month follow-up indicated that four subjects still had minor symptoms of tooth pain, headaches, and soreness and stiffness in the jaw. These individuals also had daytime bruxism, which did not benefit from the nocturnal treatment intervention. The authors contend that contingent feedback therapy may best be used as a 24-hour treatment for some subjects. This relatively easily applied intervention appears to be a promising method for the treatment of bruxism.

Clark, G. T., Rugh, J. D., and Handelman, S. L. "Nocturnal Masseter Muscle Activity and Urinary Catecholamine Levels in Bruxers." *Journal of Dental Research*, 1980, *59*, 1571–1576.

This study examined the relationship between daily stress

levels (as measured by urinary catecholamine levels) and nocturnal masseter muscle activity. A significant positive correlation was found between epinephrine and masseter activity, supporting the theory that daily stress is a prominent factor in noctural masseter activity. The authors noted large variability in muscle activity over nights. Peak nights of EMG activity were usually associated with the previous day's stresses or worry over impending problems. The observation that increases in muscle activity were frequently grouped suggests a possible cumulative stress effect, in that a particular stressor can elevate bruxism levels for several days afterwards.

Jenkins, J. O., and Peterson, G. R. "Self-Monitoring and Self-Administered Aversion in the Treatment of Bruxism." *Journal of Behavior Therapy and Experimental Psychiatry,* 1978, *9,* 387–388.

This report presents a strategy for treating bruxism using self-monitoring and self-administered aversion techniques. The subject was a 60-year-old male who reported grinding his teeth for 6 months before treatment. The bruxism was exacerbated when he was under stress. At the beginning of each session, the subject was told to imagine a stressful situation. After a baseline interval, he was requested to count the number of tooth contacts using a hand counter (self-monitoring phase). In the next phase, the subject was instructed to self-monitor and also to squirt himself with lemon juice each time tooth grinding occurred. This procedure was followed twice. The results indicated a dramatic decrease in grinding over baseline when both techniques were used together. The aversion procedure proved more effective than no treatment or self-monitoring alone. A 2-year follow-up failed to find any bruxism at all.

Sleep Disorders

Sleep, like hearing one's heartbeat, is a problem only when it is noticed. If sleep is inadequate or disrupted and can no longer "knit the ravelled ends of time," the person's ability for subsequent motor and cognitive functioning is impaired. Indeed, although one may exercise self-control and fast from food to the point of death, it is impossible to maintain a continued state without sleep. After frank organic causes have been eliminated, behavioral treatments have been applied (with varying degrees of effectiveness) to sleep disorders of several kinds—delay of sleep onset, interruption of the sleep cycle, and other disorders. A range of therapeutic tactics seem appropriate for dealing with such problems, and competent clinicians can now render a valuable service for treating this wide-ranging medical complaint.

The Efficacy of Home Sleep Recordings for Older Adults

AUTHORS: Sonia Ancoli-Israel, Daniel F. Kripke, William Mason, and Sam Messin

PRECIS: A report comparing the effectiveness of portable home sleep recordings to those obtained by laboratory polysomnograms.

INTRODUCTION: The use of polysomnography in the diagnosis and treatment of sleep disorders is widespread, and its importance is well documented. However, the use of this technique has some disadvantages. A single night's use may cost over $500, and the subject must sleep in a laboratory, an inconvenience that may reduce the generalizability of the recordings obtained to home sleep patterns. This report presented and validated the efficacy of a new sleep-recording device that can be used by patients at home.

METHOD: Twenty-four elderly subjects, eleven males and thirteen females, were recruited for this study. Their ages were between 63 and 79 years. Elderly subjects were used because detecting sleep apnea in individuals in this age range is especially important. Another sleep disorder evaluated in this sample was nocturnal myoclonus.

Sleep recordings were done using two methods. The first used the portable home recorder (PHR). The PHR can record two channels of respiration (abdominal and thoracic), one channel of wrist activity, and one channel of leg EMG. All measurements are stored on a portable analog recorder unit, which is worn on a belt and leaves the subject unrestrained. The respiratory transducers are part of a vestlike garment that the person wears and to which the analog recorder and other devices are attached. The second recording method used a laboratory polysomnograph (LR). It recorded EEG, EKG, chin and tibialis EMG, electrooculogram (EOG), and three channels of respiration (nasal, thoracic, and abdominal).

All subjects were recorded twice, once using the PHR and once using the LR. The order in which these methods were presented was randomized (therefore 50% of the subjects were measured with the PHR first and 50% with the LR first). The average PHR reading was 15 hours, and the average LR reading was 7 hours. All subjects gave a full sleep history before evaluation, which assisted in making the LR diagnoses. Each LR reading was scored on the following categories: sleep stage durations, total sleep period (TSP, defined as the time from first sleep to final arousal), total sleep time (TST), wake after sleep onset (WASO), number of instances of sleep apnea per night, and number of myoclonic leg jerks per night. For each subject, the sleep record from each machine was evaluated independently by two researchers, and a diagnosis determined. The clinical histories were not included in making the LPR and PHR diagnoses, which were based strictly on the physiological recordings. Also, during the LR sessions, portable recordings (LPRs) were made simultaneously.

The results of these analyses all indicated a strong reliability for the PHR. There were no significant differences between the different methods on the apnea indexes, indicating that the PHR method gives an unbiased estimate of the apnea index. Using the polysomnograph as the standard, the ability of the LHR to detect sleep apneas was 100%, and that of the PHR, 78%. The PHR was also determined to be effective in estimating the nocturnal myoclonus index. The sensitivity of the LPH and PHR in diagnosing nocturnal myoclonus was 100% and 85%, respectively (for a clinical criterion of more than forty leg jerks a night).

Other analyses indicated no significant differences between methods in determining TSPs computed across nights. Also, intermethod agreements for TST and WASO were significant. From these results, the authors claim that the PHR system can detect sleep apnea and nocturnal myoclonus, as well as other important sleep measures (TSP, TST, and WASO), in older adults who have primary obstructive or mixed sleep apnea.

An important issue that the authors discuss concerns the lower between-night than same-night reliabilities for sleep disorder diagnoses. It may be necessary to evaluate individuals over a series of nights in order to make accurate diagnoses. With such a need, the PHR can provide an effective and cost-effective procedure for obtaining multiple diagnostic recordings. The authors also point out that what the PHR technique loses in precision, it more than compensates for by greatly improving sampling reliability.

COMMENTARY: The authors note that the PHR method has the advantage of being more comfortable than the LR and capable of making 24-hour recordings. Although the LR can provide more comprehensive information, the efficiency of the PHR as well as its increased comfort, privacy, and convenience makes its use highly desirable. This technique can be beneficial for research investigations and for various clinical applications (such as sleep apnea screening and clinical follow-ups).

SOURCE: Ancoli-Israel, S., Kripke, D. F., Mason, W., and Messin, S. "Comparisons of Home Sleep Recordings and Polysomnograms in Older Adults with Sleep Disorders." *Sleep,* 1981, *4,* 283–291.

Paradoxical Intention in Treating Sleep Onset Insomnia

AUTHORS: L. Michael Ascher and Jay S. Efran

PRECIS: A report on the efficacy of paradoxical intention (PI) procedures for treating sleep onset insomnia.

INTRODUCTION: Deep muscle relaxation and systematic desensitization are two common techniques used in the treatment of insomnia. In some cases, however, these regimens are inadequate. The authors contend that PI can be introduced as an ancillary treatment since it is easy to apply and usually produces immediate change. PI is a behavioral technique that requires individuals to execute behaviors that appear to be incompatible with their desired goal. In the present case, this means having patients try to remain awake for as long as possible. They are asked to exaggerate the very behavior they are trying to reduce.

METHOD: The subjects consisted of five individuals, three males and two females, between 23 and 41 years of age (mean 29.8 years). The average length of their sleep difficulty was 9 years, and their average sleep onset latency was over 1 hour. Sessions were conducted weekly on an individual basis.

A 2-week baseline period was established in which subjects monitored and recorded sleep onset latency, mood when retiring, number of awakenings, and restfulness of sleep. After the baseline was established, all subjects began a 10-week training period, where they were instructed in deep muscle relaxation with an emphasis on exercise before retiring. Over successive sessions, additional techniques were added as needed (such as desensitization and covert conditioning). This procedure failed to produce any significant improvements. Following this phase, all subjects began a 2-week period during which PI techniques were introduced. Subjects were instructed to remain awake at night for as long as possible. These instructions were presented with one of two rationales: (1) Three subjects were told to do this because detailed descriptions were needed about their thoughts before they fell asleep. They were told that the previous procedure might have failed because there was not enough information on their sleep situation. (2) Two subjects were told to remain awake to perform extra relaxation exercises. The number of relaxation exercises was increased, and the subjects were required to complete all of these steps, even if it meant resisting the desire to fall asleep.

During the two sessions of this phase, subjects typically reported an inability to execute their instructions fully because they fell asleep. Upon hearing this, the therapist would express some encouragement but also suggest that the subjects redouble their efforts to accomplish their goal, to try even harder to remain awake. Most of the time of these two sessions was used to continue the regular desensitization procedures. Following this 2-week period, four of the subjects received no further treatment. One subject received another 3 weeks of the initial behavioral program with techniques added to reduce anxiety-provoking thoughts during sleep onset latency. After this phase, the subject once again received the PI instructions for another 2 weeks, at which time his treatment was terminated.

The results indicated no significant improvements from baseline to the end of phase 1 (the behavioral treatment). Significant improvements were noted from the end of phase 2 to the end of phase 3 (PI) and from baseline to the end of phase 3. It appears that PI significantly reduced the mean number of minutes to sleep onset. For the subject who received additional treatments, comparable results were found; there was a significant reduction in sleep onset latency from baseline to phase 3. When he once again received the behavioral treatment, sleep onset latency increased, but it decreased once again after PI was reintroduced. An informal 1-year follow-up revealed that all subjects remained satisfied with their sleep behavior.

The authors contend that for a small proportion of individuals, sleep onset difficulty is associated with a deteriorating ability to fall asleep. Each night, the ability to fall asleep satisfactorily is perceived as a test, with negative results reinforcing the notion that some type of disturbance is developing. The level of performance anxiety then increases as each test approaches. This anxiety disrupts and inhibits the natural process leading to sleep onset. Thus a repetitive cycle develops: The more frequently sleep difficulties are experienced, the greater the anxiety, the lesser the ability to fall asleep, and the more frequently episodes of insomnia are experienced. The more the individual tries to fall asleep, the worse the cycle becomes. PI appears to be able to break this cycle, thereby decreasing the associated performance anxiety by redefining the situation.

COMMENTARY: This article illustrates the effectiveness of PI in treating individuals with sleep onset insomnia whose condition was resistant to other treatments. Although PI was used in the context of a larger behavioral program, the results call into question the effectiveness of these other techniques (such as muscle relaxation and desensitization). Since research has shown PI to be effective with a wide variety of psychosomatic dysfunctions, it would be of interest to determine its efficacy when used alone as well as with a large subject population having sleep onset difficulties. Considering the success of the PI treatment as well as its brevity, it appears to be a very cost-effective treatment modality, suitable for wide application.

SOURCE: Ascher, L. M., and Efran, J. S. "Use of Paradoxical Intention in a Behavioral Program for Sleep Onset Insomnia." *Journal of Consulting and Clinical Psychology*, 1978, *46*, 547–550.

Biofeedback Treatment
of Psychophysiological Insomnia

AUTHOR: Peter Hauri

PRECIS: A report determining the efficacy of various biofeedback modalities, including frontalis EMG, EEG-theta, and sensorimotor rhythm (SMR) feedback, in the treatment of psychophysiological insomnia.

INTRODUCTION: Insomnia was operationally defined for the purposes of this study as being "a complaint of serious, chronic insomnia and an objectively verified shortened sleep time" without any concomitant evidence indicating a medical or psychiatric disorder. All the feedback measures used in this study have been previously shown to have some bearing on the sleep process, either by aiding a subject to become more physically relaxed before sleep or by enabling a subject to strengthen sleep-inducing cortical systems. Some major analyses made by this study addressed the amount of feedback a patient received (some of the insomniacs in this study had more training sessions than others), the degree of initial tension (as measured by anxiety tests and EMG levels taken during the screening sessions), and appropriate versus inappropriate feedback.

METHOD: A sample of forty-eight insomniacs participated in this study, all of whom met the criteria for insomnia. All subjects went through a prefeedback evaluation, where they were screened with psychological tests, interviews, and three nights of sleep in the laboratory. In the lab, polysomnographic recordings were made for each subject. (EEG leads were placed at C_3-A_2 and four channels of EMG placed to record mental, submental, frontalis, right and left anterior tibialis, two channels of eye movements, respirations, and EKG.) In the next phase, subjects were assigned to one of four feedback groups by a roll of a die: EMG, EEG-theta, SMR, and a no-treatment control group. Feedback training was performed during 1-hour sessions two to four times a week for a minimum of fifteen sessions with a mean of 24.8 sessions per patient (range from fifteen to sixty-two sessions). There were no significant differences in the number of feedback sessions between the different groups. All three of the training groups showed significant improvement over the sessions in performance on the relevant dimension.

After the feedback training, each subject's sleep patterns over three nights were reevaluated using polysomnographic recordings, home sleep logs, and interviews. After 9 months, patients in all four groups again completed home sleep logs and questionnaires, were interviewed, and had polysomnographic recordings taken for three consecutive nights. The purpose of the control group in this design was to assess the effects due to elapsed time, spontaneous remission, and random life events from prefeedback to follow-up.

Since insomniacs have a greater variability in sleep patterns than do normal sleepers, it was decided a priori to exclude from data analysis any laboratory recordings for a sleep that the subject later rated as being either "the best in weeks" or "very much worse than average" on the postsleep questionnaire. The author justifies this procedure since no systematic trend of atypical sleep was found over the three feedback groups. Of the 254 laboratory nights used in the data analysis, only 17 were excluded on the basis of these criteria.

There was also an a priori decision to classify subjects into either an appropriate or inappropriate feedback dichotomy after all data had been gathered. Underlying this approach was the view that chronic insomnia may indicate either excessive activity in the arousal system or the presence of weak, sleep-inducing systems. Both types of etiology require different modes of treatment, EMG and EEG-theta feedback being appropriate for high-arousal subjects and SMR training for low-arousal subjects. Since all subjects were randomly assigned to their respective feedback groups, some may have received clinically inappropriate feedback, while others may not have. This analysis would ascertain the effect that type of feedback has on treatment outcome when the presenting symptoms (arousal levels) of the insomnia are known.

EMG and EEG-theta feedback was considered appropriate for subjects who had either high-anxiety scores on the Institute of Personality and Ability Testing Anxiety Scales (IPAT) (a score of 8 or more), excessive frontalis EMG tension before sleep, or a sleep latency of more than 1 hour on each laboratory night but slept well thereafter. SMR training was considered appropriate for insomniacs having low anxiety (IPAT scores less than 6) or short sleep latency (less than 20 minutes) coupled with poor sleep later on (more than four awakenings per night, each lasting longer than 10 minutes, or atypical stage 2 sleep recordings). There were thirty-six insomniacs available for this analysis, fifteen classified as needing relaxation training and nine as requiring SMR training. The remaining twelve could not be clearly placed into either category. Of the fifteen needing relaxation training, ten had been appropriately assigned, while five received SMR training. Of the nine subjects judged to need SMR training, four received appropriate feedback while five received relaxation training.

The results for laboratory sleep indicated that subjects who received appropriate feedback improved their sleep efficacy by an average of over 11% after feedback, while those who received inappropriate feedback changed very little. Appropriate feedback reduced sleep latency by over 15 minutes; inappropriate feedback showed no change on this parameter. Home sleep logs indicated that subjects receiving appropriate feedback increased their total sleep time significantly more than subjects receiving inappropriate feedback. Also, correct feedback significantly decreased the number of home awakenings. It appears evident that feedback addressing needs central to an insomniac's condition results in significantly improved sleep.

EMG or theta learning did not significantly improve sleep. The authors contend that this type of relaxation training may not be a crucial parameter in sleep improvements for these groups. Rather, the cognitive components associated with such training (self-generated, monotonous stimulation) may be responsible for the results. Yet for SMR training, sleep improvement was significantly correlated to the amount of training. The authors suggest that SMR learning rather than any inherent cognitive variables is the critical factor in this type of training. The authors also suggest that further investigation into spindle production in the 12- to 16-cps EEG band may substantially increase our understanding of psychophysiological insomnia.

Finally, the more tension initially experienced by patients, the more they benefited from EMG biofeedback and the less from SMR training. The EMG biofeedback alone seemed to have a more powerful influence on sleep than did the EEG-theta learning. The authors suggest that this seemingly paradoxical finding may be attributable to an artifact in the training regimen of these two groups.

COMMENTARY: Although this study focuses on one particular diagnostic categorization of insomnia, two important points are highlighted. The first deals with the need for a more differentiated diagnosis of insomnia. As was illustrated in both this article and others presented in this volume, there are different kinds of insomnia, and each kind may have several varied yet related subcategories. More precise differentiation might enable clinicians to provide a more appropriate, more efficient treatment intervention. The second point of interest relates to the use of biofeedback. The authors rightly emphasize that feedback training can be useful in both diagnosing and treating insomnia, although it is not a panacea. It is but one part of a larger, more comprehensive approach to the treatment of insomnia. The optimal type of feedback training depends upon the nature of the presenting symptoms. Of particular interest is the potential that SMR training and its associated spindle production offers over other types of biofeedback.

SOURCE: Hauri, P. "Treating Psychophysiological Insomnia with Biofeedback." *Archives of General Psychiatry,* 1981, *38,* 752–758.

Behavioral Treatment for Insomnia

AUTHORS: Carl E. Thoresen, Thomas J. Coates, Kathleen Kirmil-Gray, and Mark R. Rosekind

PRECIS: A description of the use of a behavioral self-management technique in the treatment of sleep maintenance insomnia.

INTRODUCTION: There are two categories of insomnia: sleep onset and sleep maintenance insomnias. This paper focuses on the latter. Sleep maintenance insomnia is characterized by extended periods of wakefulness during the night (usually 30 minutes or more), early risings (to the degree that the individual receives less than 6.5 hours of sleep), and brief (30 to 60 seconds) but frequent awakenings during the lighter stages of sleep. The goals of the self-management program in treating this disorder are threefold: (1) to assess a variety of variables that may be related to a person's malfunctional sleep patterns, (2) to use these assessment findings to develop a treatment strategy geared to the individual, and (3) to enhance the sense of control that each individual has over problems that may be related to his or her poor sleep habits.

METHOD: Three subjects participated in this study. They were selected on the basis of four criteria: (1) They had at least a 1-year history of sleep maintenance insomnia, which had been impairing their daytime functioning; (2) they had no evidence of an underlying physical disorder precipitating the insomnia; (3) there were no indications of narcolepsy, nocturnal myoclonus, restless legs, or sleep apnea; and (4) baseline recordings indicated that they were awake more than 30 minutes after sleep onset or had fifteen or more arousals during sleep.

The first subject was a 27-year-old female who complained of an extended latency to sleep onset, frequent nocturnal arousals, and early morning awakenings for a period of 5 years. She frequently experienced fatigue, depression, and irritability during the day. The second subject was a 26-year-old female with a 10-year history of restless and unrefreshing sleep. She reported extended sleep onset two nights per week and frequent and lengthy nocturnal arisings seven nights per week. She experienced fatigue, depression, irritability, and headaches. The third subject was a 46-year-old male with a 14-year history of frequent nighttime arousals and an extended sleep onset. He reported chronic fatigue, depression, stress and tension, sore eyes, and tightness in the chest. The MMPI scores for all subjects were within normal limits.

Three all-night polysomnographic baseline recordings were made, including EEG, EMG, and EOG measures. Polysomnography was also performed for three consecutive nights at midtreatment 4 weeks later, 4 weeks after the termination of treatment, and at 3- and 12-month follow-ups. Each subject also completed a daily sleep diary throughout treatment and for 1 week at each follow-up evaluation. Subjects estimated minutes to sleep onset, number of awakenings, minutes awake after sleep onset, and total sleep time. Subjects also rated their degree of fatigue upon arising in the morning on a scale of 1 (not tired) to 5 (very tired).

Treatment consisted of 1-hour sessions twice weekly for

5 weeks followed by weekly sessions for another 3 weeks. Each session emphasized a specific set of skills and provided a review of progress and practice in skills learned in previous sessions. Sessions 1 to 4 were aimed at assessing the subjects' condition in order to rule out insomnia as being secondary to sleep apnea, nocturnal myoclonus, and narcolepsy. In-depth interviews were conducted to investigate the possible sources of the poor sleep habits, such as family and occupational stresses, depression, poor self-esteem, eating and exercise habits, and physical environment. Sessions 5 to 7 focused on progressive muscle relaxation, in which the subjects were trained to relax sixteen muscle groups. Each subject was given a cassette tape of instructions to practice twice daily at home, once before going to bed.

Cognitive restructuring techniques were employed during sessions 8 to 10. Individuals were encouraged to examine their personal beliefs about sleep and view their problem from differing perspectives. They received information about the basic processes associated with sleep and were taught to identify thoughts that interfered with their sleep. Finally, the alternative thoughts developed were practiced during the session to promote better sleeping patterns and enhance therapeutic progress. Sessions 11 and 12 were devoted to mental relaxation, which involved using structured fantasies to reduce excessive worrying and disturbing thoughts at night. These fantasies were mutually developed by therapist and subject and were to be used whenever the patient awakened during the night. Problem-solving techniques were the focus of sessions 13 to 16. Here subjects attempted to identify and solve issues that were still causing poor sleep. Subjects' sleep diaries were analyzed, and hypotheses were developed about factors that distinguished nights with good sleep from nights with poor sleep. These hypotheses were translated into specific strategies and later evaluated against subjects' self-reports.

Subjects 1 and 2 learned cue-controlled relaxation in conjunction with the development of a physical routine and time for going to bed. This technique teaches individuals to relax during stress-producing situations by using a subvocal command to relax in combination with rhythmic breathing. Subject 2 also learned to use this procedure to control daytime experiences of stress. Subject 3 also learned this technique along with anticipation training to manage depressive feelings during the day. This procedure requires a person to plan positive activities and to practice anticipating the enjoyment of them. Maintenance sessions were held for as long as a subject and therapist thought they were useful. These sessions focused on additional problem-solving issues and techniques.

Over the course of treatment, all subjects indicated substantial decreases in the number of nocturnal arousals and the percentage of time awake during the night. These decreases were also maintained over the course of the 3- and 12-month follow-up intervals. Self-report measures also indicated improvements in sleep patterns. Tiredness ratings also decreased over the period of the study.

The authors stress the need to document a patient's complaint completely using both physiological and phenomenological measures. Although the subjects in this study voiced similar complaints, the variables contributing to their sleep difficulties were very different and included depression, fatigue, and sleep interruption. The rate of improvement in their sleep habits also varied, perhaps because of the differences in the severity and number of their disturbances.

The authors suggest two important considerations for future research. First, sleep disturbances may result from a disruptive sleep system as well as from psychological factors. The combination of these factors may limit the value of psychological procedures alone in improving sleep maintenance insomnia, although the use of biofeedback techniques may improve the effectiveness of an intervention program. Second, the subjects' self-perception that they can change the conditions that maintain their disturbed sleep pattern (feelings of self-efficacy) may be critical to a successful treatment outcome. The two subjects in this study who rated themselves high on personal efficacy grasped the concepts underlying the treatment more easily and were more compliant with its protocol than was the subject whose score was low on this dimension.

COMMENTARY: This study describes a treatment that uses several strategies to correct the factors that maintain an individual's disturbed sleep pattern. These strategies are tailored to the person's own experiences and can be continually modified over the course of treatment. The issues surrounding feelings of self-efficacy may be important to the design of behavioral treatment, insofar as it may predict motivation and compliance with the treatment regimens.

SOURCE: Thoresen, C. E., Coates, T. J., Kirmil-Gray, K., and Rosekind, M. R. "Behavioral Self-Management in Treating Sleep-Maintenance Insomnia." *Journal of Behavioral Medicine*, 1981, *4*, 41–52.

Behavioral Interventions for Insomnia

AUTHORS: Ralph M. Turner and Robert A. DiTomasso

PRECIS: A report examining the utility of several therapeutic approaches to insomnia.

INTRODUCTION: Clinically, insomnia is defined as the chronic inability to initiate and maintain adequate sleep. Research has indicated that 10% to 15% of the population experiences mild or occasional insomnia, and another 10% to 15% complain of severe and frequent insomnia. Sleep disturbances are classified either as secondary insomnia (coexistent with physical illness or psychological disturbances) or primary insomnia (all sleep problems other than secondary insomnia). This latter classification usually manifests in three forms: protracted latency to sleep onset, interruptions in sleep during the night, and early morning awakenings. This article reviews the research literature on the effectiveness of different behavioral treatments for insomnia.

INTERVENTIONS: One major category of interventions concerns the variety of anxiety reduction approaches. From this
perspective, insomnia is seen as a heightened state of arousal
(that is, anxiety) at bedtime that interrupts the sleeping process.
Treatment centers on removing the anxiety and developing a
response that is incompatible with the aroused state, thereby facilitating sleep. Techniques included under this approach are
progressive muscle relaxation, autogenic training, biofeedback-
assisted relaxation, and systematic desensitization. Clinical applications of these techniques have indeed been shown to offer
promise for treating insomnia.

Habit restructuring is another class of approaches. These
approaches involve procedures for reassociating the bed as a cue
or discriminative stimulus for sleep. Insomnia is believed to
occur when a patient associates too many extraneous stimuli
with the bed (such as eating, thinking, or watching television).
Therapy centers on weakening these peripheral associations and
strengthening cues that are related to sleep. This is usually accomplished by having the person follow several guidelines: (1)
retire only when sleepy; (2) do not perform any extraneous activities in bed; (3) avoid daytime naps; (4) if unable to fall
asleep after 10 minutes, get up and go to another room and do
something else, returning to bed only when sleepy; and (5) set
the alarm for the same time every morning regardless of the
amount of sleep. Research using these instructions has produced substantial reductions in symptoms of insomnia. These
authors suggest that this approach be used in tandem with progressive relaxation techniques to form a comprehensive treatment approach.

The final category of therapeutic approaches is performance anxiety reduction. The most common technique in this
group is the use of paradoxical intention. The theoretical rationale for this treatment is as follows: (1) Initially something
disturbs the person's sleep; (2) the person begins to worry about
his or her poor sleep performance; (3) performance anxiety
gradually develops; and (4) this anxiety becomes the major
source of the sleep disturbance. Supporters of this approach
contend that treatments designed to assist patients to sleep

exacerbate the problem by encouraging such patients to try to fall asleep. In this therapeutic modality, the attempt is to modify the patient's cognitive focus to not falling asleep, which should then reduce the performance anxiety. Although some research findings support the efficacy of this approach, other findings show it to be ineffective. Further research is necessary to confirm the effectiveness of this intervention.

COMMENTARY: Overall, behavioral techniques have been shown to be effective in treating primary insomnia. These authors contend that the major issue is for the clinician to deterine which treatment is best for a specific patient. To do this requires a general behavioral analysis of the patient's presenting symptoms. This analysis will yield important information concerning etiology, controlling situations, and the frequency and severity of the insomnia. From this information, a comprehensive, therapeutic approach can be developed that is likeliest to have the greatest effect on the sleep disturbance.

SOURCE: Turner, R. M., and DiTomasso, R. A. "The Behavioral Treatment of Insomnia: A Review and Methodological Analysis of the Evidence." *International Journal of Mental Health*, 1980, *9*, 129–148.

Additional Readings

Alperson, J., and Biglan, A. "Self-Administered Treatment of Sleep Onset Insomnia and the Importance of Age." *Behavior Therapy*, 1979, *10*, 347–356.

The effects of two self-administered manuals on sleep latency insomnia using self-monitored records were studied. All subjects under 55 years of age were randomly assigned to one of three groups: (1) a group where members received a manual on relaxation and stimulus control treatments for insomnia; (2) a group where members received a manual recommending physical exercise and activities in bed; or (3) a self-monitor (control) group. Subjects over 55 received the relaxation and stimulus control manual. After 4 weeks, both groups of treated young subjects improved significantly more than the controls on sleep onset and quality of sleep. The older subjects improved significantly less than the younger subjects who received the same treatment on sleep latency. Also, older subjects did not significantly improve during treatment or at follow-up. This research indicates the need for more detailed investigations of sleep mechanisms and processes at different stages in the life cycle.

Cartwright, R. D., and Samelson, C. F. "The Effects of a Non-surgical Treatment for Obstructive Sleep Apnea." *Journal of the American Medical Association,* 1982, *248,* 705–709.

These researchers examined the effectiveness of a tongue-retraining device (TRD) in increasing the size of the nasal breathing passage during sleep in patients with obstructive sleep apneas. The TRD is designed to hold the tongue in a forward position by negative pressure applied to the lingual compartment of the device. It is made of soft copolymer and worn in the mouth during sleep. Fourteen male patients were tested before and after using this device. Significant improvements in sleep and significantly fewer and shorter apneic episodes were recorded when the device was in use. The rate of improvement observed with the TRD was comparable to results reported for patients who were treated surgically for this problem. Of the fourteen patients, only three rejected the device as being uncomfortable. The authors conclude that the TRD offers a viable intervention alternative for patients having a moderate obstructive apnea.

Franklin, J. "The Measurement of Sleep Onset Latency in Insomnia." *Behaviour Research and Therapy,* 1981, *19,* 547–549.

Most research in the area of insomnia relies almost exclusively on self-reports by subjects. Such measures have many flaws and introduce a source of weakness into the study. This report presents the use of a device to measure sleep onset latency that can be used in research to measure latencies objectively. The apparatus is battery operated and activated by depressing a hand-held switch that the subject takes to bed. As the subject falls asleep, the muscles in the hand relax, which allows the spring-loaded switch to interrupt the circuit and thus display the sleep onset latency. The design of the switch prevents fouling by clothes or bed linen. Research by this author has shown that the device provides a better estimate of latency than do self-reports or reports by subjects' partners.

Freedman, R. R., and Sattler, H. L. "Physiological and Psychological Factors in Sleep-Onset Insomnia." *Journal of Abnormal Psychology*, 1982, *91*, 380–389.

This research compared sleep onset insomniacs to normal sleepers on physiological and psychological dimensions. Before sleep onset, the insomniacs had a higher physical activity level than normals, but these differences became less prominent as sleep approached. Insomniacs had significantly higher MMPI scores on scales relating to anxiety, worry, and neuroticism. These authors conclude that these psychophysiological differences do not cause the insomnia. They contend that the excessive rumination characteristic of sleep onset insomniacs may be an epiphenomenon of their inability to sleep.

Healey, E. S., Kales, A., Monroe, L. J., Bixler, E. O., Chamberlin, K., and Soldatos, C. R. "Onset of Insomnia: Role of Life-Stress Events." *Psychosomatic Medicine*, 1981, *43*, 439–445.

These authors conducted an etiological assessment of insomnia with regard to the role of stressful life events. It was noted that in comparison with good sleepers, chronic insomniacs experienced a greater number of stressful life events during the year when insomnia began than they did in previous or subsequent years. These life stressors were commonly related to losses and ill health. The histories indicated more illness and somatic complaints and more childhood problems relating to eating and sleeping than found among normal sleepers. The insomniacs also reported more frequent discontent with their families as well as less satisfying relationships with them. In addition, they reported difficulties in other interpersonal relationships and in their self-concept. The authors conclude that stressful life events mediated by predisposing factors of vulnerability are related to the onset of chronic insomnia.

Cancer

Modern technology has produced aggressive measures against cancer; unfortunately, a number of medical side effects have restricted conventional therapy. Among the more troubling side effects are the reactions to chemotherapy. Not only anxiety but also anticipatory nausea and vomiting create problems for patients and thus for cancer clinic operations. Behavioral medicine has been able to offer effective therapeutic programs for such problems, as well as prevent major psychiatric crises from developing. Comprehensive assessment protocols of psychosocial variables in cancer include the role that such factors play in the etiology and development of cancers. With cautious optimism, one may speculate that a behavioral treatment program will be developed that affects the organic cancer itself.

Relaxation Training in Controlling
Adverse Reactions to Chemotherapy

AUTHORS: Thomas G. Burish and Jeanne N. Lyles

PRECIS: An examination of the value of relaxation training in controlling adverse reactions to cancer chemotherapy.

INTRODUCTION: Many patients develop a conditioned response to repeated chemotherapy treatments. Peripheral cues associated with the treatment such as the smell of alcohol or the sight of a syringe elicit anxiety, nausea, or vomiting. This report examined the ability of progressive muscle relaxation and guided relaxation imagery to reduce such conditioned responses. This procedure offers several advantages: (1) It is inexpensive and easy to learn and produces few, if any, side effects; (2) it has been demonstrated to be effective in reducing anxiety and lowering physiological arousal; and (3) the patient actively participates, thereby giving him or her an increased sense of self-control.

METHOD: Sixteen cancer patients (fourteen female and two male) receiving push injection chemotherapy treatments participated in this study. All had exhibited anticipatory emesis even though they were on an antiemetic regimen and their medication program had remained constant throughout the study. Subjects were randomly assigned to either the relaxation training group or the no-training group. Each patient participated in five sessions: one pretreatment, two treatment, and two post-treatment. These sessions were held during five consecutive visits to the clinic for the patients' chemotherapy treatment.

The pretraining session was identical for each patient and provided a baseline measure. All patients completed a Multiple Affect Adjective Check List (MAACL), and their physiological measures (blood pressure and heart rate) were recorded. Following this, patients received their chemotherapy. After this treatment session, physiological responses were once again recorded, and the patients completed another MAACL.

The two training sessions occured 45 minutes before the patients' chemotherapy injection in the treatment room. Again, the MAACL was administered and the physiological information collected. Patients were told that being relaxed would make their treatment less unpleasant and reduce the likelihood and severity of any side effects. The ability to relax was emphasized as being a learned skill that required them to participate actively in the training and to practice the techniques that they learned. After these preliminaries, the progressive muscle relaxation training began followed by the administration of guided imagery. Shortly after the imagery instructions began, the chemotherapy treatment was administered. The therapist continued these throughout the chemotherapy treatment and for approximately 5 minutes afterward. Patients were asked to practice the relaxation techniques at home daily and were provided with written instructions. Subjects in the no-treatment condition were taken to the treatment room 45 minutes before their chemotherapy treatment. During this period blood pressure and pulse rate were monitored, and the patients completed an MAACL.

During the follow-up sessions, patients were told that the therapist was not going to direct them in the relaxation training but that they were to relax on their own as much as possible using the techniques they had learned and practiced. Except for these instructions, procedures for both groups were identical to those for the pretreatment sessions.

Patients in the relaxation training condition reported feeling significantly less anxious, angry, and depressed than those in the no-treatment group. Patients and nurse ratings indicated that subjects in the training group experienced less anxiety and nausea during the chemotherapy session than the controls. However, there was no significant difference between the groups in the number of patients vomiting during the treatment sessions. At the postsessions the physiological measures indicated significantly lower systolic blood pressures for those in the relaxation training condition. The therapeutic gains posted by the training groups were maintained at the follow-up sessions.

The authors conclude that the muscle relaxation techniques were effective in reducing the negative affective and physiological side effects of the chemotherapy. The emotional distress commonly experienced by cancer patients was significantly reduced after their behavioral treatments. The authors contend that the behavioral treatment increases the feelings of self-control and self-sufficiency in the cancer patients and that these feelings may extend beyond the chemotherapy situation.

COMMENTARY: The authors attribute the effectiveness of their treatment to the reduction in distress induced by the decrement in muscle tension and the distraction from the negatively conditioned treatment setting induced by the guided imagery. Because of these two effects, patients relaxed more and worried less about their treatment, thus maintaining a lower level of subjective and physiological arousal.

SOURCE: Burish, T. G., and Lyles, J. N. "Effectiveness of Relaxation Training in Reducing Adverse Reactions to Cancer Chemotherapy." *Journal of Behavioral Medicine,* 1981, *4,* 65–78.

Systematic Desensitization in the Control of Anticipatory Emesis

AUTHORS: Gary R. Morrow and Christine Morrell

PRECIS: A report examining the efficacy of systematic desensitization in controlling anticipatory emesis and nausea.

INTRODUCTION: Anticipatory emesis and nausea, experienced by one out of four cancer patients, is resistant to antiemetic treatment. Since psychological factors are believed to be implicated in the etiology of this condition, clinicians have attempted to develop a simple and effective intervention. These researchers examine the efficacy of systematic desensitization.

METHOD: Sixty cancer patients receiving multiple infusions of chemotherapeutic drugs as their only cancer treatment participated in this study. All subjects reported having anticipatory side effects before their treatment sessions. The patients ranged in age from 19 to 76 years. Subjects were studied over four consecutive chemotherapy sessions; two were baseline and two posttreatment. Patients were randomly assigned to one of three groups.

Subjects in the experimental condition were taught systematic desensitization. Patients met with the experimenter for two 1-hour sessions in a room away from the cancer center. The sessions were held between their fourth and fifth treatments. Subjects were instructed in a modified form of Jacobsonian progressive, deep muscle relaxation techniques. The procedure took approximately 20 minutes. A hierarchy of situations in which they experienced progressive and increasingly intense anticipatory side effects was developed. Once the patients were deeply relaxed, they were instructed to imagine each of these scenes. Each scene was presented for 20 seconds and in as much detail as possible. Subjects were then told to make the scene dissolve away. If they reported remaining relaxed while they imagined that scene for two consecutive trials, the next image in the hierarchy was presented. Each patient was treated individually.

The second group received counseling sessions conducted in a person-centered Rogerian supportive context. This treatment was intended as a control for the placebo effects of the experimenters' time and attention. These sessions were conducted in the same room and for the same duration as the desensitization group. The third group received no active intervention other than the evaluation required of all subjects.

Nausea and vomiting were assessed according to patients' self-reports. The subjects also completed a Spielberger State-Trait Anxiety Scale and the Health Locus of Control.

Significantly fewer patients treated with systematic desensitization reported anticipatory nausea than patients in the other two groups. No differences were found between the two control groups. The behavioral intervention also significantly reduced the severity and duration of nausea. Desensitization also affected the frequency and severity of anticipatory vomiting.

Subjects in the treatment group reported significantly fewer episodes of anticipatory vomiting before chemotherapy than subjects in the other two groups, as well as a significant reduction in severity. Overall, the use of antiemetic medication had little effect on the anticipatory side effects.

COMMENTARY: The authors conclude that systematic desensitization is an effective intervention for anticipatory nausea and vomiting secondary to cancer chemotherapy. The effects of this approach work independently of antiemetic medications. The authors contend that anxiety reduction is not the active agent in this treatment, since subjects in the desensitization group had no greater reduction in anxiety than subjects in the other two conditions. Rather, the authors hypothesize that the treatment was effective because it gave patients a sense of increased self-control over an aspect of their treatment about which they had previously felt helpless. Further research is necessary to support this interpretation. Although the subjects were treated individually, a more cost-effective method might be the use of a group format and taped relaxation instructions to teach the muscle relaxation part of the systematic desensitization procedure.

SOURCE: Morrow, G. R., and Morrell, C. "Behavioral Treatment for the Anticipatory Nausea and Vomiting Induced by Cancer Chemotherapy." *New England Journal of Medicine,* 1982, *307,* 1476–1480.

Stress Inoculation Training

AUTHORS: Kathleen Moore and Elizabeth Mitchell Altmaier

PRECIS: A report presenting a comprehensive cognitive-behavioral model for assisting cancer patients in coping with stress associated with their treatment.

INTRODUCTION: Heightened levels of stress and anxiety in patients are common in the treatment of cancer. Predictably, patients often develop problematic behaviors associated with their treatment (such as anticipatory nausea). These authors assess the efficacy of stress inoculation training in reducing treatment-related anxiety. The intervention consists of three components: (1) an educational phase, in which patients are given a conceptual framework for understanding their responses to anxiety-producing events; (2) a rehearsal phase, in which patients are taught a variety of coping skills that employ self-instructions, and (3) an application phase, in which these new skills are tested in actual stressful conditions. The cognitive skills associated with this training include the identification and monitoring of anxiety-arousing thoughts about one's response to target situations; the generation of anxiety-reducing, coping self-statements; and the replacement of negative self-statements with coping self-statements. Behavioral techniques include deep muscle relaxation, cue and imagery control, and coping desensitization.

METHOD: Nine cancer patients at an outpatient clinic participated in this study. There were six females and four males, ranging in age from 19 to 66 years (mean age of 47). All subjects were given an initial interview, in which their degree of coping with their treatment was assessed.

All subjects received a six-session treatment package. Each session lasted approximately 20 minutes, and the authors relied heavily on home practice between sessions. The first session was the educational phase, where patients were presented with a conceptual model for understanding their stress experiences. The model used conceptualized stress in four phases: (1) preparation for the stressor, (2) confronting the stressor, (3) potentially being overwhelmed by the stressor, and (4) evaluating one's coping abilities after exposure to the stressor. Subjects were instructed to use this model in evaluating their own self-statements and how their bodies responded.

The next two sessions consisted of the cognitive phase. Here patients were encouraged to generate their own personalized coping statements. The use of personal statements was found to increase the likelihood of the patient using such statements, thereby increasing the chances for success. Subjects were then taught to substitute these positive statements for the negative ones. Thought-stopping techniques were practiced during the sessions.

The fourth and fifth sessions concentrated on physical responses to stress. Patients were instructed in progressive relaxation training. Subjects were encouraged to select a word (such as *relax* or *calm*) to repeat while relaxing their muscles. They were instructed to practice this cue-controlled relaxation technique twice daily. The second half of this phase was devoted to the imagery transformation of their target anxiety response. Subjects were instructed to develop a mental picture that included the stressor in the scene and then to convert the scene to a different context that was more positive. For example, one patient associated going to the clinic for treatment with the joyful, enthusiastic feelings she experienced when she had gone to the hospital to give birth to her child.

The final session combined all facets of the training into a consolidated package. Each patient had a strategy tailored to his or her needs.

The results of this intervention indicated that patients who were assessed as being unable to cope effectively with the treatment (on the basis of their initial interviews) reported an increased ability to cope with their treatment as well as the elimination of their anxiety-related responses.

COMMENTARY: This report represents more of a pilot study than a controlled, empirical investigation. The techniques used have been successfully employed in treating a variety of other stress-related disorders, and their application to cancer patients is promising. The authors present suggestions for future use of these techniques, including beginning the training early in the treatment regimen, issuing printed homework schedules to patients to encourage compliance, and reducing the number of sessions to three 1-hour sessions. An important consideration is the need for detailed behavioral analyses of those stimuli prompting the anxiety-related responses. The influence of secondary reinforcers is very strong and needs to be addressed in treatment.

SOURCE: Moore, K., and Altmaier, E. M. "Stress Inoculation Training with Cancer Patients." *Cancer Nursing*, 1981, *4*, 389-393.

Control of Anticipatory Emesis with Hypnosis

AUTHORS: William H. Redd, Graciela V. Andresen, and Rahn Y. Minagawa

PRECIS: A description of the use of hypnosis in reducing nausea and vomiting in patients anticipating cancer chemotherapy.

INTRODUCTION: During the course of chemotherapy, patients commonly experience fatigue, hair loss, nausea, and diarrhea, as well as vomiting, which usually becomes more intense as treatment progresses. However, some patients develop anticipatory nausea and emesis; that is, they become nauseated and may vomit in anticipation of the chemotherapy treatment. Research indicates that the incidence of this phenomenon is between 21% and 40% of all patients receiving cancer chemotherapy. It appears that through the repeated exposure to this treatment, previously neutral stimuli become associated with the aversive effects of treatment and eventually elicit the same responses as the treatment itself. In this respect, it is a model example of respondent (classical) conditioning. Conventional medical treatment of anticipatory nausea and emesis with commonly used antiemetic drugs such as Compazine and Thorazine has not proven effective. The purpose of this study was to analyze systematically the ability of hypnosis to control anticipatory emesis.

METHOD: The subjects consisted of six women between 24 and 56 years of age (mean age of 45 years). Four of the six patients were being treated for breast carcinoma, one for stage IV-B Hodgkin's disease, and one for oat cell carcinoma of the lung. The patients were selected on the basis of being observed vomiting at least three consecutive times before the chemotherapy injection. This criterion was used to ensure an observable and reliably occurring behavioral symptom against which a treatment outcome could be compared. All of these patients had received antiemetic medication without any relief from nausea and vomiting. During the hypnotic interventions, these antiemetic drug regimens were held constant.

Each patient met individually with the hypnotherapist, where the purpose and procedure for the study were outlined. The use of hypnosis was explained in social-learning terms as a means of relaxation and distraction. Patients were told that they would actually be learning a self-control technique. The actual hypnotic induction consisted of three steps. First, a fixed-point technique was used to focus the patient's attention and to aid concentration on the therapist's voice and suggestions. Second, deep muscle relaxation was induced in various muscle groups progressively from the feet to the head and back to the feet; this was repeated once. Finally, relaxation imagery was introduced in which various pleasant scenes were employed. Interspersed in this imagery were suggestions of comfort and the absence of nausea. After 30 minutes, subjects were awakened. The session was tape-recorded and the patients were instructed to listen to the tape daily so as to increase their responsiveness to hypnosis.

One week later, the patients returned to a second hypnotic session, where a trance was again induced. While in a hypnotic state, the patients were physically taken through the sequence of events preceding the chemotherapy injections.

The third session was held the day of the chemotherapy treatment. Before being placed in a trance, the patients were required to complete scale ratings of the amount of nausea experienced upon awakening in the morning and while in the waiting room. Hypnosis was then induced, and the patient was taken in a wheelchair to the chemotherapy treatment. After the injection, the patients were taken back to the hypnotherapist's office and awakened from their trances. Patients then completed ratings of nausea experienced while receiving the chemotherapy and at that present moment. This procedure was followed during each chemotherapy session until a patient had completed her prescribed number of treatments. The number of times that each patient was hypnotized varied from three to five. Three of the patients decided to forgo the use of hypnosis for one chemotherapy session. This was unplanned by the experimenters but constituted a within-subject reversal that provided additional information about the role of hypnosis in reducing nausea and emesis in the patients.

Two sources of data were used in the analyses. The first was the nurses' recorded observations of emesis while patients waited for treatment and while treatment was being administered. The second source was the patients' ratings of nausea on a polar scale with "no nausea" labeled as one anchor and "nausea as bad as it could be" as the other.

There were a total of twenty-one treatment sessions where hypnosis was used. The results indicated that anticipatory emesis was suppressed in all patients in all of these sessions. Hypnosis was effective regardless of the time in the course of chemotherapy that it was introduced (this ranged from the eighth to the fifteenth session). In the reversal sessions (those sessions where three of the patients did not receive hypnosis before chemotherapy), anticipatory emesis reappeared. When hypnosis was reintroduced to these subjects in later chemotherapy sessions, anticipatory emesis was again controlled.

The self-report nausea ratings indicated that nausea increased as the time treatment approached. This trend was drastically reversed for all patients after the introduction of hypnosis. In addition, the patients experienced little nausea both during the treatment session and when aroused immediately after chemotherapy. Hypnosis was effective whenever it was used and regardless of the severity of a patient's nausea.

Although the precise mechanisms responsible for the effectiveness of the hypnotic trance are unknown, the authors contend that there may be three components to the induction procedure that are crucial. The first may be deep muscle relaxation. Such relaxation creates feelings of pleasant calmness and brings about variations in autonomic responses that are incompatible with anxiety. The reduction in muscle activity associated with relaxation may also interfere with the sequential muscular movements necessary for emesis to occur.

Another critical factor may be distraction. By diverting the patient's attention from the eliciting stimuli and toward the therapist's suggestions, the patient is prevented from responding to the conditioned stimuli. The presence of imagery in the hypnotic induction may also serve as a distractor.

A third factor may be social demand variables (that is, implicit suggestions and instructions). Patients control their emesis in order to please the therapist. The authors believe that the influence of this factor is minimal, since similar demand variables were present when only antiemetic drugs were used.

The authors believe that the use of hypnosis in controlling anticipatory emesis may best be interpreted as an operant method of self-control. Patients are taught to evoke physiological conditions that are incompatible with severe nausea and emesis. Patients report that hypnosis restores a sense of self-control that is frequently lost over the course of a long, invasive treatment protocol. Hypnosis does have advantages as a method for counteracting this phenomenon. As this research illustrates, hypnosis is very effective and has no undesirable side effects as other drugs may (such as marijuana). It requires little training, no special apparatus, and little physical effort on the part of the subject. It can also be used to effectively control pain, anxiety, and insomnia associated with cancer.

COMMENTARY: Anticipatory nausea and emesis may be perceived as a complex conditioned response where environmental stimuli are associated with affective and physiological responses to chemotherapy and then, after repeated exposure, elicit these responses independently. The stimuli associated with the nausea and vomiting vary from patient to patient—being in a hospital; the smell of rubbing alcohol, perfumes, or cleaning agents; and even just thinking about a scheduled treatment. Even the number of treatments required to develop this condition varies across patients. In this study, its appearance ranged from after four chemotherapy sessions to after eight. Patients appear to become more sensitized to treatment, in that the intensity of their nausea and desire to vomit increase over treatments. Hypnosis appears to be an effective method for extinguishing these learned associations.

SOURCE: Redd, W. H., Andresen, G. V., and Minagawa, R. Y. "Hypnotic Control of Anticipatory Emesis in Patients Receiving Cancer Chemotherapy." *Journal of Consulting and Clinical Psychology*, 1982, *50*, 14-19.

Additional Readings

Cox, T., and Mackay, C. "Psychosocial Factors and Psychophysiological Mechanisms in the Etiology and Development of Cancers." *Social Science Medicine,* 1982, *16,* 381-396.

The authors present a comprehensive review of the research on determining contributory factors in the development of cancer. Social class, occupational, environmental, and lifestyle factors have been found to be associated with increased risks of cancer, although the relative importance of these factors has not yet been established. Recent investigations have indicated two main factors associated with an increased risk of cancer: (1) the loss of or lack of closeness to a significant other in early life (usually a parent), and (2) the inability to vent hostile affect or the abnormal release of affect. These findings have spurred interest in uncovering psychophysiological mechanisms that moderate the relationship between psychological distress and cancer. Research is increasingly implicating the immune system as the connection between the central nervous system and disease processes.

Derogatis, L. R., Morrow, G. R., Fetting, J., Penman, D., Piasetsky, S., Schmale, A. M., Henrichs, M., and Carnicke, C. L. M., Jr. "The Prevalence of Psychiatric Disorders Among Cancer Patients." *Journal of the American Medical Association,* 1983, *249,* 751–757.

These researchers randomly evaluated 215 cancer patients for formal psychiatric disorders. Assessments were made via a psychiatric interview and standardized psychological tests; the DSM-III system was used in making the diagnosis. Of these patients, 47% received a formal psychiatric diagnosis, with 44% manifesting a clinical syndrome and the remaining 3% having personality disorders. Of these individuals, 68% had adjustment disorders (13% manifesting major affective disorders, such as depression). Of those with a psychiatric condition, about 85% were experiencing a disorder with depression or anxiety as the central component. Since these authors considered the majority of these disorders as treatable, the results of this study suggest that cancer patients should be provided with ancillary treatments that address the psychological effects of their physical illness.

Nicholas, D. R. "Prevalence of Anticipatory Nausea and Emesis in Cancer Chemotherapy Patients." *Journal of Behavioral Medicine,* 1982, *5,* 461–463.

This report examined the prevalence of anticipatory emesis and anticipatory nausea (AE/AN) in seventy-one cancer chemotherapy patients. An 18.3% prevalence rate was found, with the average onset 5.12 hours before treatment. The incidence of AE/AN usually occurred at home or in transit to the clinic. Patients who complained of AE/AN also reported higher frequencies of posttreatment nausea, vomiting, constipation, and dry and itching skin than did patients not experiencing AE/AN. The author concludes that the medical staff needs to inquire about AE/AN rather than simply relying on observations made at the treatment center.

Wellisch, D., Landsverk, J., Guidera, K., Pasnau, R. O., and
    Fawzz, F. "Evaluation of Psychosocial Problems of the
    Homebound Cancer Patient: I. Methodology and Problem
    Frequencies." *Psychosomatic Medicine,* 1983, *45,* 11–21.

The Psychosocial Problems Categories for Homebound
Cancer Patients was used to determine the psychological problem frequencies for very ill, homebound cancer patients. This
instrument contains thirteen major problem categories and fifty
individual problems. The records of 570 patients were rated by
two raters (interrater reliability of .96). The five most common
problem categories were: (1) somatic side effects (30% of total
problems), (2) patient mood disturbances (15%), (3) equipment
problems (8%), (4) family relationship impairment (7%), and
(5) cognitive impairment (6%). The most frequent interventions
included (1) instructor-administered reinforcement to patient or
family, (2) no intervention for the problem, and (3) counseling
or emotional support. The authors support the greater use of
this instrument for assessing psychosocial functioning of cancer
patients.

Stress
and Hypertension

There is hardly a medical disorder that is not caused, triggered, or exacerbated by stress. Hypertension is itself a medical condition deserving serious attention, being a major concern in the study and management of cardiovascular heart disease. Drug treatment often fails because of noncompliance or noxious side effects. Similarly, the complex of social and personality variables that controls the stress-prone patient is not easily altered by quick psychotherapeutic encounters. Behavioral medicine recognizes the importance that rational health planning has assigned to this problem. Although diverse strategies continue to be tried, a lasting and effective solution is not yet at hand. Nonetheless, behavioral therapies show great promise in making major inroads into this difficult health area.

Biofeedback and Relaxation
in Controlling Hypertension

AUTHORS: Bernard L. Frankel, Dali J. Patel, David Horwitz, William T. Friedewald, and Kenneth R. Gaarder

PRECIS: An examination of the effectiveness of biofeedback and relaxation training in controlling hypertension.

INTRODUCTION: Various behavioral techniques have been used to treat hypertension, but results have been equivocal. Such conflicting results usually arise from studies with differing methodologies or levels of experimental rigor. This report presents a well-controlled study using a combination of diastolic blood pressure feedback and relaxation techniques to manage hypertension. The study was designed to provide information about carryover effects from practice sessions, comparisons of the results for treated subjects with those for untreated and sham-treated subjects, and information about compliance with home practice schedules.

METHOD: Subjects were twenty-two hypertensive individuals, twelve males and ten females, ranging in age from 28 to 63 years. All had a history of high blood pressure for 1 to 25 years. Initial baseline blood pressure values were established over a 6- to 8-week period. Subjects were randomly assigned to one of three treatment protocols. In the active treatment (AT) group, a combination of diastolic blood pressure (DBP) feedback, frontalis EMG feedback, autogenic training, and progressive relaxation exercises was given in twenty laboratory sessions over 16 weeks. The sham treatment (ST) group had twenty sessions over 16 weeks in which noncontingent DBP feedback was given. The sessions were arranged to convey a sense of success to the subjects. In the third, no-treatment group, blood pressure was measured weekly over 16 weeks. In the AT condition, subjects were to practice the autogenic and relaxation exercises on a regular schedule. Each day subjects completed a brief questionnaire designed to enhance motivation and to monitor home practice. The ST subjects were not instructed in home practice maneuvers.

None of the fourteen subjects in the AT and ST conditions showed significant decreases in blood pressure over the 4-month program. Only one subject showed a significant decrease in blood pressure during active treatment as well as further decreases during the 18-month follow-up interval. It was also noted that subjects in the ST condition reduced their blood pressure during the final six sessions as effectively as those in the AT group. The use of EMG feedback and relaxation did not produce any blood pressure reductions beyond those associated with blood pressure feedback.

The compliance rate, as determined by subjects' logs, was 91%. Subjects also reported using their relaxation skills consistently in situations that were identified as being stressful. By the end of the program, subjects in the AT group reported an increased ability to relax and cope more effectively with stressful situations. Five of the seven patients in the ST group also reported feeling more relaxed but did not report increased coping skills in dealing with specific stressors.

COMMENTARY: This study represents a well-designed and methodologically rigorous investigation into the efficacy of biofeedback and relaxation in controlling hypertension. The results did not indicate that any of the varieties of relaxation were valuable primary treatments for hypertension. The authors conclude that behavioral techniques are not useful overall but can be effective with some hypertensives. The authors contend that these techniques may be useful as supplements to management with drugs, provided that they do not divert the patient from effective medical therapy.

SOURCE: Frankel, B. L., Patel, D. J., Horwitz, D., Friedewald, W. T., and Gaarder, K. R. "Treatment of Hypertension with Biofeedback and Relaxation Techniques." *Psychosomatic Medicine,* 1978, *40,* 276–293.

Anxiety Management Training for Hypertensives

AUTHORS: Randall S. Jorgensen, B. Kent Houston, and Raymond M. Zurawski

PRECIS: An assessment of the efficacy of anxiety management training as an adjunctive therapy for individuals suffering from essential hypertension.

INTRODUCTION: Although there is no known cause for essential hypertension, research evidence suggests that psychological stress plays an important role in its development and maintenance. Anxiety management training (AMT) is a promising technique that can help patients to manage anxiety regardless of its cause, thereby interrupting the anxiety response and minimizing blood pressure elevations. Hypertensives are taught deep muscle relaxation, a response incompatible with any type of arousal. Then imagery conditioning is used to generalize the learned relaxation response beyond the treatment environment to the person's real-life situation. This intervention attempts to reduce blood pressure responses to stress as well as the resting blood pressure level of hypertensives. Since antihypertensive medications do not affect blood pressure responses to stress, the development of such an adjunctive therapy is very valuable.

METHOD: Eighteen hypertensive patients with a mean age of 54.3 years participated in this study. They were selected on the basis of having been diagnosed with essential hypertension before age 55 and having no psychiatric disturbances. Subjects were randomly assigned to either an immediate-treatment condition ($n = 10$) or a delayed-treatment control group ($n = 8$). The immediate-treatment group received AMT for a 6-week period between pretest and posttest measures. The delayed condition received AMT during the 6-week period between posttest and follow-up assessment sessions. All but one subject was receiving antihypertensive medication.

AMT was conducted weekly for 6 weeks. Each session was conducted in a group format and lasted approximately 75 minutes. The first session was directed at instructing subjects on the role that stress and tension play in promoting high blood pressure. Subjects then heard a 40-minute tape presentation of progressive muscle relaxation instructions. Afterward, the psychophysiological correlates of relaxation were discussed, and subjects were instructed to practice these exercises in a quiet setting for 15 minutes twice daily. Subsequent sessions focused on the effectiveness of this procedure in the subjects' home environment, after which subjects received 10 minutes of taped relaxation instructions. A structured rehearsal procedure was then introduced, whereby subjects were instructed to imagine a scene from their current life circumstances that produced high levels of affective arousal (for example, stress or anger). When the subjects indicated that they were tense, they were instructed to become more sensitive of the psychophysical correlates of their aroused state. They then turned their attention from the emotion-provoking imagery to initiating the relaxation response. Although the therapist initially had to help the subjects return to a deeply relaxed state, the treatment goal was to have each subject relax without any external assistance. The structured rehearsal was repeated three times each session. Subjects were also instructed to use tension as a cue for initiating these relaxation skills in the course of their normal routines.

The dependent measure was systolic and diastolic blood pressure. These recordings were made at pretest (prior to AMT), posttest (after AMT), and at a 6-week follow-up. Each measurement session consisted of three phases: The first was a baseline interval, the second phase monitored cardiovascular activity while subjects worked on the Stroop Color-Word Inference Test, and the third was a recovery period after completing the task.

The Stroop task consists of cards on which the names of four colors (red, green, orange, and blue) are printed in one of the other three colors. These words are randomly shown to the subject, who is to say the color of ink for each word as fast as possible without making any mistakes. The Stroop task has previously been shown to elicit blood pressure reactivity associated with hypertension. Subjects received 176 trials, during which the experimenter conspicuously displayed a stopwatch and recorded errors in order to enhance the stressfulness of the task. During the recovery period (4 minutes), the subjects were instructed to sit quietly.

It should be noted that at the posttest and follow-up sessions, the subjects were instructed not to use the AMT skills in order to keep the assessment sessions as comparable to real-life situations as possible. The subjects in the delayed AMT control condition received AMT during the 6-week interval between the posttest and follow-up sessions.

The results indicated that subjects in the immediate AMT group decreased their systolic and diastolic blood pressure at the baseline and recovery intervals significantly more than the control group from pretest to posttest. On the Stroop task, the immediate AMT group performed with greater variability with regard to systolic blood pressure at pretest and posttest than did the delayed AMT group. There were no differences between the two groups in diastolic pressure. The authors contend that these unexpected results may be attributable to task anxiety effects for the immediate-training group. Although such anxiety may have been present throughout the assessment session, its effects were particularly marked on the Stroop task because it required considerable effort to complete. Since the baseline and recovery periods required no effort from the subject, the authors believe that the combination of task effort and performance anxiety had an interactive effect during the Stroop task that resulted in the obtained discrepancy between the two treatment groups.

Follow-up analyses indicated that subjects in the immediate AMT condition could maintain their blood pressure decreases during each of the three measurement periods at follow-up. There were also significant decreases in both baseline systolic blood pressure and systolic blood pressure during the Stroop task from posttest to follow-up assessment periods. Subjects in the delayed AMT group had significant decreases in both systolic and diastolic blood pressure during the Stroop task and the recovery period. No such differences were found with regard to the baseline period.

COMMENTARY: Subjects' accounts indicated that skills acquired from the AMT did generalize outside of the treatment environment. Many subjects during the course of AMT also reported immediate physical and social benefits, which may have enhanced their motivation to comply with the requirements of the procedure (that is, to continue home practice of the relaxation techniques as well as to apply the coping skills in real-life situations). AMT appears to be a promising intervention for use as an adjunctive therapy for essential hypertensives. This training not only helps to reduce resting blood pressure levels but can also decrease the duration of elevated cardiovascular activity following a stressful event. It does not bring about decreases in blood pressure during a stressful event.

SOURCE: Jorgensen, R. S., Houston, B. K., and Zurawski, R. M. "Anxiety Management Training in the Treatment of Essential Hypertension." *Behaviour Research and Therapy,* 1981, *19,* 467–474.

Long-Term Application
of a Behavioral Treatment for Hypertension

AUTHORS: E. Richter-Heinrich, V. Homuth, B. Heinrich, K. H. Schmidt, R. Wiedemann, and H. R. Gohlke

PRECIS: A comparison of the effectiveness of a behavioral and a medical regime intervention for hypertension over a year-and-a-half period.

INTRODUCTION: The early stages of hypertension show a heightened autonomic and neurochemical reactivity to environmental stimuli, often associated with an increased tonic arousal level. As such, most antihypertensive medications have central nervous system blocking or sympatholytic agents. Because of the drawbacks of pharmacologic interventions, it is necessary to evaluate the effectiveness of nonphysiological treatments. Such approaches could be useful either in removing the need for medications or in reducing the dosage needed to attain the desired physical state. However, there are limitations to the exclusive use of a psychological intervention: The factors implicated in the etiology of hypertension vary from patient to patient, and a psychological treatment is not appropriate if there is physiological damage (such as ruptured blood vessels). The purpose of this report is to examine the extent to which biofeedback, relaxation training, and psychotherapy are effective in controlling essential hypertension.

METHOD: Forty hypertensives between the ages of 19 and 45 years, diagnosed as being in clinical stage 1, participated in this study. Twenty received the psychophysiological intervention and for at least 14 days before hospitalization and for the entire treatment period were free from any hypertensive medications (group 1). The remaining twenty subjects received beta-receptor-blocking agents during the treatment period (group 2). Ten subjects received talinolol and ten received propranolol (subgroups of group 2).

The therapeutic intervention was comprised of four phases. In phase 1, all subjects remained in the hospital; after all the diagnostic tests were completed (approximately 1 week), training began. First there was relaxation training twice daily, which was then combined with biofeedback procedures. Of interest was the subjects' systolic blood pressure (systolic BP), which was taken at 1-minute intervals. Aside from these two training sessions, subjects were expected to practice their relaxation techniques 20 minutes a day in their bedroom. Other features of this phase included: (1) BP recorded by the subjects three times per day, (2) circulatory and respiratory gymnastics eight times a day, (3) muscle relaxation training six times per day, (4) discussions about BP changes every training session, and (5) discussions on life-style, personal affairs, and so on. If it was deemed necessary, additional psychotherapy was instituted.

Phase 2 was begun the first 14 days after discharge from

the hospital. During this period, none of the subjects returned to work. Here BP recordings were continued thrice daily; relaxation training techniques were to be practiced at least once a day for 20 minutes and in an abbreviated form for 2 minutes in daily life situations. All subjects returned to the hospital twice a week for controlled training sessions. During phase 3, subjects returned to their employment. They still practiced their home exercises and returned to the hospital every 2 weeks for supervised sessions.

Phase 4 began 3 months after the initiation of treatment. The initial diagnostic evaluations were repeated at this point. Subjects were then divided into two groups. Subjects in the first group had showed decreases in blood pressure to less than 145/95 mm Hg, as well as manifesting significant decreases in both systolic and diastolic BP during the course of treatment. Subjects in this condition showed significant improvement over the course of the 3-month treatment; their average BP dropped from 142/93 to 134/85 mm Hg. These subjects were to continue the training procedures learned during the treatment (group 1). The remaining ten subjects were categorized as a no-treatment-success group and were placed on antihypertensive medications (group 2). This group showed no significant decreases in BP over the 3 months (average BP was 142/96 mm Hg at pretreatment and 142/92 mm Hg at posttreatment). Subjects in the first group showed a more uniform decrease in blood pressure than those in the second condition.

Comparable decreases in blood pressure were found in groups 1 and 2 using a diagnostic measure for differentiating between normotensives in clinical stages I and II. Subjects receiving chemotherapy did have significant decreases in heart rate, which were not evidenced by subjects in the behavioral treatment groups.

On a choice reaction time task, subjects in group 1 and the two control subgroups showed significant decreases in heart rate, although this effect was larger in the control groups. The decreases in group 2 were not significant. Subjects in group 1 showed decreases in tonic activation and in self-ratings of tension. All subjects were then observed for a 1-year period (evaluated at 3-month intervals), and these improvements were found to have continued. BP levels continued to decrease, and group means fell within normotensive limits. Individuals in group 1 were able to continue this regimen without any need for medications. However, in group 2, three patients had to receive chemotherapy, three others had poor compliance rates and received medications, and the remaining subjects showed borderline BP values. There was great variability in their BP recordings, which were associated with changes in their psychosocial conditions.

COMMENTARY: The authors suggest that subjects in group 2 did not successfully respond to treatment because of physiological damage caused by their hypertension; therefore, they were not responsive to a psychological intervention. The authors also note some important characteristics of subjects who had an unsuccessful treatment outcome: (1) There was more hereditary evidence for hypertension; (2) subjects manifested more neurotic tendencies on psychological measures; and (3) there were more compliance problems. The authors believe that daily training is essential in maintaining any therapeutic effects. Self-measurements of BP are also important, in that this information not only provides the opportunity to monitor treatment more closely but also serves to increase compliance and strengthen patient motivation. The results of this report clearly indicate the efficacy of this treatment with some individuals. However, as the authors note, this program is very time consuming and further research is needed to improve its efficiency.

SOURCE: Richter-Heinrich, E., Homuth, V., Heinrich, B., Schmidt, K. H., Wiedemann, R., and Gohlke, H. R. "Long-Term Application of Behavioral Treatments in Essential Hypertensives." *Physiology and Behavior*, 1981, *26*, 915–920.

Additional Readings

Caplan, G. "Mastery of Stress: Psychosocial Aspects." *American Journal of Psychiatry*, 1981, *138*, 413–420.

The author contends that there are four phases to an individual's response to a stressful event: (1) behaviors that change the stressful environment or enable the person to escape from it; (2) the acquisition of new capabilities for changing the external events and their effects, (3) the activation of intrapsychic behaviors to defend against dysphoric affective arousal, and (4) the reequilibration of intrapsychic processes in the aftermath of the stressful event. The inability of an individual to complete all four phases of the stress response can increase the person's vulnerability to mental and physical illnesses. Such a risk can be minimized if the individual receives social support in dealing with the stressful event. This support should be in the form of cognitive guidance that compensates for the inevitable impairment of problem-solving ability caused by the stress-induced emotional arousal. This guidance also facilitates the individual's ability to manage the changes produced in the person's life by the stressful event.

Gardner, E. R., and Hall, R. C. W. "The Professional Stress Syndrome." *Psychosomatics*, 1981, *22*, 672–680.

The professional stress syndrome is a condition that develops as a result of protracted stress. Common among professionals, its manifestations include disruptions in relationships, exhaustion, fatigue, headaches, gastrointestinal disturbances, insomnia, and depression. Behavioral concomitants are lability of mood, diminished frustration tolerance, and feelings of omnipotence. Unless treated early, physical and emotional disorders can develop. The authors present several strategies that can alleviate the syndrome. These include developing better peer relationships, changes in work and recreational routines, clarification of goals, and better opportunities for ventilating feelings.

Gillum, R. F., Prineas, R. J., Jeffrey, R. W., Jacobs, D. R., Elmer, P. J. Gomez, O., and Blackburn, H. "Nonpharmacologic Therapy of Hypertension: The Independent Effects of

Weight Reduction and Sodium Restriction in Overweight Borderline Hypertensive Patients." *American Heart Journal,* 1983, *105,* 128–133.

This study examined the effects of modest weight loss and sodium restriction, alone and in combination, on blood pressure in obese men with borderline hypertension. Weight, 24-hour urinary sodium excretion, and blood pressure change were measured before and after two 10-week periods of dietary intervention. The results indicated that modest reductions in weight (3.9 to 5.2 kilograms) were associated with blood pressure decreases independent of sodium intake. However, weight loss and sodium restriction were associated with substantial decreases in blood pressures for these subjects. The authors recommend a combination of these two interventions as a first step in treating hypertensives or patients at risk of essential hypertension.

Kanner, A. D., Coyne, J. C., Schaefer, C., and Lazarus, R. S. "Comparison of Two Modes of Stress Measurement: Daily Hassles and Uplifts Versus Major Life Events." *Journal of Behavioral Medicine,* 1981, *4,* 1–39.

These authors present research evidence that supports their contention that daily hassles (irritating, frustrating, distressing demands that arise in daily interactions with the environment) are more strongly related to the adaptive nature of the stress process than are major life events. They also contend that hassles are a better predictor of psychological symptoms due to stress than are major life events. These authors suggest that research approaches to understanding the source of psychological disturbances associated with stress should focus on the minor daily events in people's lives, particularly their cumulative effect on coping and behavior.

Taylor, C. B., and Fortmann, S. P. "Essential Hypertension." *Psychosomatics,* 1983, *24,* 433–448.

The authors present a review of the psychophysiological mechanisms involved in hypertension as well as common therapeutic interventions for hypertension. Although the authors support the increased usage of medications in treating hypertension, they contend that the condition requires management of the whole patient, including attention to weight, exercise, diet, emotions, rest, and relaxation. Essential hypertension is a multi-factorial disorder and should be therapeutically conceptualized as such.

Woolfolk, R. L., Lehren, P. M., McCann, B. S., and Rooney, A. J. "Effects of Progressive Relaxation and Meditation on Cognitive and Somatic Manifestations of Daily Stress." *Behaviour Research and Therapy*, 1982, *20*, 461–467.

This research compared the efficacy of meditation and progressive relaxation to self-monitoring (control state) as interventions for symptoms of stress. All subjects self-monitored stress symptoms, and their behavior was rated weekly by a spouse or roommate. The results indicated that both treatments were effective in reducing stress-related symptomatology over time. No differential effects of the treatments were observed.

Cardiovascular Disorders

Both physiology and psychology have contributed much to what we know about the heart and the cardiovascular system. As a master mechanical and electrical complex, the opportunity for errant functioning abounds. However, early studies showed that relatively simple programs of operant conditioning or biofeedback could produce changes in cardiovascular function. These studies were later refined and developed into clinical protocols used in treating specific disorders of the cardiovascular system. Added to this are the many contributions that behavioral medicine offers that can benefit public health. It is not surprising, therefore, that cardiology is one of the specialties in medicine that has been most active in supporting and collaborating with behavioral medicine.

271

Using Biofeedback to Treat Raynaud's Disease

AUTHORS: Edward B. Blanchard and Mary R. Haynes

PRECIS: A description of a biofeedback procedure based on finger surface temperature used to treat Raynaud's disease.

INTRODUCTION: Raynaud's disease is a functional disorder of the cardiovascular system in which a patient experiences vasoconstriction in the hands or feet, making the extremities cold to touch. Recent reports have shown biofeedback to be effective in treating this disease. However, difficulties in interpreting these studies arise because no systematic data are reported on the patients as they progress through the treatment, and no pretreatment data are presented. This case study addresses these deficiencies in evaluating temperature biofeedback as a treatment intervention.

CASE HISTORY: The patient was a 28-year-old female, a registered nurse, who reported having cold hands and feet "for as long as she could remember." Her mother had also had a similar condition. The patient recognized the problem as a case of Raynaud's disease during her nursing education and sought medical help without any apparent benefit. Actual episodes of painful vasoconstriction occurred about once a month.

METHOD: Treatment consisted of twenty-eight sessions lasting 40 minutes each, as well as three follow-up sessions at 2, 4, and 7 months.

Each 40-minute session was divided into three parts: adaptation, a 5-minute baseline session, and a 20-minute experimental trial. The experimental trial consisted of five different parts:

1. Baseline. For the first four sessions, the patient sat quietly and was given instructions to relax.
2. Self-control. The next six sessions were designed to control for expectancy effects and constituted a no-feedback con-

trol phase. The patient was required to try to make her hands warmer through "mental means."

3. Feedback training. For the next six sessions, the patient was given visual feedback of the difference in temperature between her hand and her forehead and was instructed to raise her hand temperature to that of her forehead.

4. Self-control. For six sessions the subject returned to the no-feedback condition to control for the effects of the feedback training.

5. Feedback training. The feedback training was reinstituted for the last six sessions.

At the conclusion of the treatment, the patient was instructed to use this biofeedback training whenever her hands felt cold. However, no home practice regimen was instituted. At the follow-up sessions, self-control and feedback training were given as boosters.

The results indicated a steady increase in hand temperature over the sessions. During baseline, the hands tended to drop in temperature and attempts at self-control yielded inconsistent results. However, the feedback training enabled the patient to increase her hand temperature consistently. Also, the latency of this response decreased over the sessions, indicating that learning was taking place with repeated trials since the patient learned to make the response more quickly. The return to self-control once again yielded inconsistent results, demonstrating dependence on the feedback situation. The final return to feedback training led to consistent increases in hand temperature, with the average increase being 3.7°F. At follow-up, the feedback training sessions led to rapid reinstatement of the patient's ability to warm her hands.

The patient reported using mental means outside of treatment to make her hands warmer when they seemed cold. Also, some transfer of the warming ability to her feet was established. Absolute hand temperature was recorded, and a considerable increase was shown from before to after treatment. The patient reported that her Raynaud's disease had mostly abated.

COMMENTARY: This study confirms previous reports that bio-feedback provides an effective treatment for Raynaud's disease. In fact, it gives even more evidence for the efficacy of biofeed-back than previous cases because of several design features: (1) There were baseline trials; (2) expectancy effects were controlled by using a no-feedback condition; (3) only biofeedback was used; and (4) systematic data show that improvement only began when feedback was introduced. Absolute hand temperature showed a reliable increase from pretreatment to posttreatment. The rapid response to booster feedback training during the follow-up sessions is also encouraging.

SOURCE: Blanchard, E. B., and Haynes, M. R. "Biofeedback Treatment of a Case of Raynaud's Disease." *Journal of Behavior Therapy and Experimental Psychiatry*, 1975, 6, 230–234.

Biofeedback Control of Ventricular Rate

AUTHORS: Eugene R. Bleecker and Bernard T. Engel

PRECIS: Patients with atrial fibrillation (AF) were trained to slow and to speed ventricular rate (VR).

INTRODUCTION: Normals can be trained to control their heart rates and to decrease beat-to-beat heart rate variability. But there has been some debate over whether patients with AF can be trained to control VR. This study proposed to determine whether patients with chronic AF can be trained to slow and speed VR and to identify some of the autonomic nervous system mechanisms that mediate the voluntary control of VR.

METHOD: Six patients with AF participated in this study. Each had a history of rheumatic valvular heart disease and was maintained on a stable dosage of digitalis for at least 3 months before the study. None had any serious neurological disorder.

Each subject was trained in a laboratory to speed and slow VR. A panel with three lights was displayed in front of the patient. The top light (green) indicated that the patient should try to speed VR, the middle light (yellow) indicated that the patient made a correct change in VR, and the bottom light (red) indicated that the patient should try to slow VR. During the first 30 minutes of an experimental session, the patient stabilized VR. Then ventricular contractions were monitored and recorded for 512 seconds (baseline period). In the last 1,024 seconds of the training period, the subject tried to control his or her VR. The yellow light remained on for as long as the VR was controlled in the correct direction. The patients were instructed to keep this light on for as long as possible.

After a series of training sessions in speeding and slowing VR, each patient was tested under alternating conditions. For four consecutive 256-second intervals, each subject was required to alternately speed and slow VR as signaled by the red and green cue lights. Then in five patients (one refused to participate), pharmacologic studies were carried out using different drugs; isoproterenol, propranolol, atropine, and edrophonium. All drug studies were performed after the training session in VR control was completed in order to investigate the mechanisms of VR and rhythm changes.

The results showed considerable differences between the fast and slow phases of the experiment for the different patients. Two subjects were more consistent in their ability to slow VR, two subjects in their ability to speed VR, and two subjects could reliably speed and slow VR. However, the most critical demonstration of a subject's ability to control VR is the ability to speed and slow VR during alternate sessions. All of the subjects differentiated between fast and slow cues in this phase of the experiment. Each patient retained differential control of his or her cardiac rate at levels that were statistically significant; two subjects retained control in 100% of the sessions.

The studies done using the autonomic drugs showed that neither isoproterenol, propranolol, nor edrophonium abolished the ability of the subjects to modify VR voluntarily. Atropine, however, abolished this ability in all but one of the subjects. But even she could not control VR as well as before. Two subjects were given more training to try to teach them to decrease the variabilities of their ventricular rates. Both were able to reduce VR variability from baseline, but neither showed any evidence of day-to-day reduction in VR variability. Molecular EKG analyses were also performed. During VR slowing, one patient generated an A-V functional escape rhythm, while another subject produced premature ventricular contractions during speeding of VR under the use of propranolol. Various anomalies of R-R intervals, QRS complex configurations, and polarity reversals were noted in the course of training under the drug conditions.

COMMENTARY: This study supports the hypothesis that digitalized patients with AF can be operantly conditioned to modify their VR. This control of VR is neurally mediated at the level of the atrioventricular node. The studies using atropine abolished this voluntary control of VR in patients with established AF. Attempts to reduce VR variability were unsuccessful because decreases in R-R variability were insufficient to produce long-term changes in VR variability. The demonstration of operant control is important because it can help to elucidate fundamental mechanisms of cardiovascular functioning and its interaction with drugs. Although this study was not designed to provide a clinical model, the importance of the findings may well lead to refined treatment programs for AF patients.

SOURCE: Bleecker, E. R., and Engel, B. T. "Learned Control of Ventricular Rate in Patients with Atrial Fibrillation." *Psychosomatic Medicine,* 1973, *35,* 161–175.

A Rehabilitation Program
for Cardiovascular Patients

AUTHORS: Susan Roviaro, David S. Holmes, and R. David
Holmsten

PRECIS: A report on the influence of an exercise-based cardiac
rehabilitation program on the cardiovascular, psychological, and
social functioning of cardiac patients.

INTRODUCTION: The rehabilitation of cardiac patients must
involve not only cardiovascular functioning but psychological
and social functioning as well. Recently exercise programs have
been used as an approach for rehabilitating cardiac patients.
This study investigates the short- and long-term effects of such a
program by assigning cardiac patients to either an intensive
exercise-based rehabilitation treatment condition or to a routine
care control condition. Five major areas were examined: (1) cardiovascular functioning, (2) understanding of heart disease and
compliance, (3) psychological functioning, (4) emotionality,
and (5) psychosocial functioning.

METHOD: Forty-eight male patients (mean age 56 years) who
had either experienced a myocardial infarction or undergone
coronary bypass surgery and who met the criteria for participation in the cardiac rehabilitation program served as subjects.
The criteria included: (1) age of 69 years or younger, (2) presence of coronary heart disease, (3) a minimum of four weeks
after a cardiac incident, (4) cardiac condition controlled by
medication or surgery, and (5) no physical or emotional problems precluding full participation in the program. Severity of
coronary heart disease did not exclude participation in the program.

    Twenty-eight patients were assigned to the treatment
group and twenty to the routine care control group. The routine cardiac care included regularly scheduled physical examinations, discussions of cardiac risk factors, the provision of dietary
information, and the presentation of a recommended program
of exercise.

The cardiac rehabilitation program lasted for 3 months. Patients assigned to this treatment met at the hospital for three 1-hour sessions a week. An exercise program for each patient was drawn up and instituted by a physical therapist, who worked closely with each patient for the first 2 months. Each session consisted of warm-up exercises, exercise to the target heart rate (which was increased 5% every 4 weeks), and maintenance of this heart rate for 3 minutes. This sequence was repeated as often as possible during a 30-minute exercise program. This exercise period was followed by a cool-down activity period, which was designed to return the patient to a resting state. During the third month, the patient regulated his own heart rate. The educational component of this program included information about coronary disease, exercise, and exercise evaluation.

Follow-up evaluations were given 4 months after the treatment session, and included appraisals of: (1) cardiovascular indexes (resting heart rate, resting systolic blood pressure, and resting diastolic blood pressure) and performance on a graded, multistage treadmill stress test, (2) understanding of heart disease (questions concerning heart disease were asked of each patient, who received points for each correct answer), (3) understanding of treatment recommendations (questions were asked concerning the patient's medication, frequency and duration of recommended exercise, and understanding of dietary recommendations), (4) compliance with treatment recommendations (a 9-point scale questionnaire was given to each patient to evaluate the degree of compliance), (5) psychological (self-perception) indexes (measures of perception of health, body concept, self-concept, and progress), (6) emotionality (measures of general anxiety, anxiety specific to heart disease, and depression), and (7) psychosocial indexes (measures of marital and personal adjustment).

Patients who participated in the rehabilitation program compared with the controls evidenced (1) more efficient cardiovascular functioning as measured by resting heart rate, resting diastolic blood pressure, treadmill exercise performance, exercise heart rate, and exercise systolic blood pressure; (2) a better understanding of heart disease; (3) a better understanding of treatment recommendations; (4) a greater reported compliance with treatment recommendations concerning medication, physical exertion, and weight; (5) more positive self-perceptions with regard to health, body concept, self-concept, and progress toward personal goals; and (6) better psychosocial functioning as reflected by decreased employment-related emotional stress, more physically demanding housework and yardwork, more frequent sexual activity, greater involvement in and enjoyment of active leisure activities, and more frequent, longer, and more strenuous routine physical exercise. These beneficial effects of the treatment program were also evidenced at the follow-up evaluations, where some patients displayed even more improved functioning over the 4-month period.

In contrast to these positive findings, the treatment did not influence resting systolic blood pressure, cholesterol levels, trait or cardiac anxiety, overall depression, perceived disruption in daily functioning, or marital adjustment.

COMMENTARY: The results of this study indicated that the cardiac rehabilitation program had beneficial effects for patients with coronary heart disease, and the treatment was equally effective for both acute and chronic patients. The authors explain that the absence of treatment effects on many of the measures can be attributed to the fact that the patients did not initially evidence elevated scores on these measures and thus there was little room for or expectation of improvement. Although it is clear that the treatment had reliable and pervasive effects, it is not clear what component or components of the treatment package were responsible for the effects that were observed. However, the salutary effects of this program were produced by a simple, low-cost, existing program that is within the staffing and equipment capabilities of most medical centers, and these findings should have wide applicability.

SOURCE: Roviaro, S., Holmes, D. S., and Holmsten, R. D. "Influence of a Cardiac Rehabilitation Program on the Cardiovascular, Psychological, and Social Functioning of Cardiac Patients." *Journal of Behavioral Medicine*, 1984, 7, 61–81.

Conditioned Acceleration and Deceleration
of Heart Rate

AUTHORS: Robert W. Scott, R. D. Peters, William J. Gillespie, Edward B. Blanchard, Eileen D. Edmunson, and Larry D. Young

PRECIS: A description of the use of reinforcement to accelerate and decelerate heart rate.

INTRODUCTION: Numerous studies have shown that heart rate (HR) can be controlled in part by using response feedback, positive reinforcement, and punishment. However, the change in HR has been rather small (1 to 6 beats per minute, or BMP) and the length of experimental trials short (5 seconds to 25 minutes). This study attempts to produce large-scale changes in HR that can be maintained over a period of days. It also examines the efficacy of two different reinforcers, commercial television programs and money.

METHOD: Three subjects participated in this experiment, a 61-year-old male psychiatric patient suffering from tachycardia and two 20-year-old male college students who participated as paid volunteers. The subjects were not informed that their HR was being measured but were told that various aspects of their internal behavior were being monitored.

Each subject sat in a reclining chair with six electrodes placed on his arms and legs. Each could control the operation of a television picture with a correct response. A correct response for subject 1 was deceleration of HR, while for subjects 2 and 3 it was acceleration of HR. The number of experimental trials needed to complete any one condition depended upon the subject's performance. All sessions lasted 40 minutes. For the first 20 minutes, the subject's HR was recorded while he sat quietly in the room; in the last 20 minutes the experimental trial took place.

The reinforcer for subjects 1 and 2 was access to the video portion of commercial television programs. The audio portion of the program was available to the subjects on a noncontingent basis. The first condition of the experimental trial was the determination of the subject's resting HR, that is, baseline. Television programming was then presented noncontingently to determine if it had any effect on HR. The noncontingent television was terminated when HR stabilized and then became contingent on the proper HR response. The subjects were told that the television picture would be on whenever they made a correct response with respect to their internal behavior and that they were to keep the picture on as much as possible. To receive reinforcement, the subjects had to change their HR by 5 BPM. Each time the criterion was met for three consecutive experimental trials, the criterion was raised another 5 BPM. This procedure continued until HR was stable at 20% from baseline. At this point, the television programming was presented noncontingently to determine the extent of the reversal of HR.

The results for subject 1 showed a decrease in HR from 87 BPM to within the normal range, averaging 71 BPM after the conditioning procedure. However, it should be noted that presentation of noncontingent television also produced a decrease in HR to 80 BPM. For subject 2 an acceleration of HR was established, from 65 BPM in baseline to 82 BPM in the experimental trial.

For subject 3, a new reinforcer, money, was presented to improve the efficiency of the original paradigm. His HR increased from 47 BPM in baseline to 63 BPM through the use of shaping and reinforcement. Presentation of noncontingent television returned HR to operant level for all subjects.

COMMENTARY: This study demonstrated large changes in HR that were maintained over long trials as well as on successive days, a finding different from previous reports. This supports the likelihood that operant conditioning and positive reinforcement can be used to develop a behavioral approach to treating certain cardiac disorders. The authors suggest that some improvements should be instituted, such as the use of additional reinforcers and the method of shaping. Also, the deceleration of subject 1's HR during noncontingent television should be investigated, since adaptation could have taken place over the trials. But this explanation seems unlikely, since a decrease of 16 BPM is unlikely to stabilize due to adaptation alone.

SOURCE: Scott, R. W., Peters, R. D., Gillespie, W. J., Blanchard, E. B., Edmunson, E. D., and Young, L. D. "The Use of Shaping and Reinforcement in the Operant Acceleration and Deceleration of Heart Rate." *Behavior Research and Therapy*, 1973, *11*, 179–185.

Additional Readings

Berra, K. "YMCArdiac Therapy: A Community-Based Program for Persons with Coronary Artery Diseases." *Journal of Cardiac Rehabilitation*, 1981, *1*, 354–360.

The need for medically supervised health and exercise education for individuals with coronary artery disease has been well established. This report describes a community-based program developed by the YMCA to meet this need. All participants are carefully screened and receive a battery of physical tests. Programs to reduce risk factors are tailored to the needs of each individual. Clients are carefully informed of their current physical condition throughout the program. Central elements of the program include learning to self-monitor angina pectoris and premature ventricular contractions. Safe and effective exercise programs also help to increase physiological functioning. This rehabilitative program has been found to be effective and therapeutic.

Freedman, R. R., Ianni, P., and Wenig, P. "Behavioral Treatment of Raynaud's Disease." *Journal of Consulting and Clinical Psychology*, 1983, *51*, 339–349.

Although there is no known etiology for Raynaud's disease, behavioral techniques have been found to be effective treatments. This report examines four different techniques: (1)

finger temperature feedback, (2) finger temperature under cold stress, (3) autogenic training, and (4) frontalis EMG feedback. Thirty-two patients received 10 biweekly training sessions. Cognitive stress management was also taught to all subjects. The results indicated that those groups receiving finger temperature feedback demonstrated significant temperature increases not observed in the other two groups. The addition of training under cold stress to temperature feedback resulted in significantly better retention of vasodilation skills at a 1-year follow-up as well as a 92.5% reduction in symptom frequency. Following treatment, subjects in this group required colder temperatures to produce an attack than those who received EMG feedback or autogenic training. The cognitive stress management techniques failed to produce any significant effect on any of the outcome measures.

Janssen, K. "Treatment of Sinus Tachycardia with Heart-Rate Feedback." *Journal of Behavioral Medicine,* 1983, *6,* 109–114.

A single-subject treatment of a 23-year-old male who had a 6-year history of tachycardia is reported. Such episodes were commonly experienced before school examinations. All organic and psychosocial pathologies were ruled out. Treatment consisted of eight biweekly heart rate biofeedback sessions. Visual and auditory feedback was presented, and the subject was required to lower his heart rate to increasingly lower levels. Results indicated a decrease in beats per minute (BPM) from 103 to 66 at posttreatment. A 1-year follow-up investigation revealed heart rate to be between 68 and 72 BPM. EMG recordings of the frontalis suggested a generalized effect of the treatment. Although more research is necessary, the author contends that this intervention would be effective in treating cardiac arrhythmias. The results also suggest that a key factor in heart rate feedback may be respiratory activity. Helping a client to learn the relationship between breathing patterns and heart rate may greatly enhance treatment efficacy.

6

Therapies
for Selected Problems
of Children

While in principle the reports of the preceding chapter apply to patients at any age, children do impose unique demands when designing a therapeutic program. Some problems begin early in life and are often seen as "diseases of children," such as asthma and hyperactivity. But more important, the cumulative effects of a disorder on a developing patient present the risk of psychological and physiological damage, which merits special attention. When intervention for any of these disorders is possible at a young age, the prognosis for personal functioning and physiological status over the long term is substantially improved. As in the preceding chapter, the separate sections address separate symptom classes, each containing diverse behavioral strategies for treatment.

Insomnia

Unattended sleep disorders in young patients can have serious social, academic, and health effects. Certain disorders are almost totally restricted to youngsters, for example, pavor nocturnus (night terror). Children are also the main sufferers of movements during sleep. Whether or not specific antecedents can be identified that give rise to such disorders, behavioral medicine techniques can offer relief. As with other medical disorders that occur in both adult and juvenile populations, sleep problems in children often require a special analytic program and therapeutic style in order to obtain meaningful clinical gains.

Effect of Sleep Deprivation on Adolescents

AUTHORS: Mary A. Carskadon, Kim Harvey, and William C. Dement

PRECIS: A study to determine the effects of sleep deprivation on young adolescents and the similarity of these effects to those on adults.

INTRODUCTION: A great amount of research has been done on the effects of sleep deprivation on adults, particularly on cognitive, motor, and psychological functioning. However, this research has focused on a particular subject population—young adult males. The purpose of this report was to examine sleep deprivation on a sample of young adolescents, both male and female, to determine if they respond to sleep loss as do adults. Such information can help to expand our understanding of sleep deprivation effects and individual differences in responses to sleep loss, especially among young adolescents.

METHOD: Subjects consisted of twelve youngsters, eight males and four females, 11.9 to 14.6 years of age (mean of 13.5). All subjects were in good health, drug free, and without a personal or family history of sleep disorders. This research was performed on groups of three or four subjects, who spent 6 days in the sleep laboratory.

Physiological recordings were made from a standard EEG, EMG, and EOG. Electrodes for these measurements were in place throughout the entire study. On either the first or second night, respiration was measured via nasal thermistors and thoracic and abdominal strain gauges. The first 3 days served as the adaptational and baseline (BSLN) periods. There was then a 1-day sleep deprivation (SD) period, and 2 recovery days (REC). On BSLN and REC days, subjects were in bed for 10 hours. All sleep periods and performance tests were conducted in individual rooms.

Performance tests were administered in three batteries each day. During SD, two additional batteries were added.

These batteries included four tests given in the same order. The first test was the Wilkinson Addition Test, a 30-minute test where subjects were to add columns of five two-digit numbers. Subjects were to work as quickly and as carefully as possible, tapping on a switch after each problem was completed. Subjects were awakened or reminded to continue working if more than 1 minute passed between switch signals. Speed of performance and accuracy were assessed. The second test was the Williams Word Memory Test. This consisted of a list of twenty-five four-letter words that were pronounced and spelled at 10-second intervals; subjects were instructed to write down each word on a separate piece of paper. After the list was presented, a technician paged through the list with each subject at the rate of 5 seconds per word. Any misspelled words had to be rewritten correctly. Each subject was then required to write down in any order as many of the words as could be remembered on a separate sheet of paper. Five minutes were allotted for this task. The number of correctly recalled words was scored.

The third test was a listening attention task designed to measure vigilance in children. This task consisted of twenty passages about animals, each averaging 10 minutes in duration. Each passage had two key words appearing 70 times. In front of the subject were two switches, one key word written on each. Every time a subject heard a key word, he or she was instructed to depress the appropriate switch. The total number of key words missed was scored. The final test was a serial attention task. Subjects were instructed to tap the two switches regularly and alternately at a steady pace for 15 minutes. Subjects were awakened or urged to continue tapping if there was a gap of 30 seconds. A cumulative score of the number of seconds subjects failed to tap the switches was obtained.

Self-ratings of daytime sleepiness were obtained at 30-minute intervals throughout all waking periods. These measures included the Stanford Sleepiness Scale (SSS) and an analog sleepiness scale. This latter scale consisted of a 100-millimeter line in which the low-value pole was labeled "very wide awake" and the opposing pole "very sleepy." Scoring was performed by measuring the distance of the subject's mark from the low-value pole. Therefore, scores closer to 0 were associated with wakefulness, and scores closer to 100 with sleepiness. A multiple sleep latency test (SLT) was given as an objective measure of daytime sleepiness; it was given six times daily at 2-hour intervals. Six SLTs were added during the SD period. Vigorous activity was suspended 15 minutes before this task. Subjects were asked to lie in bed quietly with their eyes closed and try to fall asleep. All noise and lights were eliminated. On the first day, SLTs lasted 20 minutes regardless of whether the subjects fell asleep or not. On the following days, SLTs lasted until three consecutive epochs of sleep occurred or a maximum of 20 minutes.

Throughout this study, subjects were accompanied by a technician at all times. Beverages with caffeine were not permitted. Subjects were able to participate in various physical and recreational activities. During SD, subjects were engaged in special activities to help them keep awake (such as movies, a bonfire and marshmallow roast, and a sunrise-viewing expedition).

The results indicated only one significant sex-related difference—latency to REM sleep, which was greater in males. Total sleep time and stage 4 sleep were significantly increased on the first REC night compared with BSLN and REC-2 (the second REC day). Stage 1 sleep time was also significantly reduced on REC-1 compared with BSLN and remained low on REC-2. Stages 2 and 3 did not differ significantly from BSLN on the REC days. Sleep onset latency and stage 4 sleep latency were significantly lower on REC-1 than on BSLN and REC-2. Finally, REM latency did not vary across conditions.

The data also indicated a marked impairment on the performance measures during SD, but this decrease in scores was significant for only two tests, the Wilkinson Addition Test and the Williams Word Memory Test. The authors note that there was considerable individual variability on all performance measures, but this variability was more evident on the tests given during the SD period. The authors point out that a subject's performance score was markedly lower if he or she fell asleep during a task, whether briefly or for longer periods (which required waking by a technician), compared with the scores for subjects who did not fall asleep during the task.

Significant increases in perceived sleepiness during SD were found. The SSS and analog scales were significantly correlated. These rating-scale results were quite variable during the SD period, which was attributed to daytime activities. Perceived sleepiness scores were higher after the performance test batteries than after periods of physical activity. These rating scores returned to BSLN levels after one full recovery night of sleep. SLT scores also showed a significant response to SD, but these responses differed from the subjective ratings. SLT scores declined progressively during SD until reaching a stable constant low value for the remainder of this period. There was also no variability associated with preceding activity levels. REC-1 SLT scores were significantly lower than BSLN during the first part of the day (from 9:30 A.M. to 3:30 P.M.); REC-2 SLT scores were not significantly different from BSLN.

The authors conclude that these young adolescents were able to tolerate a single night's sleep loss with few problems. The results here appear to conform to data from studies with older subjects, although differences may exist in areas not covered by this report. Decreases in performance on the test batteries were attributed to subjects falling asleep during the test rather than to a deterioration in ability caused by the deprivation procedures. This finding may be related to the variability in the self-ratings of sleepiness, which were lower after intervals of physical activity (such as volleyball or bowling). This result supports the hypothesis that to avoid sleepiness during periods of sleep deprivation, one should continue physical activities.

COMMENTARY: The SLT results indicate that a single night's sleep is insufficient to produce complete recovery from SD. The authors contend that SD produces a phase delay in one's circadian rhythm of sleep tendency. It appears that more time (two days) are necessary to reestablish this pattern. This report provides important information that can be useful in the diagnosis of sleep disturbances in adolescents and in the development of treatment interventions. Because of the similarity of reactions to sleep loss, it appears likely that treatment techniques for sleep disorders with adults can be successfully applied to children.

SOURCE: Carskadon, M. A., Harvey, K., and Dement, W. C. "Sleep Loss in Young Adolescents." *Sleep*, 1981, *4*, 299–312.

Eliminating Rhythmical Movements in Sleep

AUTHORS: S. J. E. Lindsay, P. M. Salkovshis, and K. Stoll

PRECIS: A report on the use of a response prevention technique in eliminating nocturnal head rolling in a 13-year-old boy.

INTRODUCTION: For this patient, stereotypic body movements during sleep included behaviors such as body rocking, head banging, and body rolling. Although the child remained asleep during these movements, they posed obvious potential dangers. In a survey of over 500 children between 3 months and 6 years of age, 30% exhibited some form of these rhythmical movements. The movements were especially frequent when a child was tired. A variety of techniques have been used in treating this phenomenon, including a metronome set to match the frequency of head-banging activity, overcorrection, and a light activated by the body movements. Although these movements rarely occur after age 3, this report examines response prevention training in a 13-year-old male.

CASE HISTORY: The subject was a 13-year-old male of average intelligence. He had exhibited frequent, vigorous head and body rolling at night since he was 18 months old. Each night before falling asleep, he would roll his head and shoulders from side to side, one complete cycle occurring about once every second. This occurred three to four times during sleep. The rocking could be terminated by waking the subject. The authors did not note any specific antecedent stimuli for the behavior, which began when the subject went to bed and was followed by sleep. The subject claimed that he would be unable to fall asleep without this activity. He was able to sleep for 8 hours a night and did not appear tired during the day.

TREATMENT: It was assumed that response prevention would allow the boy to learn that he could fall asleep without head rolling. Awakening the subject with an alarm when there was head rolling would be incompatible with the movements, especially if the boy had to get out of bed to turn off the alarm.

Two inflated sacs were placed under the boy's pillows. An alarm was triggered after four consecutive movements (two complete roll cycles) during the night. The boy was then required to get out of the bed and cross the room to turn off the alarm. There were four treatment phases of 6 to 16 days, each followed by a period of 7 days when sleeping behaviors were only observed. The entire intervention lasted approximately 3 months.

An average of 785 roll cycles were recorded during the initial baseline, and this was reduced to 16 by the end of the first treatment interval (16 days). By the second withdrawal phase, there were three consecutive nights free of rolling movements. Only in the fourth treatment series was there an instance of the pretreatment frequency, and that was for only one night. On that night the subject complained of not feeling well and had a fever. After that episode there were no other incidences of nocturnal movement. By the end of treatment, all rhythmical movements had ceased, and they remained extinguished at the follow-up 5 months later.

COMMENTARY: The authors note that with the curtailment of the body movements, the boy had no difficulty in falling asleep and awoke refreshed in the morning. The quality of sleep seemed to have improved noticeably. The etiology of this condition is difficult to determine, nor have the physiological mechanisms been identified that sustain sleep during the behavior. Nonetheless, response prevention techniques provided an effective intervention for eliminating these nocturnal behaviors. The rapidity with which the treatment reduced the head rolling suggests that a shorter treatment interval may be equally effective. The improvements noted here were accomplished without increasing the incidence of other sleep disturbances (such as irregular body movements during sleep) or deteriorating the quality of sleep for the patient.

SOURCE: Lindsay, S. J. E., Salkovshis, P. M., and Stoll, K. "Rhythmical Body Movement in Sleep: A Brief Review and Treatment Study." *Behaviour Research and Therapy*, 1982, *20,* 523–526.

Behavior Modification in Correcting Sleeping Behaviors

AUTHORS: Sherman Yen, Roger W. McIntire, and Samuel Berkowitz

PRECIS: A case study in which behavior modification was used to extinguish inappropriate sleeping behaviors in an adolescent.

CASE HISTORY: The subject was a 17-year-old boy who had had a history of sleeping difficulties for 2 years. The sleep problem had two components: (1) Before bedtime he would repeatedly enter his mother's bedroom to discuss his worries with her, and (2) it would take him longer to fall asleep if he could not talk with his mother before going to bed. He had been receiving conventional psychotherapy for 6 months before initiating this program but with no results. The initial interview revealed that the subject would visit his mother four to twenty times per evening, had a delay of ½ to 3 hours in sleep onset, and was taking tranquilizers every evening. The mother was very concerned about this behavior.

TREATMENT: The extinction procedure consisted of three steps: (1) The mother would no longer listen to the boy's worries before bedtime in her bedroom; (2) a special time in the evening would be reserved to discuss these troubles in the living room; and (3) if the subject visited his mother in her bedroom before retiring, the special discussion time would be canceled the next evening.

The subject kept a record of sleep latency, the things he worried about, and any sleeping medications taken. The mother recorded the duration and frequency of their special meeting times and the frequency of the subject's visits to her bedroom.

After introducing the behavior modification program, the number of visits to the mother's bedroom sharply decreased, and they were totally eliminated by the fourth week. The duration of the special times requested by the subject also decreased over the course of the treatment. The number of things that worried the subject also decreased, as did sleep onset latency. In addition, his use of sleeping medications declined. In fact, only once did the subject take any tranquilizers during the program.

COMMENTARY: The implementation of the behavioral modification program produced a dramatic change in the subject's behavior. The self-reporting and change in the mother's management of the situation appeared to be quite effective. Of interest in this study is that the entire program was maintained and monitored by the patient and his mother. As the authors note, approaching the problem with both mother and son was very effective, although it lacked the precise measurement common in the laboratory setting. The study prompts two suggestions: A behavioral modification program should include the patient's family in the program, and (2) restructuring the family routine can nurture more socially acceptable behaviors in the child patient.

SOURCE: Yen, S., McIntire, R. W., and Berkowitz, S. "Extinction of Inappropriate Sleeping Behavior: Multiple Assessment." *Psychological Reports,* 1972, *30,* 375–378.

Additional Readings

Hauri, P., and Olmstead, E. "Childhood-Onset Insomnia." *Sleep,* 1980, *3,* 59-65.

This report compared individuals with childhood onset (CO) insomnia with individuals with adulthood onset (AO) insomnia. It was found that CO insomniacs had more difficulty in falling asleep, had a total sleep time averaging 40 minutes less, and had an abnormally low percentage of phasic REM compared with AO insomniacs. The CO group also appeared to be more heterogeneous than the AO groups, exhibiting a significantly greater variability from person to person on the measured sleep variables. No differences were reported between the two groups on any pesonality dimensions, although the CO group showed more evidence of "soft" neurological impairment. Since the CO insomniacs reported less psychological stress about the onset of their insomnia, the authors suggest that these individuals may have some neurological impairment in those systems relating to the sleep-wake balance. This contention is supported by the irregular REM levels noted in the CO group.

Kellerman, J. "Behavioral Treatment of Night Terrors in a Child with Acute Leukemia." *Journal of Nervous and Mental Disease,* 1979, *167,* 182-185.

The author presents a case study treatment of a 3-year-old girl diagnosed with acute lymphocytic leukemia with a 1-month history of recurrent nightmares. Her symptomatology conformed to a clinical picture of slow-wave arousal night terrors known as pavor nocturnus. The author introduced a behavioral treatment directed at reducing the anxiety associated with maternal separation and with the medical procedures she experienced. Also involved was the reinforcement of appropriate sleep patterns. Both techniques were effective in eliminating the nightmares, and a follow-up investigation indicated no return of the symptoms. The author contends that such night terrors reflect a psychological reaction to trauma and that clinicians should be sensitive to age variables in the expression of children's anxiety.

Diabetes

The juvenile diabetic faces severe restrictions and usually a guarded prognosis. The family of the diabetic shares many of those concerns, fears, and limitations. Consequently, the potential is great for psychological problems that may lead to mental illness or exacerbate the physiological imbalances and side effects caused by diabetes. This medical problem presents a challenge for behavioral medicine, which can best assist by designing a comprehensive management effort rather than modifying any single, isolated behavior. Some of the classic illustrations of comprehensive management can be found in the literature on diabetes—one that deals with psychophysiology, family, compliance, and intrapsychic dynamics. The technological advances made by medical science will certainly allow greater control over some of the organic factors of diabetes, but they will almost certainly require the assistance of behavioral medicine to resolve the problems that result precisely because the chances of survival and gross functioning improve.

Psychological Management of the Diabetic

AUTHORS: Rudolph Bauer and Thomas J. Kenny

PRECIS: A report presenting a psychological approach to the management of diabetes in the juvenile.

INTRODUCTION: Behavioral medicine has demonstrated the monism of mind and body by establishing empirical relationships between psychological processes and vulnerability to illness. Disease may therefore represent problems in a person's ability to cope with emotional and environmental experiences. Even with regard to chronic diseases, such as diabetes, a child's symptoms can be understood as the interaction of a dysfunctioning family system and the patient's physiological vulnerability. The authors contend that in mediating any psychosomatic component of a disease, an intervention program should include the psychological treatment of the family as well as the standard medical therapy for the disease in question. The purpose of this article is to highlight some of the salient issues of a family systems approach.

TREATMENT: For these authors, disease reflects: (1) physiological vulnerability in the patient, (2) a series of stressful events in the life of the child or the parents, and (3) a dysfunctional family pattern. The family may become dysfunctional because it responds to the sick member inappropriately. The disease becomes an integral part of the family's dynamics and is therefore maintained by the system, making the disease process refractory.

Several characteristics of a psychosomatic family of a child with superlabile diabetes must be addressed by the health care provider: (1) enmeshment (the overinvolvement of family members with each other and the blurring of interpersonal boundaries), (2) overprotectiveness (too heavy a commitment and investment by the family in the care of the needy person), (3) a lack of conflict resolution (an interruption of the resolution of family conflicts and thus the prolonging of unresolved feelings because of the child's symptoms), (4) preservation of family interaction patterns to avoid change, and (5) involvement of the child in parental conflict (blaming the child's illness for all family problems).

Because of these characteristics, both the individual and the family should be treated with psychotherapy. Individual therapy with the child should center on facilitating the child's ability to cope with stress. The use of hypnosis can help teach relaxation techniques to be used when experiencing stress and to change the child's perception of self from one who is sick to one who is well. The child should also be taught how to recognize stress-producing situations and how to disengage from them. Throughout the therapy, emphasis is placed on establishing autonomy and responsibility in the child, thereby breaking down the family patterns of enmeshment.

Family therapy should be conducted weekly. It should focus on the family network involving the patient and show to the family how the patient's illness serves to maintain or break down communication among family members. In therapy, new modes of transactional patterns can be established that free the child and the family from the dysfunctional family patterns that maintain the child's symptoms.

COMMENTARY: The major thesis here is that chronic disease does not exist in a vacuum. Its existence is influenced by internal processes (physiological vulnerabilities) as well as external dynamics (family interaction). Treatment must address both areas. The approach outlined here is straightforward, with no emphasis on dynamic interpretations. Its family-restructuring techniques are a direct application of the family systems approach developed by Minuchin and offer a rapid method for managing superlabile diabetes in children and their families.

SOURCE: Bauer, R., and Kenny, T. J. "Psychological Management of Juvenile Diabetes." *Pediatric Annals*, 1975, *4*, 359–362.

The Management of Diabetes Mellitus

AUTHOR: Allan L. Drash

PRECIS: A report outlining a comprehensive approach to the management of children with diabetes mellitus.

INTRODUCTION: The incidence of diabetes is about 1.6 in every 1,000 births, and in more than 1% of all diabetics the onset occurs before 17 years of age. The clinical manifestations of insulin deficiency diabetes include polyuria, polydipsia, polyphagia, weight loss, visual disturbances, fatigue, and muscle weakness. These symptoms may be precipitated by an infection, but usually there are no obvious causal factors. The author notes that more cases of diabetes are diagnosed in the winter and spring than in the summer and fall, which he sees as consistent with the implication of viral factors in the disease's etiology. Once diagnosed, diabetics go through a predictable sequence of stages. These include metabolic stabilization (administration of insulin); the remission phase, 2 to 3 months after diagnosis, where about 90% of the patients experience a reduced dependence on insulin; and the exacerbation phase, about 6 to 12 months after diagnosis, when remission begins to wane and insulin requirements rise. This change may occur abruptly when infection or emotional stress is present. Finally, total diabetes—complete insulin deficiency—occurs between 12 and 18 months after the diagnosis. Throughout all diabetic phases, careful management of the condition is critical, especially with children and adolescents. This management goes beyond the mere administration of insulin.

MANAGEMENT: The first aspect of diabetic control is insulin administration. Twenty-four-hour urine glucose determinations should be made periodically to check on the accuracy of analyses of individual urine specimens. The insulin dose should be adjusted as necessary. Usually insulin needs increase as a child gains weight and matures sexually. Close monitoring of glucose levels is important, since, as indicated above, insulin deficiency changes significantly in the first 18 months after diagnosis. The proper adjustment of medication is necessary to avoid hypoglycemic and hyperglycemic reactions. It is also important to monitor emotional states and disease activity, because these factors significantly affect metabolic control. Physical exercise must be supervised, since the increased rate of glucose utilization may lead to hypoglycemia.

Nutritional therapy also plays an important role in managing the diabetic child. The diet should: (1) meet all nutritional needs for growth and maturation, (2) assist in achieving good metabolic control by minimizing both hypoglycemia and hyperglycemia, (3) prevent hyperlipemia, and (4) prevent obesity. The author suggests a diet in which 55% of total calories come from carbohydrates, 30% from fat, and 15% from protein. The carbohydrate calories should be derived from starch (70%) and a mixture of lactose, sucrose, and fructose (30%). In addition, the diet should reflect the food preferences of the patient in order to make the food more appetizing.

Exercise and physical fitness are other components in overall management. Increased physical fitness increases the child's ability to utilize energy efficiently, decreases insulin requirements, and minimizes complications associated with diabetes. Any exercise regimen should encourage the adoption of lifelong physical activities (such as golf, jogging, and tennis).

Emotional support and guidance to avoid or reduce emotional problems is a major challenge. A chronic disease has many consequences for the patient, family, and friends. Such pressures can lead to a deteriorated metabolic status, decreased compliance with prescribed regimens, and psychological disturbances. Depression and antisocial behaviors are frequent problems that health care professionals must be prepared to address.

Finally, there is the need to educate the patient and his or her family. The patient must assume major responsibility for both complying with prescribed regimens and participating in the therapeutic decision-making process. The family must be able to provide the necessary support systems for the patient to help foster greater self-reliance and independence. Both patient and family need to be educated about the course and treatment of diabetes. Greater sensitivity should be developed toward possible difficulties (such as vascular complications) associated with the diabetes as well as the affective state of the patient.

COMMENTARY: Managing diabetes in a child or adolescent is a multidimensional task. Attention must be devoted to a wide range of factors affecting the patient's physical status. The effective management of these factors will help to reduce the likelihood of later complications and aid in fostering a better sense of well-being in the patient. Conventional behavior therapeutic technologies are ideally suited for dealing with prevention, compliance, and self-control behaviors. They are also appropriate for treating depression and other motivational problems that arise, which may affect the medical condition of the patient.

SOURCE: Drash, A. L. "Managing the Child with Diabetes Mellitus: Practical Aspects." *Postgraduate Medicine*, 1978, *63*, 85-92.

EMG Biofeedback in the Control of Diabetes

AUTHORS: Jane E. Fowler, Thomas H. Budzynski, and Richard L. VandenBergh

PRECIS: A report examining the effectiveness of EMG-feedback-assisted relaxation in the control of diabetes.

INTRODUCTION: There is a large experimental literature that documents the effects of stress on the diabetic's condition. In this study, the authors demonstrate that training diabetics prone to stress reactions to cope more fully with the associated physiological arousal results in a stabilization of their condition as well as a decrease in their insulin requirement. The authors refer to their approach as cultivated relaxation, where EMG biofeedback allows the individual to monitor and to modify reactions to stressful events in order to maintain an optimal physiological pattern.

CASE HISTORY: The subject was a 20-year-old female with a history of diabetes since age 9. Management of her condition was uneventful until age 15, when she developed thyroiditis. At age 16 her diabetic control deteriorated, and she was hospitalized for 14 months. During this period physical or emotional stress (even position emotions) would produce keto-acidosis. Insulin doses of several hundred units per day were common, as were massive swings in blood sugar. At age 17 she received Sotalol (a beta-adrenergic blocker) and family therapy, which stabilized her condition. Medication was suspended after 15 months. Her first semester in college was marked with four hospitalizations for keto-acidosis. Emotional factors were implicated. She was hospitalized four more times during the second half of her first year and three other times in the first half of her sophomore year. Baseline observations of her condition were taken over the winter quarter of her second year in college (a 6-week period).

METHOD: The primary outcome measure for this study was the daily dose of insulin units. Urine tests and blood sugar levels were also measured periodically. A daily diary was kept to record this information as well as information on diet, exercise, medications, infections, accidents, and emotional conflicts. Two subjective measures were also employed. One was the Diabetic Scale, which provides a subjective estimate of the diabetic state. This scale was administered before each blood or urine test. Ratings were made on an 8-point scale (−4 for hypoglycemia to +4 for severe keto-acidosis) four times daily. The second measure was the Emotional Scale, which assessed general tension levels and the degree of psychological conflicts.

The training phase was conducted over a 9-week spring quarter. All measures were continued over this period. The intervention consisted of two practice sessions daily, each lasting 30 to 40 minutes. The subject used a portable EMG feedback unit (attached to the frontalis muscle and providing visual and auditory feedback) in conjunction with a series of cassette tapes containing instructions for relaxing the major muscle groups as well as for stabilizing and slowing respiration. As the subject became more proficient at relaxation during the sessions, she was encouraged to practice these skills in everyday situations that could cause her stress.

At the end of the training phase, the subject discontinued practice with the EMG apparatus and the relaxation tapes, although she continued to use her newly acquired skills in stressful situations. A follow-up period of 6 weeks' duration began 6 months after treatment was terminated. All dependent measures were assessed again during this period.

The weekly mean intake of insulin fluctuated throughout the baseline period with the peak intake occurring during her week of final examinations (103 units). The overall baseline average was 85 units daily. Significant changes began to appear in the fourth week of training; the average mean insulin intake for the last 6 weeks of training was reduced to 59 units. Of interest was the comparison of insulin units at the final exam periods for baseline and training phases (103 versus 44, respectively). Follow-up results indicated that the therapeutic gains were maintained over time. The average insulin intake for this 6-week period was 52 units. The authors suggest that these results support their hypothesis that the training not only stabilized the subject's intake but also lowered the quantity required.

Self-ratings on the Diabetic Scale correlated positively with insulin dose at a greater-than-chance level. The scores indicated that the subject's need for insulin decreased more rapidly than the rate at which the daily dose was actually adjusted. Ratings on the Emotional Scale decreased considerably from baseline during the training phase. The authors conclude that in spite of a more demanding academic schedule during the training period, the subject was less anxious and tense. She also reported that she was more able to cope with her environment and did not get upset as often as before.

COMMENTARY: Although this was only a case study, the results indicate that cultivated relaxation can be a therapeutically useful technique for controlling diabetes. It appears to have provided this subject with a more effective method for coping with the stresses in her environment, thereby reducing her emotional lability and stabilizing her diabetic condition. The reduced insulin need is a meaningful clinical achievement, suggesting that such a protocol could be a valuable adjunctive treatment strategy for diabetes. As the authors point out, this technique is relatively simple to administer and can be combined with existing forms of therapy.

SOURCE: Fowler, J. E., Budzynski, T. H., and VandenBergh, R. L. "Effects of an EMG Biofeedback Relaxation Program on the Control of Diabetes: A Case Study." *Biofeedback and Self-Regulation,* 1976, *1,* 105-112.

Psychophysiological Correlates in Juvenile Diabetes

AUTHORS: Jay D. Tarnow and Seth W. Silverman

PRECIS: A report examining the psychophysiological correlates of stress and their impact upon juvenile diabetes mellitus.

INTRODUCTION: Emotional factors have long been implicated in the etiology, severity, and course of diabetes. In particular, the influence of psychological stress upon an individual's metabolic system has been well documented. Changes in ketones, glucose, and free fatty acids can exacerbate a diabetic's condition. The authors postulate two possible psychophysiological defects facing diabetics: an augmented stress response in the metabolic system or an aberrant equilibrating metabolic mechanism. Labile diabetics respond to stress through metabolic systems, and once arousal occurs, they have difficulty in returning to their prestress homeostatic level. In this report, the authors present a psychophysiological model for stress in diabetics and provide therapeutic alternatives for managing stress reactions in juvenile diabetics.

PSYCHOPHYSIOLOGICAL MODEL: The authors note that juvenile diabetes is a psychophysiological disorder where a reciprocal relationship between affective states and disease intensity exists. Stress can effect changes in metabolic activity that result in diabetic decompensation. This deterioration can also create greater stress for the individual in its own right.

Any stressful event acts as a stimulus to the person and then is preconsciously recognized as a stressor. Such recognition changes central nervous system levels of arousal, and this arousal leads to hormonal and autonomic nervous system stimulation by the hypothalamus. Metabolic changes then arise that lead to diabetic decompensation. This result may also serve as a stressor, catching a person in a vicious cycle of arousal and physical deterioration.

The preconscious recognition of stress can serve to either increase or decrease central nervous system arousal. Here the individual may attempt to understand, integrate, or cope cognitively with the stressful event. Memories of past events or situations where stressors have been successfully mastered are evoked in an attempt to formulate appropriate and effective strategies for handling the new stressor. This "information evaluation phase" can provide such coping strategies (for example, seeking information or acting directly to reduce stress). These actions can also affect the person's perception of the stressful stimuli, which may encourage changes in central nervous system arousal.

The authors recognize that stress also has beneficial qualities, namely, motivating the individual through the process of maturation, increasing adaptive capabilities, and facilitating the development of one's potential. However, diabetes presents an individual with additional stressors not affecting healthy persons, such as dietary restrictions, insulin injections, the stigma of being diabetic or different from other children, and the embarrassment of bed-wetting.

THERAPEUTIC IMPLICATIONS: The efficacy with which the child and the family cope with the stresses associated with diabetes can have a major effect on the disease process. Of particular importance is when the diabetes is diagnosed. The family's process of accepting the disease can have important implications for its future course. At this level, the primary physician can relieve stress by providing a holistic evaluation of the patient and by developing preventive measures (such as educating the family about diet and exercise and not allowing the disease to interfere with normal development).

Group meetings for diabetics can also be helpful. They aid in removing the stigma attached to being diabetic and can reduce feelings of social alienation and increase self-esteem. In addition, they can provide the diabetic with new coping strategies and problem-solving techniques for handling stress. Because of the role that the family plays in providing the relationships necessary for normal growth and development, family therapy can help in coping with stress. By enhancing adaptive family functioning, the family can act as an effective buffer against stressors that may overwhelm the child. It can also provide a safe arena for testing new coping skills and can foster autonomy and independence in the child. Additionally, having the family accept the child's diabetic condition can increase the child's compliance with the medical regimen.

Another therapeutic alternative is psychodynamic-oriented therapy. Since past memories can be a source of stress when they are poorly mastered, this therapeutic approach can help the diabetic integrate past experiences so that they no longer act as internal stressors that increase central nervous system arousal. Problem-solving techniques and better defense capabilities can also be acquired through this approach.

Hypnosis and biofeedback can be useful by enabling the individual to modulate physiological systems and to learn new coping styles through cognitive mastery techniques. Antianxiety medications can be helpful in reducing arousal and assisting in restoring the body's homeostatic level.

The authors indicate that the most important therapeutic consideration is the multidisciplinary team approach. Such efforts have been shown to be effective in improving control, decreasing the incidence of diabetic keto-acidosis, decreasing long-term complications, improving self-concept and social adjustment, and providing long-term stability for the patient and family. Its success may be due to its ability to deal with more aspects of the stress process than other treatment modalities alone.

COMMENTARY: The authors present a model of stress that includes contemporary perspectives on the interaction between internal and external events and physiological processes. Since juvenile diabetes is perceived to be a psychophysiological disease, managing those psychological events that affect its duration and severity are central to its treatment and control. Regardless of the intervention employed, those psychosocial aspects must be considered that facilitate physiological arousal, and conditions need to be developed that minimize their effects.

SOURCE: Tarnow, J. D., and Silverman, S. W. "The Psychophysiologic Aspects of Stress in Juvenile Diabetes Mellitus." *International Journal of Psychiatry in Medicine,* 1981, *11,* 25–44.

Additional Readings

Daneman, D., Epstein, L. H., Siminerio, L., Beck, S., Farkas, G., Figueroa, J., Becker, D. J., and Drash, A. L. "Effects of Enhanced Conventional Therapy on Metabolic Control in Children with Insulin-Dependent Diabetes Mellitus." *Diabetes Care,* 1982, *5,* 472–478.

These authors instituted a 32-week, three-phase program to improve both self-regulation of adherence behaviors and insulin delivery in children with diabetes. Twenty children took part. For the first 12 weeks (phase I), behavior modification techniques were used to improve diet, exercise, urine testing, and insulin adjustment. Feedback training and parental checks were used to increase reliability. Phase II (13 to 20 weeks) was a stabilization period. Phase III (21 to 32 weeks) studied the effect of adjusting the insulin dose (once versus twice daily injections). The results indicated a significant and sustained increase in negative urine tests, but no change in levels of glycohemoglobin or fasting blood sugar. In phase III, no differences were found between the two groups.

Klusa, Y., Habbick, B. F., and Abernathy, T. J. "Diabetes in Children: Family Responses and Control." *Psychosomatics,* 1983, *24,* 367–372.

These researchers indicate the increased prevalence of psychiatric problems among the parents of diabetic children. An inability of parents to cope with a child's diabetes results in poor care for the child. The authors note that poor parental self-esteem is associated with poor control of the child's diabetic condition. Aside from impaired physical management capabilities, increased emotional stress on the child can exacerbate the diabetic condition and result in hyperglycemia and keto-acidosis. The authors contend that an important aspect of such children's treatment are interventions that also manage parental or familial psychosocial disturbances. They recommend psychiatric consultations in cases where good diabetic control is difficult to achieve.

Rose, M. I., Firestone, P., Heick, H. M. C., and Faught, A. K. "The Effects of Anxiety Management Training on the Control of Juvenile Diabetes Mellitus." *Journal of Behavioral Medicine,* 1983, *6,* 381–395.

This study examined the effectiveness of stress and anxiety management on improving diabetic control in five poorly controlled female adolescent diabetics. Anxiety management training (AMT) (which included progressive muscle relaxation training) was given to these subjects over a 2-week period, during which ratings of anxiety and stress and measures of diabetic control (urine glucose levels) were recorded. The results indicated that AMT had a beneficial effect on glucose levels (they were significantly lower and more stable) compared with baseline. The authors note that AMT had no effect on decreasing subjects' personal assessments of tension and anxiety. The authors contend that this latter finding may result from the moderating influences of complex cognitive processes.

Schafer, L. C., Glasgow, R. E., and McCaul, K. D. "Increasing the Adherence of Diabetic Adolescents." *Journal of Behavioral Medicine,* 1982, *5,* 353–362.

This study examined the effects of self-monitoring, goal setting, and behavioral contracting procedures on increasing regimen compliance among adolescent diabetics. Each technique was introduced sequentially in a multiple-baseline, across-behaviors design. A variety of target behaviors were monitored, including urine testing, exercise, and insulin injections. The results indicated that adherence was increased and maintained at satisfactory levels for two of the three subjects after the goal-setting procedures were introduced. Substantial improvement was also noticed on the metabolic indexes. The third subject did not show reliable improvement, but this may be due to the severe problems that the family was experiencing at the time of the study. Nonetheless, goal setting appears to be a promising technique for increasing adherence to a medical regimen among adolescent diabetics.

Hyperactivity

Hyperactivity in children has long been discussed by teachers and parents. It evolved as a medical problem most probably when medicine developed pharmacologic agents to control behavior and when both parents and teachers were searching for rapid, nonpsychiatric cures. As the pendulum continued to swing, not only did consumers begin to search for alternative treatments to these drugs, but pediatricians, psychiatrists, and other physicians became disquieted by their low level of success and the influence of the drugs' side effects on the social, academic, and personal growth of their patients. Combinations of biofeedback, relaxation training, and operant conditioning paradigms have demonstrated their value in providing behavioral treatment alternatives for this condition.

A Behavioral Approach to Controlling Hyperactivity

AUTHORS: Teodoro Ayllon, Dale Layman, and Henry J. Kandel

PRECIS: A description of the use of behavioral modification techniques in a school setting as an alternative to medications in treating hyperactivity.

INTRODUCTION: Hyperactivity is clinically described as excessive movement, unpredictable behaviors and an unawareness of their consequences, an inability to focus and concentrate on a particular task, and poor academic performance. The most common intervention for this condition is the use of drugs (such as Ritalin). Although a common and effective therapy, drugs may also have undesirable side effects (for example, drug dependence or a retarded academic performance). The purpose of this report is to determine if a behavioral procedure can be as effective in controlling hyperactivity as medications and if such techniques can help hyperactive children to grow educationally.

METHOD: Three subjects (two male and one female, aged 8 to 10 years) participated in this study. Each had been diagnosed as hyperactive and had been receiving medications for at least one year, and each was of average intelligence. Hyperactivity and academic performance on math and reading were measured across two academic periods. Independent observers rated hyperactive behaviors that fell into the following four categories: gross motor behaviors, disruptive noise, disturbing others, and blurting out.

Each child was observed successively for a time sample of 25 seconds. At the end of each interval, the behavior of the child was coded for the presence or absence of hyperactivity. Each child was observed about fifty times each class period (45 minutes) throughout all phases of the study.

A token reinforcement system was introduced into the classroom, and children were awarded checks on an index card by the teacher for each correct academic response during the subject period. These checks could be exchanged for reinforcers later in the day (the price of these reinforcers ranged from 1 check to 75, and they included such items or activities as candy, school supplies, and lunch in the teacher's room).

There were four phases to the study:

1. On medication. Subjects were evaluated for 17 days while on their medication. On the eighteenth day, and with physician approval, medication was stopped. Since this was the beginning of a long weekend, this allowed for the medication to clear their systems.
2. Off medication. Following this clearing period, a 3-day baseline of hyperactive behavior was determined. This phase served as the basis against which the effects of reinforcement could be evaluated.
3. No medication, reinforcement for math. This was a 6-day period when children stayed off their medication and the teacher introduced the reinforcement system for math performance only.
4. No medication, reinforcement of math plus reading. In the final 6-day phase, children continued off their medications and the reinforcement paradigm was extended to include reading performance.

Observations of hyperactivity and academic performance were maintained throughout all phases of this study.

The results indicated that when Ritalin was discontinued, hyperactivity doubled or tripled from initial levels. When the reinforcement procedures were systematically initiated, hyperactivity for all subjects decreased to a level comparable to the initial period, when the medication was being used. Academic performance, on the other hand, increased dramatically during the reinforcement program over the prior period of medication use. This was true for all subjects. These findings indicate that reinforcement of academic performance suppresses hyperactive behaviors and enhances educational performance.

COMMENTARY: The authors note that the control of hyperactivity by behavioral intervention was quick, stable, and independent of the duration and dosage level of medication received by each child before the study. The authors suggest that the continued use of medication to control hyperactivity may result in compliant but academically incompetent students. It is better that such children be given the opportunity to be drug free so as to minimize drug dependence and facilitate change through alternative behavioral techniques.

SOURCE: Ayllon, T., Layman, D., and Kandel, H. J. "A Behavioral-Educational Alternative to Drug Control of Hyperactive Children." *Journal of Applied Behavior Analysis,* 1975, *8,* 137–146.

Relaxation in the Control of Hyperactivity

AUTHORS: Freeman M. Dunn and Robert J. Howell

PRECIS: A report examining the effects of EMG biofeedback and relaxation training on hyperactivity in young boys.

INTRODUCTION: The use of EMG biofeedback and relaxation for controlling hyperactivity in boys was studied separately and in combination. Hyperactive children are overly tense, and this tension further exacerbates the symptomatology of their condition. Therefore, any attempts to reduce physical arousal should improve the ability to attend to a particular task and reduce impulsiveness.

METHOD: The subjects were ten Caucasian boys, each identified as being hyperactive. During the course of the study, no subject received medication or any other treatment for their condition.

Twenty treatment sessions were scheduled at the rate of

two to three per week. Before these sessions, all subjects were assessed to determine the level of hyperactivity exhibited under various conditions (the Bender-Gestalt Visual Motor Test and the WISC-R). Time on task and measures of concentration and accuracy were taken during a 15-minute active task (counting objects). Parents were also given a Hyperactivity Rating Scale for assessing their child's current behavior.

For the first ten sessions, no treatment was given. This was designed to measure any placebo effects associated with the intervention. During these neutral contact sessions, no references to hyperactivity were made. This period was essentially an opportunity for interpersonal relationships and play therapy with few restrictions on activity level. After these ten sessions, the children once again received an assessment evaluation. This was done to determine if any spontaneous changes had occurred and if the parents had noticed any improvements at home. At this point the experimental treatments were introduced. Children were randomly assigned to one of three groups: relaxation alone, EMG biofeedback alone, or relaxation and feedback together.

The EMG biofeedback sessions provided visual and auditory feedback of occipitofrontalis muscle activity to the subjects. The feedback was used both for training purposes and as a data-collecting instrument for the relaxation group. Each session was divided into six parts: (1) Subjects were asked to find a comfortable position in a chair; (2) the EMG was used to determine a baseline level of relaxation with no feedback given to the subject; (3) the next 12 minutes were used to implement the various treatment modalities (such as biofeedback, relaxation, or both); (4) the next 2 minutes were used to measure levels of relaxation, again with no feedback provided; (5) for the next 11 minutes, the contingency condition was reinitiated; and (6) the final 2 minutes were used to measure the subjects' state of relaxation.

The results indicated no significant improvements from preassessment to midassessment periods. The neutral intervention (play therapy) periods therefore had no effect on hyperactivity. There were significant improvements observed after relaxation training was implemented. Over these ten sessions, the subjects exhibited significantly greater levels of physical relaxation than those observed at the preassessment and midassessment intervals. These changes correlated with parents' perceptions of general at-home behavior. Parents' ratings of hypertension were significantly lower. Their ratings did not change from preassessment levels after the neutral treatment alone.

When examining the efficacy of the three modalities, the authors note some important differences. It appears that with relaxation alone, subjects learn more readily to relax but do not relax as deeply as the sessions continue. However, when EMG biofeedback is used alone or jointly with relaxation tapes, the subjects appear to learn more slowly; however, as the treatment progresses, they can relax more deeply and more consistently than those who received the relaxation tapes. The authors suggest that this difference is attributable to the greater cognitive investment necessary to master the biofeedback technique. Although progress is slower in acquiring these complex responses, it results in a more durable treatment effect. Mere relaxation can result from the natural tiring of muscles through repeated contractions and flexings. This natural process is quickly attained, but its optimal level peaks relatively fast since no real response has been learned.

COMMENTARY: This study comes to two important conclusions: (1) Biofeedback improved the ability to relax in these hypertensive children, and (2) there is strong support for the contention that muscle tension and the inability to relax contribute to and exacerbate the symptoms of hyperactivity. The treatment outlined here appears to be a simple method for controlling hyperactivity. This study was significant in that it accounted for possible placebo effects due to the initiation of any intervention as well as comparing the efficacy of two major approaches in reducing unnecessary tension in hyperactive boys.

SOURCE: Dunn, F. M., and Howell, R. J. "Relaxation and Training and Its Relationship to Hyperactivity in Boys." *Journal of Clinical Psychology*, 1982, *38*, 92–100.

Testing for Hyperactivity

AUTHORS: Soula Homatidis and M. Mary Konstantareas

PRECIS: A report on identifying measures that can discriminate between hyperactive and normal children.

INTRODUCTION: Research has produced many psychometric and observational methods that purport to differentiate hyperactive and normal children. However, there is little information on how well they do this. The major lines of research in increasing the ability to differentiate these two populations include monitoring children's responsiveness to stimulant medications (such as Ritalin), yet the validity of making such inferences from responses to specific pharmacologic medications is not firmly established. Another approach uses rating scales from parents and teachers and then factors out salient variables that differentiate hyperactives from normals. A final approach focuses on subgrouping hyperactives according to variables such as responses to treatment and symptomatology. The results of such research are mixed. This report employed a discriminant analysis of several objective and observational measures and then attempted (1) to determine the efficiency of each measure in discriminating between the two groups and (2) to select a subset of measures that together provide an effective means for classification.

METHOD: Thirteen male hyperactive children (mean age 7 years and 2 months) and thirteen normal males (mean age 7 years and 7 months) matched with hyperactives on age and intelligence participated in this study. All hyperactive children suffered from an inability to sustain attention, distractibility, poor peer interaction, and poor conduct. In all cases, the school authorities believed that the child needed special educational assistance because of the severity of the symptomatology. Each child had manifested disturbance for at least 2 years before this study.

Six major areas were examined: (1) impulse control, (2)

organizational skills, (3) attention deployment and sequencing, (4) goal directedness, (5) frustration and aggression, and (6) self-concept. A total of twenty-seven different measures were included in the analyses. Cognitive impulsivity was assessed by both the Matching and Differentiating Familiar Figures tests. Motor activity was measured by two tasks: having the child walk a 6-foot line and having the child draw a 6-inch line, first at a normal pace and then with the instruction to go "as slowly as possible." The dependent variable was the difference in time required to perform the task under the two sets of instructions. Also, each child was observed alone in a room by an assistant who noted the amount of motility exhibited by the child. Field independence/dependence was measured by the Children's Embedded Figures Test; planning and organizational focus was measured by the Porteus Maze Test; and goal direction, sustained attention, sequencing, and distractibility were measured by the Jumbled Numbers Game.

Frustration tolerance and aggressive behavior were assessed via observations. Children were left alone for a 4-minute period in a playroom that contained, among other things, a Bobo punching doll. During this period any aggressive behavior toward the doll was monitored (to establish the basal aggression level). The child was then given a task to perform during another 4-minute period. The task consisted of the child trying to open a wooden Chinese puzzle box for a piece of candy inside it. Any aggression toward the doll was recorded in this situation (aggression during a frustrating task). The observers measured task persistence, goal directedness, and off-task behaviors in two different ways. The first was the amount of time that the child spent in opening the puzzle box described above. The second was the amount of time the child worked on a difficult maze in the Porteus Maze Test. (This maze was done after the Porteus test was completed.) The child had 5 extra minutes to work on a maze taken from the 14-year-old level. Finally, self-concept was measured by the Primary Self-Concept Inventory. Three subtests were analyzed independently: personal, social, and intellectual self-domains.

All subjects were tested individually during the two 30-

minute sessions. A 1- to 2-week period elapsed between sessions. In each session, the same tests were presented, although their order varied across subjects. Interrater reliabilities for observations ranged from .85 to .94 with a mean of .88.

The results indicated that of the twenty-seven measures employed in this study, only nine were found to be potentially significant discriminators. The single best discriminator was the error score on the Jumbled Numbers Game, followed by the test age on the Porteus Maze Test and the errors score on the Matching Familiar Faces Test. Further analyses were performed to determine the subset of measures that best differentiated between the two groups of children. It was found that the combination of errors on the Jumbled Numbers Game test, test age from the Porteus Maze Test, and basal aggression scores were able to classify the children into their previously determined groups with 100% accuracy. Because of the relatively small samples, the authors urged caution in interpreting the results.

COMMENTARY: The authors point out that increasing the ability to differentiate hyperactives from normal children will not only be beneficial in the diagnosis and treatment of hyperactives but in reducing sampling discrepancies in future research studies. Such sampling anomalies may explain some of the discrepant findings present in the literature. This report is important because of the emphasis placed both on diagnostic and treatment considerations. No treatment, however elegant or rigorous, can withstand evaluation if the diagnosis is faulty. Behavioral treatment for hyperactivity rests on the presumption that the health condition is reliably discerned. This report indicates how to increase that reliability.

SOURCE: Homatidis, S., and Konstantareas, M. M. "Assessment of Hyperactivity: Isolating Measures of High Discriminant Ability." *Journal of Consulting and Clinical Psychology,* 1981, *49,* 533–541.

Additional Readings

Hampstrad, W. J. "The Effects of EMG-Assisted Relaxation Training with Hyperkinetic Children: A Behavioral Alternative." *Biofeedback and Self-Regulation,* 1979, *4,* 113–131.

A multiple-baseline study of six hyperkinetic children assessed the effectiveness of EMG-assisted relaxation training on acquiring self-regulatory skills to decrease hyperkinetic behavior. Descriptive verbal feedback on the subjects' performance was provided in addition to continuous auditory feedback. Post-training results indicated significant gains for subjects on visual motor tasks. EMG activity decreased for all subjects. The therapeutic gains were maintained at follow-up. Improvement was also noted both in the home and school environments. The EMG feedback was found to be effective, but no significant effect was found for the verbal feedback. From teacher and parent observations, four subjects for whom medications had been recommended before treatment were judged not to need the medications at follow-up.

Robinson, P. W., Newhy, T. J., and Ganzell, S. L. "A Token System for a Class of Underachieving Hyperactive Children." *Journal of Applied Behavior Analysis,* 1981, *14,* 307–315.

This study examines the effectiveness of a token system that reinforced academic achievement (reading and vocabulary performance) in a class of hyperactive children. Students earned tokens by successfully completing two tasks that involved learning to read and the use of new vocabulary words and two tasks in which the student served as the proctor to another child who had not yet completed those tasks. Tokens could be exchanged for time to play on a video game. The introduction of this program increased the completion rate of tasks for this class four to eight times over baseline. All subjects improved their academic performance after the introduction of this token system.

Shouse, M. N., and Lubar, J. F. "Operant Conditioning of EEG Rhythms and Ritalin in the Treatment of Hyperkinesis." *Biofeedback and Self-Regulation,* 1979, *4,* 299–312.

These authors examined the effectiveness of sensorimotor rhythm (SMR) operant conditioning in treating hyperkinesis.

Contingent changes in SMR were noted in three of the four children studied and were associated with similar changes in classroom assessments of motor inactivity. The combination of medications and SMR training produced physiological and behavioral improvements that exceeded the effects of drugs alone and were sustained with SMR training after medications were withdrawn. These improvements were absent in one subject, who was highly distractible and unable to learn the SMR task. The authors note that the pretraining levels of SMR accurately reflected the severity of subjects' original motor deficits as well as their susceptibility to both drug and behavioral treatments.

Fecal
Incontinence
and Enuresis

Fecal incontinence and enuresis were originally the bane of re-tarded populations. The health and general quality of life for these people required that bowel and bladder functions be properly controlled. Thus, effective protocols to insure such control were developed and implemented by using various behavior modifications. These protocols continue in use today, not only for populations with special needs but also for children who soil or wet without documented physiological cause. In still other cases, mentally and intellectually normal children face problems of incontinence as a result of complications from other diseases, disorders, and handicaps. Behavioral medicine procedures for these children have incorporated the original protocols that reliably establish body control. These procedures are being increasingly accepted and integrated into standard medical practice, often as the treatment of primary choice.

Follow-Up Evaluation
of an Inpatient Bowel Training Program

AUTHORS: Sharon Dietrich and Gary Okamoto

PRECIS: A report assessing the effectiveness of an inpatient bowel training program for children with neurogenic dysfunctions.

INTRODUCTION: This study presents the findings of a follow-up investigation of the effectiveness of an inpatient bowel training program. This program, in conjunction with other programs aimed at improving personal hygiene habits and motor skills, attempted to control fecal incontinence in children with a variety of neurological disorders. Before their child's discharge, parents were instructed in techniques for maintaining this regimen while the child was at home. The program involved both a parent and the child and included teaching regularity, the gastrocolic reflex, medication use, dietary manipulation, and anorectal stimulation. This report had three important goals: (1) to obtain evidence for the effectiveness of the inpatient training regimen over a long time period (evaluations were collected an average of 1.2 years after discharge), (2) to establish the compliance rate with the program in the home environment, and (3) to document the factors contributing to parental changes or modifications of the training protocol.

METHOD: Fifty children were used in this follow-up investigation. There were twenty-eight males and twenty-two females with a mean age of 13.5 years. Twenty-one children had acquired spinal cord lesions from injury, transverse myelitis, or tumor; twenty-seven had meningomyelocele; and two had a repaired imperforate anus. The mean age at hospital admission was 12.1 years (range 4.3 to 18.1 years). A mixed open-and-closed questionnaire was used to gather information about clinical status, bowel program in use, and personal attitudes and opinions.

The authors found that 58% (twenty-nine) of the cases

modified their bowel regimens without direct recommendations from their physician. Only 16% (eight) had their programs changed by the hospital program staff. However, from discharge to follow-up, the mean duration of the bowel program decreased significantly from 41.2 minutes to 32.4 minutes. Also, most bowel programs in the hospital were conducted at 8 A.M.; scheduling at home was quite variable. The use of bowel stimulants also greatly decreased from 72% (thirty-six cases) to 56% (twenty-eight cases) from discharge to follow-up.

This bowel management program appeared to be very successful. There was a significant decrease in the number of bowel accidents from discharge to follow-up, and the longest duration of continence increased significantly. The group with the best level of continence was usually older and female, had a high level of motor paralysis and spastic anal tone, and was disabled by acquired spinal cord lesions. However, in all cases a socially acceptable level of continence was attained.

As was previously mentioned, 58% of the families modified their program after discharge. The authors list four reasons that parents gave for these changes. First, parents found the regimen schedule too restrictive for their schedules. Also, the duration of the program was decreased. Both of these modifications appeared to have no effect on program success. Second, because of their expense many families limited the use of suppositories and related paraphernalia. Third, some families noticed increased incontinence in their child after discharge and altered the program until a more acceptable level was attained at home. Finally, many families believed that dietary manipulations were as effective as medications in stimulating bowel movements and in forming solid stool. However, parents preferred avoiding foods that were associated with diarrhea and loose stool rather than encouraging the consumption of high-fiber foodstuffs and liquids, as the hospital staff had recommended.

The authors contend that the total management of incontinence must involve frequent contact between parents and the outpatient staff. The children should be encouraged to participate in these clinical discussions and decisions to maximize their sense of involvement in their self-care.

COMMENTARY: The results of this study should be incorporated into future programs in order to make them more effective and adaptable to family routines. The authors suggest six guidelines for a successful continence regimen: (1) Scheduling, routine, and consistency are the foundations of any sound management program; (2) at discharge, a home program should be recommended that is workable for the family and their home routine; (3) the use of medications and supplies should generally be considered as a temporary measure in order to minimize the economic burden; (4) dietary recommendations should emphasize not only the intake of high-fiber foods and liquids but also the avoidance of foods associated with diarrhea and loose stool formations; (5) specific attention should be given to those aspects of the program found offensive to the parents (such as manual evacuation); and (6) any modifications in the program should be introduced in a logical, stepwise manner so as to avoid multiple changes at one time.

SOURCE: Dietrich, S., and Okamoto, G. "Bowel Training for Children with Neurogenic Dysfunctions: A Follow-Up." *Archives of Physical Medicine and Rehabilitation*, 1982, *63*, 166–170.

Treatment of Fecal Incontinence with Biofeedback

AUTHOR: Arnold Wald

PRECIS: A study of the use of biofeedback in treating fecal incontinence in children with meningomyelocele.

INTRODUCTION: Meningomyelocele is an open neural tube defect that occurs in 1 to 4 of every 1,000 live births. Its most devastating psychosocial effect is neurogenic anal impairment. Fecal soiling elicits intense criticism from peers, which is quite injurious to self-esteem. This problem is implicated as a major contributing factor to the poor social adjustment of many children suffering from meningomyelocele. For this reason, bowel management programs are a crucial component to any rehabilitation program. This study examines the effectiveness of biofeedback in training these children to achieve continence.

METHOD: Eight children, four males and four females ranging in age from 5 to 15 years (mean 8.6 years), were involved in the biofeedback training. They were selected on the basis of interest in the program, their ability to ambulate without assistance, and the frequency of solid stool incontinence. All were unable to show external and sphincter responses reflexively or on voluntary command as determined by anorectal manometry. All had some rectal sensations (threshold of 60 milliliters). All subjects had been on other bowel programs (such as dietary alterations, the use of suppositories and enemas, and timed defecation), all of which had little or no effect on their incontinence.

The three-balloon system of manometric recording was used to measure the internal and external anal sphincters and the proximal rectum. During an initial evaluation, the author recorded: (1) the presence or absence of reflexive contractions of the external sphincter, (2) the presence or absence of reflexive internal sphincter contractions, (3) the smallest volume of rectal distension necessary to produce internal sphincter relaxation, (4) the smallest volume necessary for the subject to sense rectal distension, (5) the presence of fecal impaction (suggesting overflow incontinence), and (6) the presence or absence of perianal sensations using a pinprick.

One to four weeks after this evaluation, the treatment program was initiated. Anorectal manometry was repeated and compared with the previous performance. Children were shown a correct manometric tracing of internal and external anal sphincter responses and then were instructed to experiment with different responses until they were able to increase pressure on the external sphincter balloon. Visual manometric feedback was given throughout this procedure. Verbal reinforcement was given for all correct responses. Once the subjects were consistently able to produce the correct response, they were taught to synchronize external sphincter contractions with perceived rectal distension. Once such synchronization was established, visual feedback was withdrawn and the process repeated. Rectal distension began at 50 milliliters and was decreased in 10-milliliter decrements until the subject's threshold of sensation was reached. After this session, subjects were instructed to practice the learned techniques daily and to maintain a diary of incontinent episodes. All children received at least one booster session from 1 to 6 weeks later.

Four of these children had significant decreases in the frequency of fecal soiling after treatment. Two were completely continent, one had improved by 90%, and one by 75%. These children continued to improve and exhibit increased confidence in matters relating to bowel control. These results were obtained on follow-up evaluations conducted 3 to 12 months after treatment termination. Of the four children who showed no improvement after biofeedback, three had impairment of the threshold of rectal sensation. The fourth was not able to master the techniques even after receiving two treatment sessions. Neuromuscular testing revealed weakness and poor development of the pelvic girdle, although the child could perceive stool present in the rectum.

Based on the results of this investigation, the author suggests that normal thresholds for rectal sensation and normal internal sphincter relaxation are good prognostic indicators for benefiting from this program. Four of the five children who met these criteria had a successful outcome. For the one who did not, an inability to master the technique of increasing sphincter pressure was believed to be the cause of failure. The author also suggests that the level of neuromotor deficits can serve as a general guide to selecting promising candidates, since no subject who responded well to treatment had a deficit proximal to L-5. The best indicator of a favorable outcome appears to be anorectal manometric findings. The prospects for a good response to treatment can be assessed after the first treatment session. However, these are only general guidelines that need further research to be refined.

COMMENTARY: This report describes the effectiveness of bio-feedback in controlling fecal incontinence in children. The procedures outlined here are simple and rapidly learned and often produce dramatic results. The prognostic guidelines suggested by the author can help in identifying candidates most likely to benefit from a biofeedback intervention. An important area of future investigation is to determine the influence that such an intervention has on later psychosocial adjustment.

SOURCE: Wald, A. "Use of Biofeedback in Treatment of Fecal Incontinence in Patients with Meningomyelocele." *Pediatrics*, 1981, *68*, 45-49.

Biofeedback for Fecal Incontinence in Meningomyelocele Patients

AUTHORS: William E. Whitehead, Lynn H. Parker, Bruce J. Masek, Michael F. Cataldo, and John M. Freeman

PRECIS: A study of the use of sphincter EMG biofeedback to control fecal incontinence in patients with meningomyelocele.

INTRODUCTION: Previous research has shown that in meningomyelocele patients, fecal incontinence is due to few or no contractions of the external anal sphincter when the rectum is distended. Commonly, such patients are subjected to a protocol of enemas or suppositories to keep the rectum clear. This procedure is effective in only about 40% of such patients. Since biofeedback has been effective in controlling fecal incontinence in adults, these authors applied a modified form of biofeedback training with meningomyelocele patients in an attempt to decrease their incidence of incontinence.

METHOD: There were eight subjects in this study, ages 5 to 15

years, all of whom had a lifelong history of severe fecal incontinence secondary to meningomyelocele. All manifested manometric evidence of impaired external anal sphincter function.
No subject had appropriate bowel movements.

The treatment plan consisted of four phases. First, a diagnostic procedure was employed to assess the reflexes of the internal and external sphincters and the threshold for subjective
feelings of rectal distension. The manometric device was fash-
ioned from a hollow cylinder that had two balloons attached to
it. The first, a doughnut-shaped balloon, was surrounded by
the internal anal sphincter when inflated with 10 milliliters of
air; the second, a pear-shaped balloon, was surrounded by the
external anal sphincter. A third balloon was inserted through
the cylinder to distend the rectum. The sensory threshold for
rectal distension was determined by ascertaining the smallest
amount of rectal distension necessary for the patient to report a
sensation. If a patient was inconsistent in his or her responses, a
forced-choice test was used, in which the person was required to
identify which of two volumes of air was injected in ten trials.
A patient was considered to have subjective sensation at a particular distension level if he or she was correct on at least 80%
of the trials.

In the second phase, subjects were taught to make appropriate contractions of the external sphincter. With most patients, this was done without rectal distension. Patients monitored their behavior with polygraph tracings. Verbal support
and reinforcement were given for responses in the desired directions. After contractions were produced, patients received verbal
encouragement so that they would increase the strength and
duration of external anal contractions. Gradually the verbal responses were decreased as subjects became more competent in
their contractions.

The third phase concentrated on a feedback procedure to
develop contractions of the external anal sphincter following a
distension of the rectum. Distension levels began at the subjective threshold determined earlier, and 5- to 10-milliliter increments of air pressure were introduced up to a 60-milliliter distension level. These increments depended on an appropriate

response by the subject at the previous level. Subjects were encouraged to initate a contraction as soon as a distension was sensed and to maintain it for the duration of the relaxation response of the internal sphincter. Verbal encouragement was given during this procedure. This task was intended to enable subjects to synchronize internal and external sphincter responses as well as to simulate the normal duration and strength of external sphincter contractions. Visual feedback from the polygraph tracings was also provided.

The fourth phase was an extension of the previous phase with the exception of the visual feedback. Air was injected into the apparatus at variable intervals and without verbal cues. Patients now had to depend solely on subjective sensations to know when to begin appropriate rectosphincteric responses. Verbal reinforcement was initially provided but gradually reduced as patients became more capable of responding.

Each training session lasted from 60 to 90 minutes and had approximately forty training trials per session. Between sessions, patients were encouraged to practice external sphincter contractions five times daily in order to strengthen the muscle. Each subject received between two and six sessions. Training was terminated when a subject either completed all phases of the study successfully or spent two consecutive sessions at the same phase.

Subjects and their parents were instructed to record incontinent episodes, appropriate toiletings, and evacuation procedures for 1 week before training, during training, and for 4 weeks after the termination of the training. Treatment was terminated after the first few sessions for two subjects because they were unable to produce any external sphincter contractions with or without rectal distension. It should be noted that these subjects were also the youngest of all subjects (5 and 6 years of age).

The authors concluded that seven of eight subjects could sense rectal distension within normal limits. The final patient, the 5-year-old, reported no sensation under 40 milliliters of distension, but the authors were not sure that he understood the task. The results indicated an increase in the strength of voluntary contractions of the external anal sphincter over the course of the treatment session.

By the end of treatment, five of the six subjects were completely continent, and the sixth had a greatly reduced occurrence of incontinence (from a baseline of forty-two to fifty-six times per week to seven times per week). Two of these five patients received only two phases of the treatment. Five of the six discontinued the use of enemas and suppositories. The remaining patient continued such a regimen, but still remained continent during a 1-week hiatus. Follow-up interviews conducted from between 13 to 24 weeks after treatment indicated that subjects were still maintaining drastically reduced levels of incontinent occurrences from pretreatment levels.

The authors note that there are two important differences in fecal incontinence between patients with meningomyelocele and patients with adult-onset incontinence resulting from peripheral nerve injury. First, the sensation of rectal distension is very good for the former group of patients but often impaired for the latter. Second, rectal distension somewhat weakened external sphincter contractions in the meningomyelocele subjects but severely weakened or extinguished contractions in the adult group. The authors contend that meningomyelocele patients either have a weaker external sphincter than adults or had never learned to contract the external sphincter in response to distension, while adults had learned this response but were unable to execute it adequately.

COMMENTARY: Traditional biofeedback training in this area has been sensory oriented; patients were requested to respond to large volumes of rectal distension, which were then gradually reduced. The procedure outlined previously is more of a response-shaping procedure. This approach was to teach subjects to contract the external sphincter without any distension or with a small amount of distension. The amount of subsequent distensions was then gradually increased. The authors believe that the best discriminator for determining who would benefit from biofeedback training is sensitivity to bowel distension. The more sensitive a person is to this sensation, the likelier a biofeedback approach such as this is to be successful. It is also of interest that since two of the subjects achieved continence after only two phases of treatment, a shorter training period as well as a simpler training procedure may be sufficient for some meningomyelocele patients to control their fecal incontinence.

SOURCE: Whitehead, W. E., Parker, L. H., Masek, B. J., Cataldo, M. F., and Freeman, J. M. "Biofeedback Treatment for Fecal Incontinence in Patients with Meningomyelocele." *Developmental Medical Child Neurology*, 1981, *23*, 313-322.

Additional Readings

Barmann, B. C., Katz, R. C., O'Brien, F., and Beauchamp, K. L. "Treating Irregular Enuresis in Developmentally Disabled Persons: A Study in the Use of Overcorrection." *Behavior Modification*, 1981, *5*, 336-346.

The purpose of this study was twofold: (1) to develop a shortened version of the Foxx and Azrin toilet training program for use with developmentally disabled children and (2) to assess the efficacy of parents as the primary agents of behavioral change. The training technique consisted of administering an overcorrection procedure for inappropriate voiding. Positive reinforcement was given for correct toileting behavior and for the absence of any soiling episodes. The results indicated that the introduction of the overcorrection procedure brought about immediate decreases in enuretic behavior and the elimination of "accidents." The methods used here appear to constitute an effective home program for controlling enuresis in disabled children.

Bollard, J., Nettelbeck, T., and Roxbel, L. "Dry-Bed Training for Childhood Bedwetting: A Comparison of Group with Individually Administered Parent Instruction." *Behaviour Research and Therapy*, 1982, *20*, 209-217.

Traditional dry-bed training (DBT) involves a complicated schedule of tasks and is time consuming. These authors assessed the efficacy of DBT by training parents in small group meetings. These meetings saved the therapist time both in explaining the program and following up on the children's progress. These group sessions also offered individuals sharing a common problem the opportunity to discuss with each other important issues. The technique removed the needs for (1) having a stranger enter the child's house for the evening and (2) finding trained personnel to work night hours on a regular basis. The authors also compared DBT using a urine alarm with training without an alarm. The results indicated that DBT was effective when handled by a trained parent. Subjects reached criterion (14 days without an accident) on the average of 5 days faster than subjects in a study where a professional therapist was used. DBT without the alarm produced significant decreases in bed-wetting but failed to eliminate the symptoms completely. The alarm makes the procedure more effective, and it motivates the parents to comply with the treatment program.

Bornstein, P. H., Sturum, C. A., Retzloff, P. D., Kirby, K. L., and Chong, H. "Paradoxical Instruction in the Treatment of Encopresis and Chronic Constipation: An Experimental Analysis." *Journal of Behavior Therapy and Experimental Psychiatry*, 1981, *12*, 167–170.

In this study, the authors used paradoxical intention as a treatment intervention for a 9-year-old boy with daily encopresis and constipation. The subject was instructed to go into the bathroom every hour, pull down his trousers, and sit on the toilet for 5 minutes. He was to act as if he had to make a bowel movement but *not* to allow it to occur. During the 11 weeks of this protocol, the child significantly improved in proper toileting over baseline, and the incidents of soiling ceased. These treatment effects were maintained at a 1-year follow-up. In addition to the efficacy of this treatment approach, it is relatively brief and simple. The authors contend that this technique avoids the aversive consequences common to other behavioral and medical treatment interventions.

Finley, W. W., Rainwater, A. J., and Johnson, G. "Effect of Varying Alarm Schedules on Acquisition and Relapse Parameters in the Conditioning Treatment of Enuresis." *Behaviour Research and Therapy*, 1982, *20*, 69–80.

This report examined the efficacy of varying conditioning schedules on the acquisition of appropriate toileting behaviors and relapse rates for 178 enuretic children. Five alarm schedules were compared: 30% to 59%, 60% to 69%, 70% to 79%, 80% to 89%, and 90% to 100%. All schedules less than 100% (continuous reinforcement) were variable ratio (VR). It was found that children who experienced multiple wettings per night (MW) took twice as long to acquire the proper behaviors than nonmultiple wetters (NMW). For NMW children, the optimal reinforcement schedule was the 70%-to-79% VR (only a 10% relapse rate). For MW children, the 60%-to-69% VR schedule produced the lowest relapse rate (42%). Continuous reinforcement was the worst protocol for the MWs. Although older children experienced more relapses than younger children, the 70%-to-79% VR alarm schedule eliminated any age differences. The results indicate that optimal VR reinforcement schedules vary according to the category of the enuretic child.

Asthma

In addition to general theories about the dynamic and psycho-somatic approaches to asthma, a number of behavioral strategies that are largely atheoretical have been advanced that show promise in treating and rehabilitating this respiratory condition. In the adult, a variety of chronic pulmonary disorders may present similar patterns of symptoms, but in children such symptoms invariably indicate asthma. Asthma is precipitated by various organic and psychological stressors, and patients can attempt to discover effective tactics for preventing the onset of an attack or for aborting one that has already begun. These tactics include stress management, biofeedback procedures for improved pulmonary functions, and improved compliance with a medical regimen. Although no single treatment stands out as being superior, the complex of behavioral medicine technologies for the assessment and treatment of asthma constitutes an important addition to options of the primary care physician.

Classification and Treatment Issues of Asthmatics

AUTHOR: Gregory K. Fritz

PRECIS: A summary of diagnostic and treatment issues relating to childhood asthma.

INTRODUCTION: Psychologists are interested in asthma because of the psychological variables that affect the course of the disease and the psychosomatic processes that affect the person. The incidence of asthma in children under 15 years of age is estimated at 5% to 10%; boys are affected two to three times as frequently as girls. Since asthmatics constitute a heterogeneous population, there is a need to develop a detailed classification system as well as a need to develop intervention techniques that are effective for all. This report presents an overview of both a diagnostic framework and a therapeutic approach.

DIAGNOSTIC CLASSIFICATION: There is a lack of explicit diagnostic criteria for differentiating asthmatics. Four groups have been defined in terms of different features:

1. Intrinsic versus extrinsic asthma. In this widely employed distinction, extrinsic asthma refers to individuals who have a strong allergic basis to their condition. For such asthmatics there are a family history of allergy and positive skin tests, and their condition is seasonal. Intrinsic asthma lacks seasonality, and attacks are usually precipitated by infections.
2. Response to separation from parents. This characteristic is usually noticed among some individuals with intractable asthma. Individuals commonly respond extremely well to separation from their parents: Separation does not precipitate an attack; rather, improvement may occur. Somehow the parent-child dynamics maintain the child's asthmatic condition. However, there are no known family characteristics that differentiate children who respond to parental separation with asthmatic attacks from those who do not.

3. Response to suggestion. It has been known for some time that some asthmatics respond with bronchoconstriction to an inhalant of saline if they believe it is an allergen known to cause their attacks. Research has found that such individuals have an airway that is hyperactive to methacholine and histamine challenges. These patients were also found to be emotionally labile.

4. Panic-fear response level. Research has indicated that high levels of nonspecific, characterological anxiety is related to longer hospital stays, more frequent hospitalizations, and more intensive use of oral steroids. Low panic-fear scores were related to increased rates of hospitalization also. Mid-range levels of anxiety were associated with more adaptive coping styles for monitoring disease activity and responding to professional care. The author notes that this measure of anxiety still must be evaluated with a young asthmatic population.

TREATMENT INTERVENTIONS: The author notes that definitive studies are lacking of the efficacy of various interventions, although some evidence is available. The most basic intervention is education, that is, making patients aware of their disease, medical treatment, and the reasons for the life-styles mandated by their condition. Such information can increase compliance and reduce feelings of helplessness in patients. Research has indicated that such a program can profoundly influence the frequencies of hospitalizations, emergency room visits, and school days missed. The author contends that given the cost-effectiveness of such a program, it should constitute the first line of intervention with asthmatics.

Several clinical situations indicate the need for further psychological evaluation. These include: (1) symptoms that are unresponsive to conventional medical treatment, (2) acute asthmatic attacks that appear precipitated by episodes of stress, (3) parents and/or patients that are unable to perceive physical improvement and may even seem to need the illness, (4) an inappropriate attitude by the patient toward the asthma (either overly anxious or indifferent), and (5) a case that regularly elicits unexplained feelings in the primary care physician, such as anger, rejection, or protectiveness.

The most common behavioral intervention is relaxation training, which consists of teaching the child progressive muscle relaxation techniques and guided imagery. Results of research on this treatment are equivocal. Biofeedback training in tandem with relaxation seems to improve the results. Systematic desensitization techniques appear to be more successful. The critical issue here is to determine which patients will respond best to which treatment and how long such therapeutic gains can be maintained.

Another approach can be individual and/or family therapy. Although asthma itself is not an indicator for psychotherapy, such an intervention can be very useful for individuals whose central problems are psychological in nature. The most intensive psychological treatment is hospitalization in a psychosomatic unit. These treatment options are reserved for patients whose symptoms do not respond to any other interventions and whose overall functioning is disrupted by the asthma. The treatment program usually includes individual therapy, behavior modification, and family sessions. The goals of the program are individually developed, and a multidisciplinary approach is necessary.

COMMENTARY: Asthmatics are a heterogeneous population, and much research is needed to develop more precise diagnostic categories and more effective treatments. Although current research does not provide us with any proven techniques, it has indicated promising areas of investigation. This report describes important diagnostic issues and treatment techniques. One pressing need is to translate many of the diagnostic scales used with adults into a form usable with children. Although the same patterns found in adults may be found in children, different clusterings of specific items could be found. Because results obtained with adults may not generalize to children, such additional efforts are necessary.

SOURCE: Fritz, G. K. "Childhood Asthma." *Psychosomatics,*
1983, *24,* 959-967.

Cardiac Acceleration in the Treatment of Asthma

AUTHORS: Anne V. Harding and Kevin R. Maher

PRECIS: A description of the use of heart rate biofeedback as a
therapeutic intervention for decreasing airway resistance in
bronchial asthmatic sufferers.

INTRODUCTION: A characteristic of bronchial asthma is a nar-
rowing of the airway. Physiologically, this is due to an increase
in vagally smooth muscle tone in conjunction with the resulting
edema of the airway mucosa. The symptoms may be exacerbated by bronchial smooth muscle hypertrophy in a predisposed hyperirritable airway. Although research has been done
using direct airway biofeedback, results are inconclusive. The
authors propose an intervention that centers on the physiological mechanisms of the attack itself, namely, the vagally moder-
ated increases in bronchomotor tone, which are early symptoms
of the asthmatic response. Direct conditioning of vagal functioning is difficult and impractical. However, focusing on other
systems that are anatomically related to vagal innervation (in
particular, the heart) is possible. This research was designed to
determine the effect that biofeedback-assisted voluntary cardiac
acceleration can have on the tonus of vagal fiber to the lungs, as
measured by peak expiratory flow rates (PEFRs). Such an acquired ability may provide asthmatics with a useful way of
countering asthmatic attacks.

METHOD: Sixteen asthmatic subjects and twelve normal control subjects (matched on age and height) were studied. The criteria for selection for the asthmatics included a history of

asthma with recent episodes, no other concurrent disease or history of heart disease, and not receiving steroid therapy. Asthmatics were prescreened for suggestibility by evaluating their responses to placebo inhalants under suggestions of both bronchoconstriction and bronchodilation. Highly suggestible individuals were excluded from the study. All subjects refrained from using asthma medication for at least 4 hours before each training session.

Heart rate feedback was provided by an analog rate meter positioned at a subject's eye level. PEFR measurements were obtained 15 minutes before and immediately after each training session. All subjects were blind to the nature of this measure in order to reduce any suggestibility effects. The basic procedure consisted of having subjects sit in a small, air-conditioned cubicle for 2 minutes. Then, with their eyes closed, they received recorded instructions. The experimental group was informed to accelerate their heart rate. The instructions were followed by a 1-minute interval during which the feedback equipment was activated and a baseline heart rate response was obtained. This was followed by fifteen training intervals of 45 seconds, which were separated by 60-second rest periods with eyes closed. Recordings of heart rate were made on trials 1, 5, 10, and 15.

Subjects in the control group received one session as outlined above with the exception that they were instructed to maintain a steady heart rate. Experimental subjects received sufficient training to achieve an individual asymptotic level of cardiac acceleration. This level was determined by examining the learning curves for each subject within and across sessions and was defined as the maximum cardiac rate achieved during training. Subjects reached asymptote between two and five sessions. Control subjects received only one training session. Experimental subjects were also given stethoscopes to use when practicing cardiac acceleration between training sessions. The normal control subjects received only one session of cardiac acceleration; their training was otherwise identical to the training given the asthmatic experimental group.

Following the biofeedback sessions, all asthmatic patients were required to maintain a diary of their asthma episodes for 2 weeks (actual posttest recording periods lasted several weeks for most patients). These individuals were instructed to keep track of attack frequency per week, medication usage per week, and medication usage per attack. Experimental subjects were made aware of the results of their training at the conclusion of their last session, as well as changes in their PEFR readings over the course of training. The physiological mechanisms underlying these changes were explained to them briefly, and they were requested to use the techniques that they had learned (increased heart rate) whenever they felt a tightness in their chest as a strategy to avoid an asthmatic attack. If cardiac acceleration was unsuccessful, they were to resort to their customary use of medication.

The results indicated that the asthmatic control and experimental groups were equivalent on the suggestibility variable. These groups did not significantly differ on pretreatment baseline heart rates or PEFR values. Further analyses noted a significant increase in heart rate and PEFR values for the experimental group over the controls. Control subjects also significantly lowered their heart rate from the baseline to postsession. On the self-report measures, experimental subjects showed a significant improvement at posttest on all three indexes. The number of asthmatic attacks per week decreased significantly, as did weekly medication usage and the amount of medication used per attack. The control subjects showed no such changes. In comparing the asthmatics to normals on heart rate level and rate of acquisition of the acceleration response, there were no significant differences. However, asthmatics had significantly lower airway flow rates than normals, even though the asthmatics were symptom free during training sessions.

The authors conclude that the major hypothesis of this study was supported. Specifically, biofeedback-assisted voluntary cardiac acceleration does produce changes in airway resistance that may result from a generalized change in vagally mediated bronchiolar smooth muscle tone (there was a significant increase in PEFR readings for the asthmatic subjects across trials). Although it is not possible to influence vagal innervation of the lungs directly, increasing voluntary control over related vagally medicated functions can generate an effect that generalizes throughout the entire system.

COMMENTARY: Because of the decrease in the number of asthmatic attacks reported by the experimental group, the authors contend that the acquisition and continual practice of the acceleration response can have the long-term benefit of providing a prophylactic strategy. Not only does this response reduce the severity of an asthmatic attack, but continual practice may mediate vagal efferent activity in the bronchioles and thus reduce the number of physiologically initiated asthmatic responses. Yet, as the authors note, further research is necessary to determine the durability of this response. This research does offer an interesting approach to both the treatment and control of bronchial asthma and warrants further rigorous experimental study.

SOURCE: Harding, A. V., and Maher, K. R. "Biofeedback Training of Cardiac Acceleration: Effects on Airway Resistance in Bronchial Asthma." *Journal of Psychosomatic Research*, 1982, *26*, 447–454.

Behavior Modification in the Treatment of Asthma

AUTHORS: Neil J. Yorkston, Elke Eckert, Richard B. McHugh, Dennis A. Philander, and Malcolm N. Blumenthal

PRECIS: A comparison of the effectiveness of verbal and practical desensitization methods in improving lung functioning in bronchial asthma patients.

INTRODUCTION: The purpose of this study was to compare two desensitization techniques with relaxation procedures alone. Verbal desensitization, which has been shown to be effective and have long-lasting effects, is designed to teach patients to think calmly about their asthma (since an asthmatic attack can be brought about in some patients by simply thinking about their illness). Durable results are obtained by having individuals become desensitized to as many internal stimuli (thoughts and symptoms experienced during an attack) and external stimuli (precipitating circumstances) as possible. The authors examined another internal stimulus for asthma sufferers, expiratory effort, which has been overlooked. The practical desensitization techniques used attempted to accommodate subjects to increasing expiratory effort without raising associated anxiety, a factor that may exacerbate their condition.

METHOD: Twenty-eight subjects (twenty-three women and five men, with a mean age of 45 years) took part in this study. The mean duration of their illness was 23 years (range from 17 to 66). None of the subjects had smoked within 5 years of the study, and none had any related, complicating diseases such as emphysema, cardiac failure, or infections. All subjects were first given a pretreatment interview, where a detailed record of symptoms, associated thoughts, and antecedent circumstances to the attacks was compiled. Each subject also completed the Eysenck Personality Inventory. Subjects were then randomly assigned to one of three conditions and then underwent 2 weeks of baseline study, 3 to 4 weeks of treatment, and 2 weeks of follow-up treatment.

Treatments were given for six 1-hour sessions over the 3 to 4 weeks. Of the twenty-eight patients, eighteen were receiving steroids and ten were not. Subjects were randomly distributed over the three experimental groups. The first condition was the relaxation-only group, in which nine subjects were taught to relax in a comfortable reclining chair and listen to simple suggestions. While remaining relaxed, these subjects were told to imagine themselves in progressively more uncomfortable situations. No reference was made to the subject's asthmatic condition or to related circumstances. Suggestions were limited to relaxation; no direct suggestions of improvement were made.

The verbal desensitization group had ten subjects, who were also taught to relax using the above procedure. These subjects were then instructed to differentiate between neutral statements (which did not influence their relaxed state) and statements that did make them feel uncomfortable (after which they were to return to their relaxed state). During the verbal desensitization process, the subjects listened carefully to a graded progression of stressful statements about asthma. Once they were able to remain relaxed at one level, they progressed to a more descriptive level until they were able to remain calm while listening to a standard description of asthma. The subjects were also desensitized, statement by statement, to a complete description of their own worst asthmatic experience.

There were nine subjects in the combined verbal and practical desensitization condition. During the first two sessions, the subjects again learned how to relax using the aforementioned procedure. The remainder of the sessions were allocated equally between verbal and practical desensitization procedures. The former followed the same protocol as for the previous group. The latter had subjects gradually accustom themselves to increased expiratory effort without provoking anxiety. The authors used an apparatus that could increase resistance to a subject's expirations. This device consisted of a tube connected to a blow-bottle containing colored water; the outflow tube was 1 meter in height. The subjects were encouraged to progress at their own rate and to blow into the tube and sustain a column of water as high as possible.

An allergist and a psychiatrist assessed each patient before and at the end of the study. The allergist was blind to the experimental condition of the subjects. Each patient was rated as either improved, no change, or worse. Forced expiratory volumes were obtained at each assessment by the allergist. Peak flow readings were recorded by the patients five times daily and then averaged to yield one daily reading. These recordings were performed for 2 weeks pretreatment and posttreatment. Subjects also recorded symptoms and drug usage day and night. The symptoms were categorized as either of the upper or lower respiratory tract and were graded on an 8-point scale, ranging from 1 (no symptoms) to 8 (severe symptoms requiring hospitalization).

Of the subjects receiving steroids, significantly more improved following desensitization procedures than improved following relaxation alone. There were no differences between the verbal and practical desensitization groups. For subjects in the nonsteroid group, there were no significant differences among the three conditions (this effect may be due to the relatively small number of subjects in these conditions, a total of nine, compared with the eighteen in the steroid group). Subjects in the steroid group who received desensitization also showed improvement in daytime and nighttime respiratory tract symptoms according to their subjective ratings, and they reported less use of medications compared with steroid-using subjects in the relaxation only condition.

According to the overall mean score for all subjects (13.64) on the Eysenck Personality Inventory that measures neuroticism, this sample was more neurotic than the general population. There was a positive correlation between neuroticism and peak flow change that approached significance.

COMMENTARY: The use of the new type of desensitization did not appear to improve the asthmatic condition any more than the conventional verbal desensitization technique. There were no significant differences between the verbal and practical behavior modification groups. It also appears that medications (steroids) may play an important role in contributing to the success of the behavior modification techniques. Desensitization was successful only in those patients on steroids. The implication of this factor and of the degree of neuroticism for the therapeutic improvement of asthma patients requires further investigation. Nonetheless, systematic desensitization can be an effective intervention for the control of asthma, regardless of whether a verbal or practical approach is employed. This finding, if confirmed, makes sensitization a major adjunctive treatment option for primary care physicians who manage asthmatic disorders for all age ranges.

SOURCE: Yorkston, N. J., Eckert, E., McHugh, R. B., Philander, D. A., and Blumenthal, M. N. "Bronchial Asthma: Improved Lung Function After Behavior Modification." *Psychosomatics*, 1979, 20, 325–331.

Additional Readings

Hill, D. J., Shelton, M. J., Hosking, C. S., and Turner, M. W. "Growing out of Asthma: Clinical and Immunological Changes over 5 Years." *The Lancet*, 1981, 2, 1359–1362.

Over a 5-year period, asthmatic children with bronchial reactivity to a seasonal allergen (pollen) were studied. Changes in symptoms and drug usage were correlated with changes in the levels of serum antibodies to the allergen. The authors noted that the clinical severity of the asthma significantly declined over the course of the study and that this occurred concomitantly with significant decreases in serum antibodies. Children with bronchial reactivity to ryegrass pollen showed no change over the course of the study. These authors contend that long-term perennial allergen exposure promotes immunological hyposensitivity, while intermittent seasonal allergen exposure is related to persistent immunological hypersensitivity.

Nickerson, B. G., Bautista, D. B., Namey, M. A., Richards, W., and Keens, T. G. "Distance Running Improves Fitness in Asthmatic Children Without Pulmonary Complications or Changes in Exercise-Induced Bronchospasm." *Pediatrics*, 1983, 71, 147–152.

These researchers examined the effect of a long-distance running program on children with severe chronic asthma. Subjects ran 4 days a week for 6 weeks, the distance gradually increasing to 3.2 kilometers. Clinical status and the need for treatment did not change. It was found that episodes of exercise-induced bronchospasm were reduced and fitness significantly improved. Other physiological indexes did not change (resting pulmonary function and ventilatory muscle strength). The authors conclude that distance running is a safe activity for asthmatic children that can increase general fitness while they continue to receive therapy.

Staudemayer, H. "Parental Anxiety and Other Psychosocial Factors Associated with Childhood Asthma." *Journal of Chronic Diseases*, 1981, 34, 627–636.

The effects of childhood asthma on the children's parents were assessed by five psychosocial factors derived from a questionnaire given to 159 mothers and 70 fathers. The results indicated that parental anxiety was related to (1) the amount of debilitation experienced by the child, (2) the father's perception of manipulation by the child, and (3) the mother's self-perception of overprotectiveness. There was no relationship between good family communication and level of debilitation, but the author noted that these results should be interpreted cautiously. Overall, the results indicated that parental anxiety is related to the medical manageability of the asthmatic child. The author suggests that this measurement procedure should be administered routinely as a matter of course in clinical practice to assist physicians in their therapeutic decisions.

Author Index

347

Subject Index